The Marginal Cost and Pricing of Electricity

THE PLANNING AND CONSERVATION FOUNDATION

The California Planning and Conservation Foundation is a non-profit organization dedicated to environmental research and education. The Foundation's areas of activity have included water quality, citizen participation, energy conservation, electricity pricing, biodynamic French intensive gardening, and land use planning. PCF research projects are funded by private contributions and foundation grants.

The Planning and Conservation Foundation
717 K St., Suite 209
Sacramento, California 95814
(916) 444-8551

The Marginal Cost and Pricing of Electricity

An Applied Approach

Charles J. Cicchetti
William J. Gillen
Paul Smolensky

A Report to the National Science Foundation
on behalf of the Planning and Conservation Foundation
Sacramento, California

Ballinger Publishing Company • Cambridge, Massachusetts
A Subsidiary of J.B. Lippincott Company

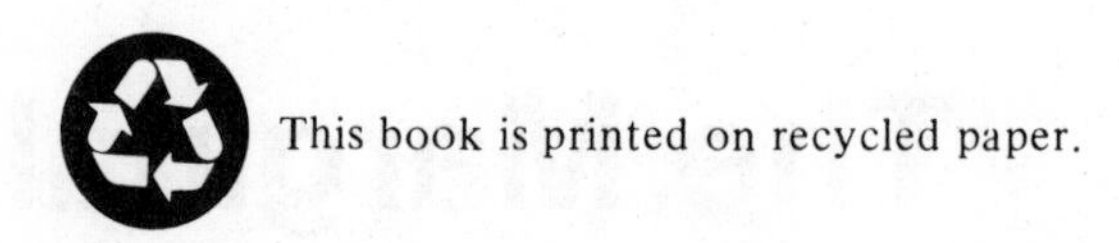

This research was made possible by National Science Foundation grant #SIA 74–24370. The opinions, findings, conclusions, or recommendations expressed in this report are those of the authors and do not necessarily reflect the views of the National Science Foundation.

Additional Support for Appendix B, as well as earlier work by the authors of this report came from the Environmental Defense Fund and the Rockefeller Foundation.

International Standard Book Number: 0–88410–612–8

Library of Congress Catalog Card Number: 77–2312

Printed in the United States of America

Library of Congress Cataloging in Publication Data

Cicchetti, Charles J
The marginal cost and pricing of electricity.

"A report to the National Science Foundation on behalf of the Planning and Conservation Foundation, Sacramento, California."
1. Electric utilities—United States—Costs. 2. Electric utilities—United States—Rates. I. Gillen, William J., joint author. II. Smolensky, Paul, joint author. III. United States. National Science Foundation. IV. Title.
HD9685.U5C528 338.4'3363'620973 77–2312
ISBN 0–88410–612–8

Dedication

To Pat, Carol and Nina

Contents

List of Figures

List of Tables

Preface

The purpose of this study has been to provide a practical guide for analysis of the marginal cost structure of electric utilities for the particular purpose of designing electricity tariffs. Necessarily, this is not a layman's guide; but neither does it presuppose an extensive background in electrical engineering, economics or related fields. The study is intended for those who have a working familiarity with electric power systems and who desire a general, but less abstract, discussion of the marginal cost structure of electric power systems than has heretofore been available. This group will consist largely of those who participate as utility representatives, regulators or intervenors in the process of designing tariffs. Given the volume of text that follows, liberally laced as it is with arithmetic, tables, graphs and computer output, we expect that we will reach our intended audience by a process of self-selection.

The objective selected, of course, influences the approach to any problem, and here we concentrate on those features of marginal cost structure that might as a practical matter be accounted for in tariff structure. Analysts with other objectives might properly ignore what will be critical points for this study, while others may find our presentation grossly oversimplified for their purposes. The designing of turbines and the designing of tariffs are quite different matters, but doing a proper job of either requires a familiarity with the same basic cost framework.

Tariffs should reflect, insofar as practicable, the principal variations in marginal costs (loosely, the extra costs of an additional unit of output). The tariffs of any particular electric utility will depend, however, on a number of considerations other than marginal cost, "revenue requirements," for instance, about which it is not possible to say much with generality. These other considerations are ad hoc and are appropriate for discussion only after one has determined something about marginal costs. Accordingly, the reader will find that the following discussion pertains to the determination of marginal costs from the perspective of tariff design, and that the rendition of a marginal cost structure into a particular set of tariffs is left to the analysis of each particular case, with only a few general remarks at the conclusion of this report. We will be satisfied if we have provided a means of finding the benchmark and methodology for such tariffs. We will be especially satisfied if the informed reader comes to agree that, in the general case, the analysis is neither particularly difficult, nor very expensive, to execute.

For a brief summary of this report, the reader may refer to the introductions to Sections I and II and to Chapter 7. The balance of the report is organized in the following manner: Section I is a generalized description of the approach to marginal cost: its determinants, sources of variation and calculation; Section II consists of three illustrative case studies in which this methodology is applied; Section III is a computer algorithm with a user's guide for the computation of marginal costs and related processes. The principle purposes of the computer program package are to organize the data for convenient, low cost determination of marginal cost structure, and to provide a means for rapid testing of the importance of the various inputs to the final result. There follow three appendixes. Appendix A presents the results of a survey of manufacturers of equipment that may be useful in implementing marginal cost pricing. Appendix B is a consideration of experimental design for testing the hypothesis on which marginal cost pricing is premised. Appendix A is included because we have not seen the results of such a survey presented elsewhere except in anecdotal form, and Appendix B is included because several millions of public funds are being or are about to be spent on projects designed to test the efficacy of marginal cost pricing. Efficient design of such experiments is a very complicated matter, but one of great importance if such experiments are to prove worthwhile. Appendix C is a listing of the computer programs discussed in Section III. The listings are in Fortran V and are available from the National Technical Information Service.

In many respects, this project is the product of several years of interest and involvement in the controversial subject of electric rate structures, an experience we have shared with our friend and colleague, Edward Berlin. His continued participation in this project was precluded by his appointment to the New York Public Service Commission, but much of what is useful in these pages is an enduring mark of our association.

Ralph Turvey, presently with the International Labor Organization, collaborated with us at several important stages of this work, especially the Wisconsin case study. He directed the initial work in Wisconsin and provided early advice for the California case studies. Having set us on the right track, however, he returned to Europe and cannot be held responsible if we have strayed from it. Professor Turvey, whose range of interests and contributions in diverse fields confirms that economics is a discipline of broad applicability is not only the foremost English-speaking authority on our subject, but one of the finest teachers and patient friends it has been our pleasure to encounter. His earlier works (*Optimal Pricing and Investment in Electricity Supply* [London, England: George Allen and Urwin, Ltd., 1968] and *Economic Analysis and Public Enterprises* [London, England: George Allen and Urwin Ltd., 1971]) are classics in electricity pricing theory, practice and policy. We strongly recommend them to any serious student in this field.

Bill Press, presently director of planning and research for the state of California, was an important catalyst for this study and did much to facilitate its execution. Bruce Smith of the National Science Foundation encouraged us to persist with what then seemed endless red tape before we could get down to serious work, and we are glad now that he did. Vernita Aigner conducted the metering survey appended to this report, along with Nancy Sugden, who also did much of the administrative work; if we have avoided an editorial disaster, it is only her doing.

Dennis Aigner contributed his expertise in experimental design. His advice to the Federal Energy Administration on this subject is the first policy benefit of our collaboration on this study. Stan Hamre of the Wisconsin Office of Emergency Energy Assistance helped with the programming and description of the computer programs. This is his first work in this field but we suspect it will not be his last. We also have a debt of long standing to Donald N. De Salvia of Syracuse University and William Vickrey of Columbia University. Both contributed greatly to our understanding of the marginal cost structure of the electric power industry at a very early stage of our study.

Perhaps our greatest debt is owed to the three utilities that agreed to participate as our case studies. Homer Vick and James Miller of Wisconsin Power and Light Company, Ken Mellor and Dean Park of the Sacramento Municipal Utility District and Harrison Call of the Los Angeles Department of Water and Power greatly increased our understanding of the design, planning and operation of electric power systems. We made frequent and substantial demands on their time and energy. They were generous and we are grateful.

All of those named above, plus the Edison Electric Institute, Thomas J. Graff of the Environmental Defense Fund, Bridger Mitchell of the Rand Corporation, National Economic Research Associates, J.W. Wilson and Associates, and the Wisconsin Electric Power Company, provided very helpful comments on the draft manuscript.

Working for one author is bad enough, but Barb Feggestad had to contend with three of us. It would not have been possible to finish the draft manuscript without her help. Special thanks are also due Alice Wilcox, Jean Arnold and Jackie Forer, whose skill and patience enabled us to meet our publication deadline.

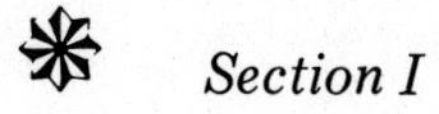

Section I

An Overview

Introduction

Within the past few years, the design of electricity rate structures has become a subject of considerable interest and controversy. A substantial part of this interest is evoked by proposals to price electricity according to the structure of marginal costs.* Simply put, marginal cost pricing means charging consumers a price that reflects the additional costs to the producer of an additional unit of consumption. The plainest contrast to marginal cost pricing is average cost pricing. To illustrate, if some units of electricity cost 2 cents to produce and others cost 8 cents, a marginal cost tariff would charge those amounts respectively; an average cost tariff would charge 5 cents for each of them.

While most electricity tariffs in the U.S. are based on some variant of average cost pricing, few are as simple as our illustration. Neither would a marginal cost tariff often be as simple as two numbers. In fact, there are several factors that influence the cost of electricity supply, and the objective in efficient tariff design is to reflect at least the most important of these in prices. For example, electricity can be supplied more cheaply at high voltage than at low voltage. Similarly, consumer demands for electricity at certain times may require producers to expand production facilities in order to sustain an adequate level of reserve capacity, whereas at other times consumer demands can readily be met with existing plants that would otherwise be idle.

*See W. Huntington, "The Rapid Emergence of Marginal Cost Pricing in the Regulation of Electric Utility Rate Structures," 69 *Boston University Law Review* 689 (November 1975).

Other determinants of the cost structure are power factor* and the location and density of consumers. Needless to say, the complete structure of marginal costs can be fairly complicated. Still, the totality of electricity consumers can be divided into a few large groups for which the conditions of electricity supply (i.e., the marginal costs) are similar, so that for any one such group there may be only one or two things (and perhaps three in the case of the very largest consumers) on which the price of a unit of electricity consumption will depend.**

A certain simplicity in tariff design is important because the purpose of marginal cost pricing is to signal to consumers what the effect on the producer is of a change in consumer behavior. Consumers then decide whether it is worth it to them to pay the price (or reap the savings) equivalent to what it will cost (or save) the producer to supply a bit more (or less) electricity. That is not to say that consumers *care* what the producers' costs are; rather that the decisions of consumers and producers are brought into harmony by the basic symmetry of prices and costs.

Notwithstanding the relatively recent interest in marginal cost pricing for electricity in the U.S. and the decades of discussion of the subject in professional economic journals, there have been few practical applications of marginal cost analysis for electric utilities. The most interesting work in this regard has been limited to efforts of the Electricité de France (the French national utility), the Central Electricity Generating Board and the electricity industry in Great Britain and several studies conducted under the auspices of the International Bank for Reconstruction and Development. The intention here, therefore, is to provide a descriptive methodology, with examples, of how a marginal cost analysis might be done.

In the analysis that follows we will be looking at various aspects of the electricity production process. The main features of an electricity production system are generation capacity, transmission and distribution capacity, and fuel or a substitute such as water or even sunlight. Together these comprise the system that produces a flow of energy measured in kilowatt hours (KWH). From the point of view of the consumer, kilowatt hours are usually a homogeneous commodity. One is like another, whether it is used for light, heat or work.

**Power factor* is defined as the ratio of the amount of power, measured in kilowatts, used by a consuming electric facility to the apparent power measured in kilovolt-amperes (KVA).

**"Time of day pricing" and "peak load pricing" are frequently used as more descriptive surrogates for the more technically correct term "marginal cost pricing." While the timing and the frequency of peaks and valleys of consumer demand *usually* correspond to variation in marginal cost, that need not be true in every case. For that reason, we prefer the latter expression.

From the point of view of the utility (and its more sophisticated consumers), however, kilowatt hours are quite heterogeneous. What makes them different is the subject of our inquiry.

Throughout, our concern will be the economic effect on the entire power production system of consumer demands for electricity. If consumer demand increases or decreases, what happens to total system costs? Demand for additional KWH may require greater outlays in one portion of the system and simultaneously lesser outlays in another portion, or demand for additional KWH may entail both a capital outlay and a savings in operating expenses. The effect on system costs is the combination of all these. Thus, it is incorrect to draw a categorical equivalence between capacity and capital costs on the one hand, and energy and operating costs on the other. It is a frequently encountered accounting convention that capital costs are "capacity costs" and operating costs are "energy costs." In fact, additional capacity may sometimes be acquired without additional capital outlays, and additional energy sometimes does require capital investment. The point to remember is that marginal cost is measured and determined by a change in *system* costs. The cost accounting conventions that have evolved in regulatory proceedings on utility tariff design are not always appropriate to the task at hand here.

Similarly, the conventional forms of electricity tariffs themselves are, at least initially, disregarded here. We do not begin by asking the marginal cost of serving, say, commercial versus residential consumers. Such a distinction might later turn out to be appropriate, but we do not suppose it in advance. Rather, the perspective here is that of the system planner who faces choices and makes decisions about the long-term configuration of the system, and that of the system dispatcher whose responsibility is the day-to-day operation of the system. The question will be: If consumers choose to take more or less electricity, what will happen to the costs of maintaining and operating the utility system?

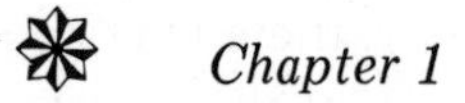

Marginal Generation Capacity Costs

The cost components of electricity supply are most conveniently broken down into capacity costs (which is further divided into generation, transmission and distribution capacity), energy (or running) costs and customer costs. In this overview section, we consider the determination of the marginal cost of each component. This chapter considers marginal generation costs.

By definition, marginal cost is the change in total cost that results from a change in output. In this section, "output" means kilowatts of generating capacity, and marginal generating capacity cost is measured by the effect on system cost of a change in the level of capacity available to produce energy. The "change" is as between possible alternative scenarios for the future. In the simplest case, the alternatives are simply to provide extra kilowatts in the future or not to provide them. In the case of electricity supply, however, the situation is more complex, and usually involves a choice between providing additional kilowatts in, say, 1986 or providing the same number of additional kilowatts at an earlier time, say 1985. In short, system planners usually adjust for expected changes in consumer demand by bringing forward or deferring various plants that make up a generation capacity expansion plan. An example of such a plan for the Wisconsin–Upper Michigan System, a joint planning group of utilities, is provided in Table 4–1.

Marginal generation capacity costs will often be measured by the costs of accelerating this plan if demand is increasing or, correspondingly, deferring it if demand is decreasing. Note that, conceptually, accelerating and deferring the expansion plan are simply opposite sides of the same coin. In practice, however, there may be important differences in the cost consequences of the two alternatives, so which we take as the appropriate measure of marginal costs should depend on the characteristics of each particular case. In addition, lest it is not already clear, this business of moving an expansion plan forward or back amounts to the same thing as adding or removing small increments of capacity (usually in the form of gas turbines) from the construction schedule. We will return to this subject again, but it is helpful to note the equivalence at the outset.

Marginal generating capacity cost and its calculation is best looked at from the perspective of the electric utility system planner, the individual charged with seeing to it that adequate capacity will be available to meet consumer demand in the future. The planner's analysis begins with the forecast of future demand. The forecast usually spans the next ten to twenty years, with expected demand estimated at intervals of six months to one year. A plan or schedule of new plants is then drawn up in which the objective is to provide the least-cost combination of peaking, intermediate and baseload units that will satisfy the expected increment to demand (with an allowance for reserves). If the forecast changes significantly, the expansion plan will also be changed. However, since some elements of the plan can only be altered at considerable cost, if at all, certain elements of the plan will be more or less fixed for the next few years.

The planner will take into consideration not only the extent of present commitments, but also the size and duration of the anticipated increment to demand, the composition of the existing generating plant, the availability of surplus power elsewhere in the region, the cost and availability of capital, legal and regulatory constraints, and some other considerations. Subject to these constraints, the planner will have a number of options. Marginal generating capacity cost will be determined according to which alternatives or combination of alternatives the utility actually chooses. Let us turn then to the various ways in which a utility may provide additional capacity.

Perhaps most often, anticipated additional demand is met by taking the existing plan for expansion and accelerating it. A plant previously planned to come on line in 1983 is brought forward to 1982. In some cases, a whole sequence of plant additions is adjusted. Sometimes, however, the present expansion plant is not adjustable. This might be due to long lead times and already tight construction schedules. Or, a particular plant may be a joint venture with other utilities that will not acquiesce in the acceleration. In such cases, relatively small gas turbines may simply be inserted into the planning schedule, or short-term purchase agreements may be negotiated with other utilities.

If the source of the additional capacity is power purchased from other utilities, marginal cost estimation is straightforward; it is the price paid for the new capacity. Just what that price is may require careful reading of a complex contract, but that, in any event, is the place to look. Note, too, that we are talking about *prospective* contract terms, not the terms of existing contracts unless they are subject to renegotiation and modification. If a utility is already bound to a contract to buy or sell power in the future, it is in a position analogous to having already built a power plant. A utility is, for the most part, stuck with its past decisions and commitments, and the relevant question pertains to the area in which it still has some flexibility. Thus, the question will be not, What is the price of kilowatts under our contract with the neighboring utility? but, If we agree to buy more (or less) what will it cost (or save)? The answer to this last question will also be the answer to, What is the marginal cost of additional generating capacity?

Alternatively, small adjustments to the expansion plan are frequently made by adding gas turbine peaking units. Here, too, marginal cost determination is relatively straightforward in that gas turbine units do not ordinarily produce fuel savings, as is the case with larger, more efficient intermediate and baseload units. Marginal generating capacity cost is simply the annuitized cost of the unit itself (plus an allowance for losses and reserves as discussed below).

FUEL SAVINGS

Addition of the larger coal-fired and nuclear plants is another common case and presents a more complicated problem. The reason is that larger, more efficient generating plants have two distinct effects on a utility system. First, they provide more capacity. Second, by virtue of greater efficiency they displace some of the existing plants in the dispatching schedule.* In fact, they may be so much more efficient that it would be economical to build them even if the capacity were not needed! What we observe then is a situation where the capital costs of the unit are greater than the net addition to system costs. In other words, there may be a capital outlay of $100 million,

*It is not always true that new capacity is more efficient than existing capacity. Overall efficiency is not simply a matter of economy in fuel-to-electricity conversion, but depends also on the emissions constraints under which plants operate. Stricter emissions standards may reduce or eliminate an operating efficiency edge that newer plants would otherwise have.

but the net effect on system costs, which, to repeat, is how we measure marginal cost, is less than $100 million because of fuel savings.

To grasp the source of these fuel savings, imagine a system operating at some point in the future. The system consists of a multitude of generating units, each of which has different running costs. The system is optimally dispatched so that the less efficient units are run as little as possible and the more efficient units are run all out. If the expansion plan is brought forward a year, some of these more expensive units can either be run even less or perhaps retired early. Generation from the newer, more efficient plant displaces them. This is a savings that must be shown as a credit against the cost of the newer plant.

The amount of the savings will vary depending on the particular type of plant that is being brought forward. If it is a gas turbine peaking unit, for example, there are little or no fuel savings to be realized. Gas turbine plants, while cheap to build, are expensive to run and are thus unlikely to displace anything in the dispatching schedule. Nuclear plants, on the other hand, are extremely expensive to build, but run quite economically. In fact, nuclear (and other baseload) plants, while expensive to build, are often selected because they produce very considerable savings in system running costs—enough to offset the higher initial costs of construction.

In practice, calculating these fuel savings will be a relatively simple matter. A computer simulation of the future operation of the system is run twice; once with the new plant on line in year n (as originally planned), and again with the plant on line in year $n-1$ (as accelerated). The period of the simulation is, ideally, the entire lifespan of the new plant; but in any case, at least long enough to exhaust any significant difference between total fuel costs as a result of having the new plant on line a year sooner. The amount of the fuel savings to be deducted from capital costs is the present value of the difference in total fuel costs over the life of the plant. In the event that simulation programs are not available for a particular system, a respectable estimate of fuel savings can usually be made by the system dispatchers based simply on their intimate knowledge of how that system works and is planned to work in the future. Two additional points to note are that (1) new baseload plants frequently have a "teething period" in which they are broken in, and the number of kilowatt hours presumably increases during each of the years of a plant's life, which is why the analysis must span more than one year; and (2) exactly the same analysis applies if the accelerated expansion plan includes a reshuffling of more than one plant (as in the Wisconsin case study below.)

BRINGING PLANTS FORWARD*

Given an engineering estimate of the capital cost (in current dollars) of building a new plant, the question is, What will it cost to have that added capacity a year sooner? Further, since the increment to capacity is caused by an increment to consumer demand that is taken to be permanent, we must also allow for replacing the new plant when it wears out a year earlier than otherwise. For example, if the capital cost of an additional KW of generating capacity were $100, and a plant lasted twenty years, then as demand increased a utility would expect to make a $100 per KW investment every twenty years (disregarding inflation). It is this entire series of plants that is brought forward.

What we wish to determine, therefore, is the value of the *difference* between two time series, one commencing in year n and another commending in year $n-1$. If the plant never wore out, the difference would be determined by the applicable interest rate, i,** times the capital cost. But since the investment deteriorates with time and use, matters are more complex. The cost of moving the first plant forward a year is i, the interest rate, times the capital investment. The cost of moving its replacement forward some years hence, say from the twenty-first year to the twentieth, and the next from the forty-first to the fortieth, and so forth, is a cost of i in each of these years. What we need, therefore, is the present value of that series. So the i's for each twenty years must be discounted to yield a present value. The diagram below, in which the vertical lines represent plant construction and replacement, illustrates the discounted time series to be evaluated, using twenty year intervals and capital costs of $100 per KW.

*Accelerating or decelerating the construction schedule is a useful approach to marginal cost estimation. It is *not* the *only* approach. See also pages 62 and 73.

**The choice of an appropriate interest or discount rate is as difficult and debated a matter in principle as it is in practice, filling many scholarly journals with debates on the fine points of the argument. In the simplest terms, for pragmatic reasons the rate selected should reflect the "opportunity cost of capital." This is estimated by taking a weighted average of all debt and after corporate income tax return to equity for society as a whole. Such a measure is believed by some to reflect society's valuation of current consumption versus future returns of production benefits. In addition, the interest rate may also be appropriately varied depending on expectations about future technological progress as discussed below. For a general discussion, see Krutilla and Cicchetti, "Evaluating Benefits of Environmental Resources with Special Application to the Hells Canyon," 12 *Natural Resources Journal* 1 (1972).

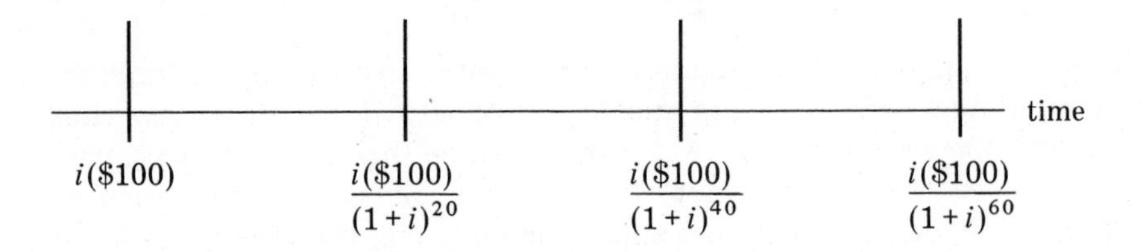

Carried on continuously, the present value of the series may be expressed as $\frac{i}{1 - 1/(1+i)^n}$, where n is the interval between replacements. The reader may be relieved to realize that this expression is the commonplace "capital recovery factor," i.e., the same expression that is used to amortize or annualize a lump sum amount (or to calculate a monthly mortgage payment, for example). Thus if we were to have an interest rate of 10 percent, a plant life of thirty years, and a capital cost of $100 per KW, we have $10.61. To this we must add an additional year's operation and maintenance expenses and deduct the fuel savings, if any, discussed above.

Sometimes, an adjustment to the generation expansion plan will involve not a single plant with a single set of capital and other fixed costs, but more than one plant. In our Wisconsin case study, for example, accelerating the system expansion plan would entail moving two plants forward. For a variety of reasons peculiar to that system, these two plants are linked in the construction schedule; that is, they are regarded as a single plant and are physically interdependent. One would not be accelerated or deferred without the other. The difficulty arises from the fact that the two plants have different annual costs and different effects on system fuel costs ($12.13 per KW per year in one case and $25.16 in the other). Since neither by itself is an accurate reflection of marginal generating capacity cost (i.e., neither plant is inframarginal), the most appropriate measure of marginal cost appears to be a weighted average of the two, which comes to $21.24 in this case.

Although it happened in the Wisconsin case study that the two plants considered were linked in the planning schedule, such will not always be the case. For example, acceleration of the expansion plan may consist of adding a gas turbine unit in year n as well as bringing forward an intermediate load plant from year $n + 6$ to year $n + 5$. In such a case, it would be appropriate to discount the annual costs per KW of the intermediate load plant from year $n + 5$ to year n before taking the weighted average.

RESERVE MARGINS

Having determined the marginal cost at the generator of producing an extra KW, this figure must then be adjusted upward to allow for the desired reserve margin, which reflects the valuation a utility or its regulator places on avoiding disruptions of service. If the reserve margin is 15 percent, and the computed cost of new capacity is $10.61 per KW per year, the cost of additional capacity including reserves is $10.61 × (1 + 15%) = $12.20.*

LOSS MULTIPLIERS

It is important to note that the cost of an additional KW of capacity at the point of generation will not equal the cost at the point of consumption because there are losses in transmitting and distributing power to less-than-generation voltages. Marginal generation costs per KW must be grossed up by loss multipliers appropriate to the various levels of service voltage—a matter deferred for consideration in Chapter 2.

There is an additional approach to marginal cost estimation that will be appropriate more frequently than one might suppose, i.e., in cases where there will be no effective capacity constraint for the next several years. The size of the generating plant planned for the future may be quite large relative to present capacity needs. Demand is expected eventually to grow into the size of the additional plant, but for a number of years in the meantime, there will be substantial excess capacity. Moreover, the plant may not be "accelerable," so it does not make much sense to talk in terms of bringing the plant forward a year.**

The usual way in which a utility accommodates this kind of "lumpiness" in the supply schedule is to sell off the extra capacity during those years in which it is available. If demand in the potential seller's area were to increase so that less capacity than otherwise is available for sale, then the cost of the selling utility (and its consumers) is the

*Similarly, if the analyst knew the actual economic losses associated with shortages, this number could be multiplied by the probability of an outage. This is an approach suggested by the French school of tariff design. However, in practice the number is usually determined by inference, and differences in types of supply shortages with respect to length, location and severity will make estimation mostly subjective. Accordingly, we recommend using the reserve margin as an implicit weight that can be used to reflect the extra capacity that is built to avoid or minimize the risk of shortages.

**Our second case study, Sacramento Municipal Utility District (SMUD), is such a case.

revenue foregone on the averted sale. Marginal cost, therefore, is the selling price of excess capacity.

The second case in which interutility selling price is the appropriate measure of marginal cost is that in which there are no plans at all to increase capacity, the existing plant being more than adequate for future needs. Again, the cost of holding excess capacity is the net revenue foregone on sales of this excess capacity. Sales are forgone only when local uses require the available capacity, and therefore the cost of additional local demand is the net revenue that would have been received had the local demand not existed.

During the course of this study, we encountered strong resistance on the part of one of the cooperating utilities, SMUD, to the use of contract prices for the sale of surplus capacity and energy as the measure of marginal cost. The objection, as we understand it, is not that marginal costs have been misconstrued, but that the use of marginal costs *thus determined* is inappropriate for designing tariffs. For example, suppose Utility A can at a given time produce KWH at a marginal cost of 3 mills, and can sell that energy at 10 mills to Utility B. Obviously, Utility A will not sell to its own customers at more than 10 mills, so the question is, At what price should it sell to its own customers if not at the 10 mills we suggest? Whatever intuitive conclusion appeals to the reader, it is clear that Utility A's customers will as a group have to contribute more to the total annual revenue requirement than would have been the case had the sales been made at the full market price. A revenue requirement that might have been reduced by 10 mills will instead be reduced by a lesser amount. This is a subsidy that increases in proportion to energy consumption* and that is extracted from those whose pattern of consumption tends to make possible a lesser total cost operation. To us, at least, this is dubious policy that presents problems that vanish if *individual* consumers are offered electricity at prices that equal the opportunity costs to *all consumers*—namely, 10 mills.

TECHNOLOGICAL CHANGE

One further factor might be considered. The supposition above, namely the taking of a constant annuity, implies the absence of technological progress in generating equipment. That is, it suggests that no less costly way will be found to provide generating capacity in the future than is presently available. Those familiar with the history of

*Not total energy consumption, but consumption during the hours when the 10 mill market price prevailed.

technological progress in the electric utility industry will recognize that, at least until recently, that would have been a serious error.

For the present and foreseeable future, even disregarding the effect of inflation, the prognosis for technological innovations leading to lesser generating capacity cost is speculative. There are plausible arguments both ways. No doubt there will continue to be some improvements in generating technology.

On the other hand, the real cost of generating capacity (i.e., the cost net of purely inflationary effects) appears to be rising. These are countervailing, but not strictly offsetting, considerations. In the absence of better information, our preference is to assume constant costs. In any case, note that the expectation of future technological progress tends to increase marginal costs in the present, since by building today we in effect pass up the opportunity to exploit tomorrow's technological innovations and incorporate them in plant design. For the analyst who wants to include technological progress as a factor, we suggest a simple rule: raise the discount rate used in the calculation of marginal cost by the expected annual improvement in technology.

THE DISTINCTION BETWEEN PEAK AND OFF-PEAK SERVICE

Additional capacity is not ordinarily needed to meet demand for additional energy (KWH) at all times. Demand for additional KWH at some (often most) hours can be met with existing capacity. It is necessary to determine those hours during the year when an additional KWH demand would require additional capacity. We have already determined what it will cost *if* it occurs, and we must now determine the value of the mathematical expectation that it will occur during a particular hour.

Conceptually, this expression is p($ per KW); that is, the probability that additional demand will require additional capacity during a particular hour, times the cost per KW if it does occur. It will be obvious that the ps (the probabilities) are not equal for all hours of the year.

Sometimes, for example late at night, there is considerable spare generating capacity and the ps are extremely low—virtually zero. Other times, hot summer afternoons, for example, there may be very little extra capacity and the ps are relatively high. In addition, no one knows precisely when peak demands will occur (i.e., which particular hour of the 8,760 hours in a year will be *the* peak), so peak days, of themselves are of little interest. What we wish to identify are the hours of the year during which additional demands are *likely* to require new capacity and how this likelihood varies between different groups of hours, in order to calculate marginal costs that can be used as a basis for designing tariffs. How sophisticated we make the analysis depends largely on how much complexity we will tolerate in tariffs.

Before we consider even the simplest case, we must be clear on what we are trying to define. The hours of system maximum demand, alone, are not a sufficient criterion for defining the peak period since capacity availability also varies during the year due to maintenance requirements, other outages and seasonal deratings. What is relevant, therefore, is *demand in relation to supply*. Since both demand and supply change during the day and year, we are interested in the margin between them. Low probabilities are associated with wide margins and high probabilities with low margins. For example, a utility with a distinct summer peak may have twice as much demand during the summer as during the winter, but because of interutility connections, seasonal variation in hydro availability, winter maintenance outages, and so forth, may also have half as much capacity available in winter as in summer. Thus, on a seasonal basis, the demand-supply margin may be the same throughout the year.

When loss of load probability studies are available, as they usually are, these can be examined to determine the value of the ps, with some grouping and simplification perhaps being required. In a simple case, we may find that there is no reasonable expectation of demand exceeding available capacity during any of the year's nighttime hours, weekends or during the daytime hours of any nonsummer month. However, as to the remaining hours (summer days), additional capacity costs might be incurred because demand may exceed supply during any one of them. If there were 700 such summer daytime hours, the cost per KW can be converted to a KWH basis by taking $\frac{1}{700}$ times the cost of an additional KW of capacity to estimate the cost of any KWH during the peak period.

It must be stressed that we are speaking of available capacity, for it is quite possible during times of scheduled maintenance or obligatory contract sales to other utilities that even a relatively low demand will approach the capacity limits of the available system. A rule of thumb that may be appropriate when loss of load probability studies are not available, or for some reason are inappropriate to the task, is that the peak period should be identified as those hours during which demand would exceed available capacity less reserves in the absence of new capacity. The idea here is that system capacity is increased in order to maintain the reserve margin, so demand that threatens to penetrate this margin is what makes additional capacity necessary and defines the peak period.

It is evident that the process of identifying the hours in which additional demand will require additional capacity is not precise, not least because we are concerned with future demand and supply patterns, not historical ones. What will be appropriate in any particular case will depend on the characteristics of the given system. "Shoulder" periods may be identified during which there is a significant but lower value of expected additional cost than for "peak" periods. Likewise, there may be almost no hours when the probability should be treated as absolutely zero.

The three case studies provide illustrations of how the marginal costs of generating capacity are imputed to various time periods in various cases.

FINAL QUALIFICATIONS

Much has been said in this chapter to qualify the application of a rather simple notion. On the one hand, the extra capacity cost of producing an additional unit of energy (a KWH) is very small, or zero, if excess capacity is expected to be available. On the other hand, if an increase in demand is likely to cause the utility to speed up its construction plan, the extra cost is equal to the additional costs required to move part of the system plan forward, less any savings that such an action will cause. Similarly, if a reduction of demand results in net savings from postponing or slowing down a system plan, this can also be considered as the marginal cost of generating capacity.

Some changes in demand may be structural in nature. The taste of an entire service area may change, for instance, with the introduction of air conditioning. All customers who reach a certain level of income and/or who move into the area may be expected to demand this service. Under such circumstances, the marginal cost of such a structural change in demand may mean that a whole series of demand-induced forward shifts in construction plans may result. Under such circumstances, the calculation of the marginal cost relative to a "moving target," that is, the upward sloping expected consumption schedule, may more accurately indicate marginal cost than a calculation done with respect to a single point in time and level of demand. Such a calculation will produce a larger measure of marginal generating cost because a successive "chain reaction" of plant acceleration all discounted to the first such change will be included.

In the computer package discussed below, this very special case is offered as an option. It must not be confused with the case in which more than one plant is physically interdependently related to another. In the calculation of marginal operation costs, such plants are treated as one, since the system planner considers them this way. This latter option is also a case considered in the computer package.

Marginal generation capacity costs are calculated in current dollars. It is important to note, albeit perhaps obvious, that if inflated dollars are used to estimate the costs of plants "moved" forward or "delayed" some years into the future, these must be discounted to the present before calculating marginal costs. A related matter is that the calculation of marginal costs for a change in present demand that will not affect costs for the utility to some point in the future is actually calculated by considering the change in the future time stream of costs. This estimate is made using current construction costs and an assumption that large capital investments can be disaggregated into pieces as small as a KW. To those who prefer using actual future capital costs in the amount and at the point they will be incurred, we repeat our earlier statement that these be discounted to the present to remove the effects of anticipated inflation. If the rate of interest used to discount future costs exceeds the expected inflation rate, this approach will lead to lower marginal generating cost estimates, and vice versa.

❋ *Chapter 2*

Marginal Transmission and Distribution Costs

The purpose of this chapter is to describe the process by which one determines the marginal costs of transmitting and distributing electric power. What are the additional costs of transmission and distribution that are caused by additional demand of consumers for electric power? The answer depends on the cost of physical facilities for transmission and distribution, on the stage or voltage level at which the consumer ties in with the system, and on when the additional demand occurs.

A transmission and distribution system can be considered as an integrated single network that brings energy from generators to consumers. Other than the distinctions made below, these two portions of the service system do not need to be separated. As a system, it consists basically of a network of lines and of transformers and switching stations. Lines are classified according to the voltage at which they carry power, and transformers by the volt-amperage by which power is reduced from one voltage level to another. Figure 2–1 is a simplified sketch of such a network. Note that there are transformer substations each of the voltage levels.

The size and capacity of the network depends largely on the maximum KW it will be required to transport at an instant in time. However, the maximum demand on one part of the network does not necessarily coincide with the maximum demand on other parts. For example, system maximum demand may be expected to occur during summer afternoons, perhaps due to a large air conditioning load. There may, however, be some part of the transmission and distribution system where the maximum consumer demand occurs during

Figure 2–1. A Simple Schematic of a Utility Transmission and Distribution Network

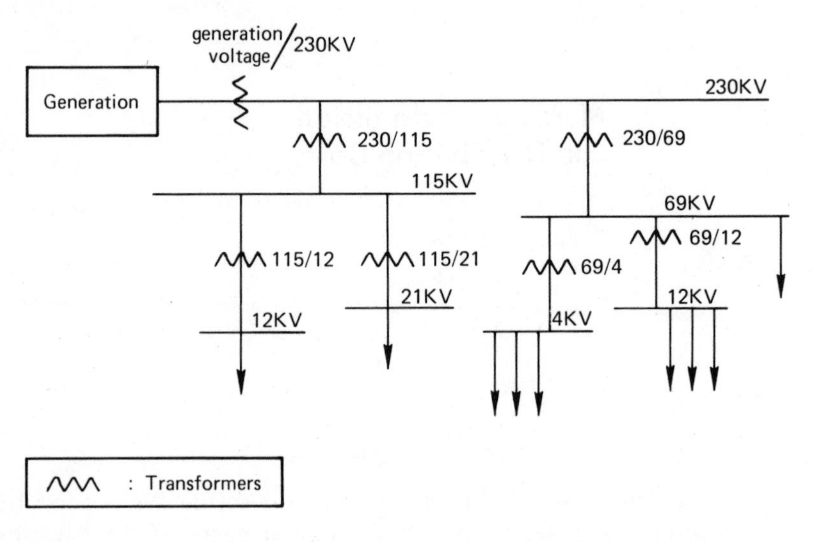

winter evenings, perhaps due to a concentration of space heating on that segment of the network. Overall, transmission and distribution maximum demands tend to coincide with the maximum generating demand, but in any particular case it is desirable to inquire into the matter of diversity in maximum demand on various parts of the transmission and distribution network.

LOSS MULTIPLIERS

A KW of capacity drawn at a point downstream on the transmission and distribution network requires that more than one KW be produced upstream. The greater the distance and number of steps (voltage changes) traversed, the greater the loss in efficiency. The explanation lies in electrical line resistance and copper and iron losses in transformation. In brief, the farther downstream the consumer, the greater the cumulative losses from the point of generation upstream.

Losses in transmission and distribution affect not only marginal capacity costs, but also marginal energy costs. Since the treatment of losses is similar both in the case of capacity and of energy, both are considered here, although the application of energy loss multipliers is deferred until Chapter 3.

The basis for the distinction between losses as a determinant of capacity costs and as a determinant of energy costs is that losses are a variable function of, among other things, the level of load on the system at a given time. In the case of capacity, the concern is with an *expanding* transmission and distribution system that serves a given level of system maximum demand. The size of the transmission and distribution network, and the associated losses, will depend on the level of system maximum demand. For purposes of estimating capacity-related losses, we will be interested in the ratio of KW input to KW output at whatever level system maximum demand happens to be. However, with respect to energy-related losses, matters are different. There, we are concerned with the flow of energy through an *existing* system. The energy loss is a function of load—not a particular load such as system maximum demand, but whatever the load happens to be at the time the energy is drawn. The capacity-related losses are no longer relevant, since they are estimated only for a single load level that happens to occur only about once a year. Moreover, the purpose of the latter estimate was to gauge the effect on various components of system capacity—lines, transformers, generators, etc.—of consumers' maximum coincident demand. Energy losses, in contrast, are estimated for the purpose of accounting for the variable quantities of fuel that have to be consumed in order to supply energy at one time (and voltage level) in comparison to supplying it at another time.

AVERAGE LOSS MULTIPLIERS FOR CAPACITY

Average losses at system peak equal the ratio of KW input to KW output at each stage or voltage level. Thus, referring to the right hand side of Figure 2–1, the ratio $\frac{\text{KW input}}{\text{KW output}}$ can be computed from generation to high voltage (69 KV) consumers and to the high side of the 69/12 transformers. The loss multiplier for service to primary distribution customers (12 KV) equals the ratio of $\frac{\text{KW input}}{\text{KW output}}$ from the high side of the 69/12 transformers to 12 KV consumers and/or the high side of secondary distribution transformers, times the loss multiplier at the upstream stage. Similarly, the loss multiplier for secondary distribution equals the ratio of $\frac{\text{KW input}}{\text{KW output}}$ from the high side of the distribution transformers to low voltage consumers, times the multipliers at the two upstream stages. These figures can be conveniently arranged as in Table 2–1.

Table 2–1. Average Losses at Time of System Peak

	Simple	*Cumulative*
Stage 1	A_1	A_1
Stage 2	A_2	$A_1 \times A_2$
Stage 3	A_3	$A_1 \times A_2 \times A_3$

$$\text{Where } A_i = \frac{\text{KWH input}}{\text{KWH output}} \text{ at stage}_i$$

MARGINAL LOSS MULTIPLIERS FOR ENERGY

Marginal loss is the derivative of energy input with respect to output, $\frac{\text{d KWH input}}{\text{d KWH output}}$. Electrical energy loss is a function of current (I) and resistence (R) such that

$$\text{loss} \approx I^2 R$$

The value of the derivative of this function ($2IR$) thus depends on the level of demand, R being a constant. Accordingly, losses must be computed separately for peak and off-peak loads, and for each voltage stage of the network.

Table 2–1 can be expanded to include energy-related losses. For any particular system, Table 2–2 should have as many rows as there are voltage levels at which customers are served. For energy losses there should be as many cumulative loss columns as there are readily distinguishable periods of demand levels. For the purposes of using marginal costs to design tariffs the number of periods will correspond to the number of separately priced time periods.

The problems that arise in computing loss multipliers arise not from conceptual difficulties, since the basic relationship of losses, current and resistance are well known, but in deriving the multipliers from data that happens to be available in a particular case. The basic loss equation is

$$\text{loss} \approx I^2 R$$

More precisely, total losses are the sum of no load (iron) losses and $I^2 R$ (copper) losses. For simplicity, we employ the $I^2 R$ approximation to total losses.

Table 2–2. Capital and Energy Loss Multipliers

	Average Loss Multipliers for Capacity (Demand) at Time of System Peak $\frac{KWH\ input}{KWH\ output}$		*Marginal Multipliers for Energy* $\frac{d\ KWH\ input}{d\ KWH\ output}$			
			Peak Periods		*Other Times*	
	Simple	*Cumulative*	*Simple*	*Cumulative*	*Simple*	*Cumulative*
From generation to high voltage consumers and high side of distribution substations	a_1	a_1	b_1	b_1	c_1	c_1
From high side of distribution substations to primary voltage consumers and high side of line transformers	a_2	$a_1 \times a_2$	b_2	$b_1 \times b_2$	c_2	$c_1 \times c_2$
From high side of line transformers to low voltage consumers' meters	a_3	$a_1 \times a_2 \times a_3$	b_3	$b_1 \times b_2 \times b_3$	c_3	$c_1 \times c_2 \times c_3$
		Where: $a_i = \frac{KWH\ Input}{KWH\ Output}$ at $stage_i$		Where: $b_i = \frac{d\ KWH\ Input}{d\ KWH\ Output}$ at $stage_i$		Where: $c_i = \frac{d\ KWH\ Input}{d\ KWH\ Output}$ at $stage_i$

Most frequently, the loss measure that utility engineers have available is percent losses of $\frac{\text{loss}}{\text{load}}$. Before we describe the appropriate loss-to-load ratio required for capacity and energy loss multipliers, we should note that the loss multiplier for capacity is not $\frac{\text{loss}}{\text{load}}$, but $\frac{\text{KW input}}{\text{KW output}}$. A simple conversion, $1/(1 - \frac{\text{loss}}{\text{load}})$, which equals $\frac{\text{KW input}}{\text{KW output}}$, produces the desired result.

Recall that the average loss multiplier for demand is based on system peak demand, and that the marginal loss multipliers for energy are based on demand during peak and off-peak periods. The loss-to-load ratio, however, is based on the average total demand. Given the average total demand, we can estimate average losses at peak and marginal losses on and off peak from the I^2R relationship. To illustrate, let us suppose average total $\frac{\text{loss}}{\text{load}} = 0.011$, with an average load of 1100 MW. Since

$$\text{loss} \approx I^2R$$

where I is current or load and R is resistance, then,

$$R \approx \frac{\text{loss}}{I^2}$$

$$\approx \frac{\text{loss}}{I} \div I$$

We know that $\frac{\text{loss}}{I} = 0.011$, so that the constant $R = 0.00001$. By substituting system maximum demand, e.g., 1800 MW, for average demand, we can now estimate average losses at maximum demand as follows:

$$[\text{loss} \approx I^2R] \text{ yields } [\frac{\text{loss}}{I} \approx IR]$$

since $I = 1800$ MW and $R = 0.00001$

then $\frac{\text{loss}}{I} = 0.018$

This is converted to the average loss multiplier by simplifying $1/(1 - \frac{\text{loss}}{I})$:

$$1/(1 - 0.018) = 1.0183.$$

For energy, we need marginal losses, or $\frac{\text{d loss}}{\text{d load}}$. With loss $= I^2 R$, marginal loss $= 2IR$. Using the same values for I and R as used in the example above, the marginal loss multiplier on peak is $1/(1 - 2IR)$:

$$1/(1 - 2(1800)(0.00001)) = 1.0373.$$

If the load off peak were 800 MW, the energy loss multiplier would be 1.0163. The figures used to represent loads during peak and off-peak periods should be the weighted average load in each period.

One further observation may spare the reader some confusion in comparing average and marginal loss multipliers in practice. Logically, one expects the on-peak energy multiplier to be greater than the off-peak multiplier; and further expects the average multiplier for demand to be less than the marginal multiplier for energy on peak. In practice, the first observation will hold, but the second may not. The reason for this apparent anomaly is that the average multiplier for demand uses the actual system peak demand, the highest value of I; whereas the marginal multiplier for energy on peak uses a weighted average of the Is during the entire period. These calculations are presented in the case studies of Section II.

CALCULATING MARGINAL TRANSMISSION AND DISTRIBUTION CAPACITY COSTS

Recall that the objective is to calculate marginal costs and in the process to relate additional units of transmission and distribution capacity to demand at each voltage level. Due to the losses described above, the total demand perceived upstream at the point of generation will exceed the arithmetic sum of the demands at each voltage level of consumer demand. Demand forecasts are not always available by voltage level, and therefore, it may first be necessary to estimate these from the system maximum demand that is forecast. This can be accomplished by estimating the coincident maximum demand at each voltage level and dividing by the average cumulative multiplier for that voltage level.*

*Coincident maximum demand may be estimated by dividing annual KWH generation at each level by the product of approximate load factor for each stage of transmission and distribution times 8,760 hours per year.

To illustrate, suppose the following data is available:

Annual generation at voltage level$_i$	= 525600 MWH
Load factor at voltage level$_i$	= 60%
Cumulative average loss multiplier	= 1.05.

Then

Coincident maximum demand at voltage level$_i$ =
525600 MWH ÷ (8760 Hours × 0.60) = 100 MW
Demand at voltage level$_i$ = 100 MW ÷ 1.05 = 95.24.

A similar calculation is made for each voltage level of service.

The types of facilities serving each voltage level may be grouped according to the consumers they serve. For example:*

High voltage consumers	138 KV transmission line 69 KV transmission line transmission substations
Primary voltage consumers	The above, plus 12 KV distribution line distribution substations
Low voltage consumers	The above, plus line transformers

Likewise, MW demand can be expressed in terms of voltage levels, so that demand at the highest level is the sum of demand at the next lowest level plus losses, and so on to low voltage demand. In this manner, KW demand and transmission and distribution facilities are arranged in a comparable form.

There are two possible approaches to relating changes in demand at each voltage level to changes in the transmission and distribution system. One is to use the actual expansion plan (exclusive of replacements) for the period for which marginal costs are to be determined, say five to ten years, and take, for example, first differences between line miles or KVA of transformer capacity added, and additional KWs forecast. Thus, if the additional KW forecast at high voltage over the period is 100 megawatts, and the miles of additional 230

*The line voltages used are for illustration only. Each system will have its own configuration of lines and substations.

KV transmission line planned is thirty miles, then the MW demand at high voltage per line miles added is simply 3.3.

A similar calculation may be made for each type of line and transformer substation. One difficulty with this approach is that the estimated factors may be distorted because there are facilities that will have to be built, but that have not yet been planned.

A second approach is to rely on the factual historical data (perhaps together with the expansion plan for the next few years) and to do a simple linear regression of the form

$$\begin{matrix}\text{Total miles} \\ \text{(or KVA)} \\ \text{installed}\end{matrix} = a + b \begin{bmatrix}\text{KW demanded} \\ \text{at voltage level}_i\end{bmatrix}$$

The coefficient, b, of course, is the additional transmission and distribution capacity added per additional KW demanded. Any difference between this approach and the former should be explainable in terms of over or underbuilding of transmission and distribution in the recent past or expected in the near future. Ad hoc adjustments in any particular case may be appropriate and are recommended for the peculiarities of different systems. Both alternatives are included in the computer package presented in Section III.

With physical quantities known, it is possible to calculate marginal cost per KW of additional transmission and distribution facilities. First, capital cost per unit (mile or KVA) of each of the components of the network must be obtained. Next, the marginal capital cost of transmission and distribution per KW of increased demand must be converted to an annual basis. This is accomplished by taking the annuitized capital cost, plus annual operation and maintenance cost, and multiplying it by the miles (or KVA) per KW. These costs are then summed up for each of the components associated with a given stage of the transmission and distribution network, and multiplied by the cumulative demand loss multipliers, giving the marginal annual transmission and distribution cost per KW demanded at time of system peak at each supply voltage.

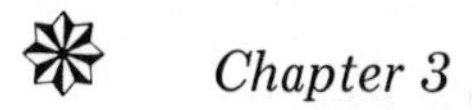

Chapter 3

Marginal Energy and Customer-Related Costs

MARGINAL ENERGY COSTS

The first two chapters were concerned with marginal capacity costs, or whether an increment of demand for energy (kilowatt hours) will require expansion of the existing plant generating capacity (kilowatts) and the transmission and distribution capacity that is shared with other consumers. In this chapter we are concerned with the cost of operating or running the existing plant a bit more (or less) to provide additional energy and with the related costs of adding a new customer. There are two principal determinants of system running costs: the level of load (demand) on the system at a particular time, and the voltage level at which the energy (KWH) is taken.

Load level is important because a utility system consists of a number of generators, each of which requires a different quantity of fuel input to produce a kilowatt hour of output. The ratio of heat input to energy output (the heat rate) may also vary for a particular unit, increasing as load increases. Running costs increase in a similar manner. System dispatchers schedule the various units in such a way as to minimize running cost at current load level. This practice is known as economy dispatch.

Total operating costs are minimized subject to the constraint of meeting a particular load that may develop. Mathematically, this problem is solved using a Lagrange multiplier, lambda (λ). Formally:

$$\text{Minimize } Z = F(EC) + \lambda(L_i - Q)$$

where

$$
\begin{aligned}
&\text{Total running cost} && = TRC = F(EC) \\
&\text{Energy cost} && = EC \\
&\text{Marginal energy costs} && = MEC = \frac{\partial TRC}{\partial Q} = F/(EC) \\
&\text{Output} && = Q \\
&\text{Load at a particular time}_i && = L_i \\
& & \lambda & = \text{Lagrange Multiplier}
\end{aligned}
$$

The necessary condition for cost minimization is:

$$\frac{\partial F(EC)}{\partial Q} - \lambda \qquad = 0$$

$$\therefore \text{ set marginal energy costs } = MEC = \lambda$$

There can be as many values for λ as there are hours in the year. Hence, we will be interested not in all the possible values of λ, but in the pattern of systematic variation in λ over seasonal and diurnal cycles. What, for example, is the level of λ during summer days, summer nights, weekends, springtime, etc.? It won't be the same during all summer daytime hours, but the variance among those hours will usually be less than between those hours and, for example, winter nighttime hours. Thus, the first criterion for grouping the 8,760 values of λ is that the variance within cells should be less than the variance between cells. In addition, the hourly groupings should be contiguous,* if this information is to be used for designing tariffs.

The number of periods (groups) should also be reduced to a manageable number. The value chosen to represent each period should be the weighted average of all the values of λ during the period. In practice, the weights should be based upon the loads expected during each hour in a period.

CUSTOMER COSTS

A further component of the costs of operating a utility system is, for the vast bulk of consumers, not specifically related to KW or KWH

*That is, summer evenings from 7 P.M. to 8 P.M. and winter mornings from 5 A.M. to 6 A.M. is not a sensible grouping even if λ is exactly the same during these sets of hours.

usage. This is the so-called customer cost or the cost of patching or connecting a consumer into the utility network, which includes sundry billing and metering costs, the cost of the service drop (the wire from the distribution line to the point of consumption) and to some extent the line transformers on the distribution system. For the most part these costs are not marginal in the same sense as the generation, transmission, distribution and running costs discussed above. They do not vary "a bit more or less" according to the level and quantity of electricity demand. They are either incurred in a lump sum or not at all, depending upon the use of the individual consumer.

The appropriate treatment of customer-related costs is to charge a periodic rental rate adequate to fund the replacement of the equipment when it has outlived its usefulness. The difficulty is in drawing the line between customer-related costs and KW-related distribution capacity costs that are collective in nature. The capacity of the distribution system depends both on the aggregate level of load on each section of the distribution network and on the number of consumers on it. Our judgment is that this complexity is best dealt with on an ad hoc basis, but we note in any event that it is a problem of minimal importance in fact.

One thing to note is that the capacity-related and customer-related distribution cost *cannot* be easily separated merely by doing a multiple regression of the form:

$$\begin{bmatrix}\text{KVA transformer}\\ \text{capacity}\end{bmatrix} = a + b_1 \begin{bmatrix}\text{number of}\\ \text{customers}\end{bmatrix} + b_2 \begin{bmatrix}\text{demand at}\\ \text{distribution}\end{bmatrix}$$

If this relationship were known, b could be used to measure the extra costs of adding customers. However, the number of customers and the demand on the distribution system are themselves very highly correlated. Chances are that the mechanics of the estimating procedure will provide a perfectly arbitrary ascription of the KVA capacity to the two causal variables.*

Customer-specific determinations should be made where there is a clear distinction among heterogeneous customers in a single category, for instance, urban and rural residential consumers or industrial users of widely different characteristics. In fact, customer-related maximum demand may be important for high voltage customers.

*See, W.J. Baumol, *Economic Theory and Operations Analysis* (Englewood Cliffs, N.J.: Prentice Hall, 1965), p. 220.

SUMMARIZING MARGINAL COST BY TIME OF USE

In this chapter two additional cost components were introduced. One is entirely individual customer related and does not vary by time of use. The main purpose of the three chapters that are included in this first section is to analyze and measure the costs that vary on the basis of time of use for the collective or shared system of generation, transmission and distribution.

In Chapters 1 and 2, marginal capital costs per KW of customer demand were described based upon the effect of an increase (or decrease) in demand that would cause an acceleration (or postponement) in the system's construction schedule. For those hours of the year in which we can be reasonably certain that increases in demand will not affect the generating and/or transmission and distribution capacity construction schedule, a zero marginal capacity cost is appropriate. In others for which the probability of demand exceeding supply (thus producing a loss of load) is significantly high, the marginal capacity costs are calculated as described in Chapters 1 and 2.

The final step in analyzing costs is most important, because it leads to the realization that a kilowatt hour of energy is not a homogeneous commodity from the cost standpoint. There are several ways of incorporating this simple fact into the final calculation that must be made before tariffs can be designed. Each of the 8,760 hours in the year is not equally likely to have a level of demand that exceeds the available supply of generating and transmission capacity. We are talking here about demand relative to an expected or anticipated supply, not the nameplate generating capacity of the system in question. Scheduled plant maintenance and repair, of which one has prior knowledge, will mean that certain units are unavailable during certain times of the year. These schedules must be brought into the calculation of the probability of a loss of load; that is, the probability of demand approaching or exceeding the capacity of the electric utility.

In determining the time pattern of this probability of demand exceeding supply, it is important to assign the cost of expanding the electric utility system (that is, the marginal cost of generation, transmission and distribution capacity) to those hours for which the likelihood of demand exceeding supply is great relative to those hours of the year for which it is small. For some electric utility systems there might be some intermediate or shoulder periods for which the probability is not quite as great as for those hours that we might identify as peak as opposed to those hours that we might identify as off peak.

There is no simple generalization that can be made in advance to fit every individual electric utility system in the United States.

If we have done all of the above, we can calculate for those hours that are similar in terms of high, low and intermediate probability of loss of load the cost of running the system expected to operate during those periods and assign the marginal generating and transmission costs to peak hours on either a kilowatt or kilowatt hour basis (depending upon whether we want to perform an additional step of division). In addition, we can determine transmission costs at different voltage levels and customer costs further down the distribution system.

These steps are demonstrated in the case studies discussed in the following section and additional subtleties are raised. By way of summary, the eleven following logical steps outline the marginal cost of electricity analysis presented in Section I.

1. Calculate the marginal generating cost per KW of demand;
2. Apply loss multipliers to convert to a per KW basis at each voltage level;
3. Divide by the number of hours in a year in which loss of load probabilities are high to convert marginal generating costs to an energy or KWH basis for each type of time period analyzed (e.g., peak, off-peak, intermediate or summer weekday, etc.);
4. If intermediate periods are utilized, divide the number of such hours by their probability of loss of load first and separate from the peak period in step 3;
5. Calculate the marginal transmission and distribution capacity costs for each voltage level;
6. Apply loss multipliers to each preceding step in the supply system in order to determine the full cost per KW of transmission and distribution at each voltage level;
7. Repeat step 3 to convert KW costs to an energy or KWH basis for each type of time period analyzed, (e.g., peak, off-peak, intermediate or summer weekday, etc.);
8. Calculate the weighted average marginal energy cost for each type of time period analyzed;
9. Apply marginal energy loss multipliers to calculate marginal energy cost at each voltage level;
10. Sum the marginal generation, transmission and distribution, and energy costs per KWH at each voltage level and for each time period;
11. To complete the cost analysis, calculate any remaining segregated customer-related cost for the typical customer served at each voltage level.

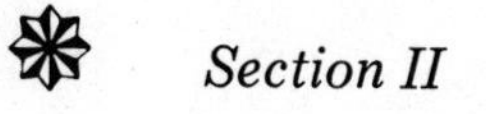

Section II

Case Studies

Introduction

In order to demonstrate the application of the methodology described in Section I, three case studies of utilities are presented in this section. A data base was established for each utility, and marginal costs were determined from these data. For each case study, the computational process is described in detail. It varies somewhat among the three utilities depending on the characteristics of the particular system.

Each of the cases purports to be a realistic representation of the marginal cost structure of that system. However, some of the data were necessarily only the "best guess" of the true value of certain variables. In many cases, such informed estimates are regularly employed by utility engineers in planning and operating a system, the cost of better information not being worth the price. In all the cases studied here, the utility engineers agreed that their estimates were reasonable and that the likely magnitude of error would not significantly distort the analysis. Needless to say, a still better picture of each system's marginal cost structure could be obtained by the expenditure of more time and effort, but for most purposes, even a rough guess is better than implicitly setting some values equal to zero. Moreover, the reader who has the facilities to use the computer program MARGINALCOST (described in Section III) will have the capability to input a range of values for most variables so that sensitivity analysis is readily available. In other words, the analyst will be able to determine whether finding out the precise value is worth the effort, based upon the sensitivity of the final result to a reasonable range of values.

Whether such an investment would be worthwhile is a matter of judgment, and *none of the utilities can give assurance that the quality of the estimated data is adequate for certain purposes, for example, the design of tariffs actually to be placed in effect by regulatory commissions in the service area served by them.*

A NOTE ON GENERALIZABILITY

Marginal cost is a tool for the analysis of choices. The choices available to particular utilities, of course, vary and so, therefore, do their marginal costs. In selecting these three utilities, we have tried to pick systems that, among them, show the most important differences in the sort of choices that various utilities may face.

Wisconsin Power and Light Company (WP&L), for example, is largely a stream generation system. Its additional capacity will be a combination of coal-fired and nuclear units. Sacramento Municipal Utility District (SMUD), on the other hand, derives a substantial share of its energy from hydro sources. Its additional capacity will be nuclear. Los Angeles Department of Water and Power (LADWP) is also a mixed hydro-thermal system, but it plans no additional capacity at all—at least not for avoiding capacity shortages. The effective constraint there is total energy availability; not peak load capacity, of which it has a significant excess.

WP&L is probably the case most representative of the U.S. electric power industry. The analytical approach that applies to it will apply to most U.S. electric utilities. SMUD is included because it represents systems with significant hydro availability, which, although declining relatively as a generation source, still account for about 15 percent of total U.S. electricity generation. Moreover, natural gas, which accounts for an additional 20 percent total U.S. generation, is conceptually very much like water due to the shortage of natural gas nationally. In contrast to both of these systems, LADWP is in some respects a special case. Its binding constraint is energy, not capacity. At present, there are few U.S. utilities in this circumstance. In the future, there may be many more, particularly if the optimistic projections for marginal cost pricing and its consequences come to pass.

In short, these case studies represent:

- A fairly typical case;
- A less typical but still significant case;
- A case that is somewhat atypical, but that may be more common in the future.

By analogizing from one or a combination of these systems, other analysts should be able to treat any electric utility system in the U.S.

The results of the case studies are summarized in the tables at the end of each study: WP&L, Table 4–10, page 60; SMUD, Table 5–5, page 73; and LADWP, Table 6–8, page 85.

 *Chapter 4*

Case Study A: Wisconsin Power and Light Company

WP&L is an investor-owned electric and gas utility that serves a 16,000 square mile area in southern and central Wisconsin. It is part of the Wisconsin–Upper Michigan System (WUMS), a joint planning and dispatching entity comprising a number of the utilities in the area. Its type distribution of customers is as follows:

Residential	185,398
Rural	48,225
Commercial	28,596
Industrial	635
Other	905
REA Cooperative	26
Municipal Utilities	32
	263,817

Electricity sales in 1974 were approximately 5,154 gigawatt hours, with a peak load of 1,015 MW in summer and 992 MW in winter. Installed generating capacity was 1,260 MW, of which 221.5 MW were gas and oil-fired peaking units. WP&L electricity generation by type of plant in 1974 was as follows:

Hydro	4.2	percent
Coal	71.9	”
Natural Gas	0.1	”
Oil	4.8	”
(continued)		
Nuclear	13.3	percent
Purchases	5.8	”
	100.0	”

In the ten years prior to 1973, maximum annual demand had been growing at a rate of 8.8 percent per year. For the next ten years, the expected growth rate is 6.4 percent. The current forecast for 1985 maximum demand is 2,015 MW, which is 12 percent less than was forecast a year ago for 1985.

Of the three case studies in this section, WP&L is the utility most representative of the industry as a whole. It is a medium-sized utility, having a diverse mix of customers and generating equipment, and growing (in terms of MW demand) at a rate close to the national average. For these reasons we have used it for the computer applications of Section III.

MARGINAL GENERATION CAPACITY COSTS

On average, the Wisconsin–Upper Michigan System (WUMS), of which WP&L is a member, plans to have an installed capacity in each year that is 15 percent higher than the projected peak. The plans for WUMS and its four member utilities are summarized in Table 4–1.

A large change in the projected demand would, if time were available, be likely to affect the expansion plan. Indeed, the present one differs from that promulgated two years ago, when predictions of demand were much higher (and when expectations about fuel and utility prices were very different). The difference is shown in Table 4–2, which indicates clearly that a large reshuffling of the plan was involved. For smaller postulated changes in projected demands, however, in circumstances uncomplicated by energy crises, it can be assumed that if sufficient time were available, the expansion plan would be modified more simply by merely postponing or bringing forward some of the additions to capacity. Such additions, as Table 4–1 makes clear, are planned to come on line in most future years.

Consider, for example, an increase in the demand projected for 1980. It might be met by increased purchases from outside WUMS, but the cost of these cannot be foreseen. Thus, we will suppose that it would be met by bringing forward by one year a 400 MW intermediate load range (ILR) unit previously scheduled to come on line in 1981, and we now investigate the cost consequences of this for the system. (An exactly parallel approach could be applied to investigating the cost consequences of the case—possibly a more realistic one—where a reduction in projected 1981 demand resulted in a postponement by one year.)

Table 4–3 shows that the capital cost of such an ILR unit would be about $\$(388 + 10) \times 400{,}000 = \$159{,}200{,}000$, and that its annual fixed operation and maintenance cost would be about $680,000. These, like *all* cost figures presented, are in 1975 prices.

The extra cost from bringing forward the unit by one year is approximately equal to the product of the capital recovery factor and its capital cost (i.e., its annuitized capital cost), plus one year's fixed operation and maintenance cost. Taking a thirty year life and a 10 percent interest rate, the extra cost would be

$$(0.10608 \times \$159{,}200{,}000) + \$680{,}000 = \$17{,}567{,}816.$$

Against this there is a saving to be considered. We are seeking the net effect on total system costs of adding to capacity in 1980 without subtracting from it in other years. Since the unit will have a variable cost of $7.70 per MWH sent out while existing units already on the system will have costs of up to $15, one of the net effects of bringing it forward will be to run it to displace the more expensive MWHs from these other units earlier than otherwise.

The preferred method used to obtain the present value of the extra fuel savings thus obtained by bringing forward the timing of new units is to use a simulation model of the operation of the system over a period of years. The model is run twice, the only difference in the inputs being the date at which a particular new unit is assumed to come on line. The effect of the change on total system fuel and variable operation and maintenance costs can then be obtained from the two sets of outputs of the model.

Table 4–4, which gives the results of some simulation runs, shows the present worth in 1980 of the resulting savings to be $7,505,000. The subtraction of these from the net extra cost calculated above gives a net addition to system costs of $17,567,816 – $7,505,000 = $10,062,816. Dividing by 400 MW gives the net cost as $25.16 per KW.

Table 4–4 also shows the fuel savings from bringing forward Koshkonong Number 1 from 1983 to 1982 as $7,050,000. Its capital cost per KW being $476 + $10.56, its fixed 0 and M per KW being $1.50, and its capacity being 172 MW*, the resulting 1982 cost of an extra KW is

$$0.10608 \times (476 + 10.56) + 1.5 - \frac{7{,}050{,}000}{172{,}000} = \$12.13.$$

The fact that this is less than half the figure for an ILR oil-fired plant shows that the expansion plan is nonoptimal based upon the wisdom

*WP&L's share of the unit.

Table 4–1. Capacity-Demand Data (1975–1985)

	Wisconsin Power and Light				*Wisconsin Public Service Corporation*				*Madison Gas and Electric*			
Year	*CAP*	*DEM*	*% RES*	*ADD*	*CAP*	*DEM*	*% RES*	*ADD*	*CAP*	*DEM*	*% RES*	*ADD*
1975	1400	1090	28.4	207 COL 1	1287	910	41.4	205 COL 1	491	360	36.4	115 COL 1
1976	1400	1190	17.6		1287	956	34.6		491	375	30.9	
1977	1400	1320	6.1		1287	1026	25.4		491	400	22.8	
1978	1680	1425	17.9	280 COL 2	1417	1099	28.9	130 COL 2	608	423	43.7	117 COL 2 →
1979	1651	1540	7.2	−29 Retire EDG 1&2	1417	1168	21.3		608	446	36.3	
1980	1651	1660	0.5		1417	1254	13.0		608	470	29.4	
1981	2051	1790	14.6	400 ILR	1717	1337	28.4	300 ILR	608	496	22.6	
1982	2051	1930	6.3		1717	1422	20.8		608	523	16.3	
1983	2223	2060	7.9	172 KOS 1	1861	1508	23.4	144 KOS 1	665	551	20.7	57 KOS 1
1984	2395	2180	9.9	172 KOS 2	2005	1591	26.0	144 KOS 2	722	581	24.3	57 KOS 2
1985	2395	2260	6.0		2005	1685	19.0		722	613	17.8	

Continued Below →

Abbreviations:
CAP capacity
DEM demand
% RES percent reserves
ADD capacity added (or retired)

Power plants:
COL 1&2 Columbia 1&2
EDG 1&2 Edgewater 1&2
ILR Intermediate Load Range Unit (unspecified)
KOS 1&2 Koshkonong 1&2
Oak C Oak Creek
GT Gas Turbine (unspecified)
PP 1&2 Pleasant Prairie
LS Lake Side

Table 4–1. continued

	Pool				Wisconsin Electric Power Company				Wisconsin Upper Michigan System			
Year	*CAP*	*DEM*	*% RES*	*ADD*	*CAP*	*DEM*	*% RES*	*ADD*	*CAP*	*DEM*	*% RES*	*ADD*
1975	3178	2360	34.7	527 COL 1	3603	3168	13.7		6781	5528	22.7	527 COL 1
1976	3178	2521	26.1		3653	3287	11.1	50 Oak C	6831	5808	17.6	50 Oak C
1977	3178	2746	15.7		3653	3440	6.2		6831	6186	10.4	
1978	3705	2947	25.7	527 COL 2	3873	3593	1.7	220 GT	7578	6540	15.9	527 220 COL 2 GT
1979	3676	3154	16.6	−27 Retire EDG 1&2	4093	3752	9.1	220 GT	7769	6906	12.5	220 GT EDG 1&2
1980	3676	3384	8.6		4673	3913	19.4	580 PP 1	8349	7297	14.4	580 PP I
1981	4376	3623	20.8	700 2 ILRs	4673	4080	14.5		9049	7703	17.5	700 2 ILRs
1982	4376	3875	12.9		4968	4250	23.6	−285 LS 580 PP 2	9344	8125	15.0	580 −285 PP II LS
1983	4749	4119	15.3	373 KOSH 1	5545	4424	31.8	527 KOS 1 50 GT	10294	8543	20.5	900 KOS 1 50 GT
1984	5122	4352	17.7	373 KOSH 2	6072	4608	38.0	527 KOS 2	11194	8960	24.9	900 KOS 2
1985	5122	4558	12.4		6072	4799	32.5		11194	9357	19.6	

Table 4–2. Wisconsin–Upper Michigan System

1973–1975 Generation Expansion Plan

Year	*Demand Difference (in MWs)*	*Additions*
1975	433	+ 50 Oak Creek
1976	577	– 50 Oak Creek +500 turbine
1977	646	+500 turbine
1978	767	–220 turbine
1979	898	+500 coal –220 turbine
1980	1,047	+300 coal –580 Pleasant Prairie +350 turbine
1981	1,201	+950 nuclear –700 Intermediate Load Range Unit
1982	1,391	+950 nuclear –580 Pleasant Prairie 2
1983	1,614	+350 turbine +300 coal –900 nuclear

Source: Wisconsin Power and Light Company

of hindsight. In other words, the emphasis on nuclear capacity would have been far greater had the rise in oil prices beginning in 1973 been foreseen. But what marginal costs would have been with a better crystal ball is irrelevant. Since the ILR unit and the nuclear unit are linked in the planning schedule and would be brought forward together in response to an increase in demand, the marginal cost of a KW of capacity in the first half of the 1980s is a weighted average of the marginal cost of each plant, the weights being their relative contributions to new capacity. That is,

$$\$25.16 \times \frac{400}{572} + \$12.13 \times \frac{172}{572} = \$21.24.$$

Again, this figure represents marginal costs with nonoptimal plant mix, but with pool economies due to joint planning and construc-

Table 4–3. Generation Cost *(1975 Prices)*

	Generation
Nuclear	Capital cost including: Step-up $476 KW + 345 KV transmission $10.56 KW Variable O and M .05¢ KWH Annual fixed O and M $1.5 KW
Intermediate Load Range	Capital cost including: Step-up and scrubber $388 KW + transmission $10 KW Fuel Cost .69¢ KWH Variable O and M $1.7 KW
Base load coal	Capital cost including: Step-up and scrubber $410 KW + transmission $10 KW Fuel cost .60¢ KWH Variable O and M .065¢ KWH Annual fixed O and M $1.65 KW
Turbine	Capital cost including: Step-up $125 KW + transmission $1 KW Fuel cost (oil) 3.6¢ KWH Variable O and M .48¢ KWH Annual fixed O and M 10¢ KWH

Source: Wisconsin Power and Light Company

tion. If we had known when the commitment to the ILR unit was made that fossil fuels prices would leap, and if nuclear plants did not require extended lead times for construction, marginal costs would be different: much closer to $12.13 than to $21.24.*

Gas turbine costs have not been used in these calculations because there are none in WP&L's plan that could be brought forward. The prices at which it could buy or sell firm power to other utilities in various years, on the other hand, will affect marginal costs, but cannot be predicted.

WP&L's planned reserve margin for 1980–1985 as shown in Table 4–1 is only 7.37 percent, as compared with 18.65 percent for WUMS as a whole. Presumably, if these plans are realized, WP&L will have to pay other members of the pool something for the reserve capacity with which they provide WP&L. If so, the cost to WP&L of providing for an extra KW of demand will exceed 1.073 × $21.14.** For the sake of illustration, we suppose the cost to be the same as if it provided itself with a 15 percent margin, i.e., 1.15 × $21.24 = $24.43 per KW. Thus, we have a reasonable measure of the marginal annual generation cost per KW of demand.

*"For all sad words of tongue or pen, the saddest are these: 'It might have been.' " It applies as equally to marginal cost analysis as to other affairs.

**That is, the average marginal cost of reserve capacity.

Table 4–4. Fuel Savings Based on Simulation *(Total System Running Costs (thousands)*

	Year	*Base Case*	*Change Timing*	*Difference*	*Present Value Difference in 1980 $*	*Present Value Difference* in 1975 $*
Move ILR unit from 1981 to 1980						
	1980	$122,538	$115,710	$6,827	$ 6,827	$5,102
	1981	135,195	131,661	3,534	3,213	2,401
	1982	155,588	155,584	4	3	2
					$10,043	$7,505
Move Koshkonong #1 from 1983 to 1982						
	1982	$155,588	$148,851	$6,737	$ 6,737	$4,480
	1983	174,976	170,726	4,250	3,864	2,570
	1984	189,786	189,786	0	0	0
	1985	208,090	208,090	0	0	0
					$10,601	$7,050

*Netting out 6 percent annual inflation assumed in the simulation.
Source: Wisconsin Power and Light Company.

In order to determine the cost of an additional KW demand at the various service voltages, loss multipliers must be applied. These are shown in Table 4–5. Since we assume that generation capacity expands in equal proportions with transmission and distribution capacity expands in equal proportions with transmission and distribution capacity, it is average loss multipliers that are appropriate. Using the figures in Table 4–5,

1.051 × \$24.43 = \$25.68 for high voltage supply,

1.102 × \$24.43 = \$26.92 for primary voltage supply,

1.151 × \$24.43 = \$28.12 for secondary voltage supply.

Extra capacity is required to match an increase in demand when, without it, the reserve margin would be reduced by the demand increase, thus increasing the risk of failure of supply. Furthermore, it is not known in advance when the peak of adjusted demand in relation to available capacity will occur. Thus, it makes sense to regard the costs just calculated as costs that have a certain unit probability of arising in *all* the hours in the year when this condition could occur. These, as noted in Table 4–5, are included in the period from 8 A.M. to 10 P.M. on weekdays other than holidays, totaling 3,500 hours per year. (These may not all be equally likely to be the peak hour for demand in relation to capacity; the peak thus defined is perhaps more likely to occur in summer than in winter. Nonetheless, for simplicity, this complication will be ignored.) Hence, the mathematical expectation of marginal generating capacity cost per KWH during the 3,500 hours is \$25.68/3,500 = 0.734¢ for high voltage supply. For primary voltage supply it is 0.769¢, and for secondary voltage supply it is 0.803¢.

The calculation of an equal mathematical expectation of marginal cost of a KW for all the 3,500 hours may involve an oversimplification. The argument has been that:

- The net reserve margin for WUMS is relatively constant over the whole year;
- The loss of load probability is proportional to the reserve margin;
- The working of WUMS is such as to equalize the loss of load probability for the constituent utilities.

However, the third of these points is a bit crude. Suppose that the first two are correct, but that WP&L has a higher winter margin while the rest have a higher summer margin. On these assumptions, any loss

Table 4–5. Loss Multipliers: Wisconsin Power and Light

	Average Multiplier for Demand at Time of System Peak†		*Marginal Multiplier for Energy*†			
			*Daytime Weekdays**		*Other Times*	
Stage	*Simple*	*Cumulative*	*Simple*	*Cumulative*	*Simple*	*Cumulative*
From generation (net) to high side of distributor SS and HV consumers	1.051	1.051	1.036	1.036	1.031	1.031
From high side distributor SS to high side of line transformers and primary voltage consumers	1.049	1.103	1.037	1.074	1.032	1.064
From high side line transformers to LV consumers' meters	1.044	1.151	1.033	1.110	1.029	1.095

†An average multiplier is KWH input to a stage of the transmission and distribution system per KWH output from it. A marginal multiplier is the derivative of KWH input with respect to KWH output.

*From 8 A.M. to 10 P.M., five weekdays per week, less ten holidays, thus including 3,500 hours each year.

Source: Wisconsin Power and Light Company.

of load that does occur is more likely to be borne by WP&L consumers if it happens in the summer and less likely if it happens in winter. But this does not introduce any seasonal variation in marginal costs. An increase in demand *anywhere* in WUMS will either require more capacity or will increase the probability of loss of load *somewhere* in the system. In either case, this is a marginal cost, so that any variations in its geographical incidence create no seasonal variations in marginal costs in any one of the participants in WUMS.

MARGINAL TRANSMISSION AND DISTRIBUTION COSTS

The expansion of transmission and distribution capacity is related to the growth of peak demand at each voltage level. The demand at each voltage level is the demand of consumers served at that level plus the loss multiplier times the demand at the next lowest voltage level. For 1969 the coincident maximum demand at each voltage level was as follows:

Demand at secondary voltage	366 MW
Demand from primary voltage customers	187 MW
Demand from 34.5/69 KV voltage customers	113 MW

With demand of secondary voltage customers at time of system peak equal to 366 MW, plus 187 MW demand from primary voltage customers, the total demand on the primary system was (366 × 1.044) + 187 MW = 569 MW. Likewise, the demand at high voltage was (569 × 1.049) + 113 MW = 710 MW. These figures were obtained by estimating annual KWH consumption for the main consumer classes broken down by voltage level and applying guesstimated load factors to each, thus relating consumption to their demand at time of system peak instead of to their own maximum demand.

Using the figures in Table 4–6, it is now possible to calculate the following regressions to determine the physical relationship between a change in facilities and a change in demand or the inverse of the marginal physical products:

138 KV pole miles = 471.93 + .00031 (KW Demand at 69/34.5 KV)
$R^2 = 0.86$

69 KV pole miles = 881.57 + .00058 (KW Demand at 69/34.5 KV)
$R^2 = 0.79$

Table 4–6. Transmission and Distribution Capacity and Demands at Time of System Peak

	1969	1970	1971	1972	1973	1974	1975	1976	1977
138 KV pole miles	644	720	740	766	766	773	800	800	857
69 KV pole miles	1,388	1,219	1,356	1,359	1,408	1,466	1,519	1,549	1,600
34.5 pole miles	725	796	808	739	643	616	—	—	—
12.4 KV pole miles	14,776	14,997	15,233	15,474	15,721	15,932	16,100	16,300	16,500
MVA Trans. SS	1,213	1,246	1,361	1,528	1,415	1,640	2,000	2,000	2,000
MVA Dist. SS	935	1,254	1,313	1,246	1,313	1,338	1,385	1,485	1,577
MVA line trans.	1,338	1,437	1,547	1,666	1,821	1,995	2,160	2,325	2,590
No. line trans.	78,143	81,029	83,067	86,819	90,687	94,596	98,300	102,000	105,700
Demand at low voltage, MW	366	401	427	457	500	480	547	610	670
Demand of PV consumers	187	175	204	234	260	255	244	256	297
Demand at primary voltage, MW	569	594	650	711	782	756	815	893	996
Demand of HV consumers	113	121	130	142	162	173	182	195	211
Demand at 69 and 34.5 KV, MW	710	744	812	888	982	966	1,037	1,132	1,256
Sys. Max. Dem., MW	747	782	853	934	1,032	1,015	1,090	1,190	1,320

Source: Wisconsin Power and Light Company

Note that in principle the amount of "generation-related" 138/69 KV line should have been omitted, the regression only taking into account the "load-related" mileage, since the former is properly included along with generation costs:

MVA transmission SS = 31569.3 + 1.66 (MW Demand at 69/34.5 KV)
$R^2 = 0.83$

Multiplying the three slope coefficients with the relevant unit costs from Table 4–7 and adding

$$\begin{bmatrix} (0.00031 \times \$6590 \text{ for 138 KV line}) \\ + (0.00058 \times \$4553 \text{ for 69 KV line}) \\ + (1.66 \times \$1.77 \text{ for substations}) \end{bmatrix} = \$7.62$$

gives the marginal annual cost per KW of high voltage transmission capacity. In fact, this estimate is probably high (by about 4 percent), since it fails to account for diversity among the peaks on various parts of the transmission network. This could be accounted for either by dividing $7.62 by the diversity factor, or by using noncoincident maximum demands in the regression equations. For present purposes, we will assume the diversity factor is 1.0 and proceed.

For the primary system, the following regressions are derived from the data in Table 4–6:

KVA distribution SS = 68729 + 1.13 (KW demand at primary voltage)
$R^2 = 0.769$

12.4 KV pole miles = 12545 + 0.00416 (KW demand at primary voltage)
$R^2 = 0.947$

For low voltage, the estimated regression equation is:

KVA line transformers = − 212878 + 4.21 (KW demand at low voltage)
$R^2 = 0.965$

The large negative intercept and the implied low utilization ratio make 4.21 an implausible coefficient for marginal cost. The most likely source of bias in the estimate is that the number of line transformers added reflects both the additional load of existing customers and the increment to load from adding new customers. The latter is properly related to customer costs, not to distribution capacity costs, as a function of added demand for KW. The bias is at least partially

Table 4–7. Transmission and Distribution Cost *(1975 Prices)*

Item	*Unit*	*Capital Cost*	*Annualized Equivalent*	*O and M*	*Annual Cost*
138 KV line	mile	$60,000	$6,365	$225	$6,590
69 KV line	mile	$40,000	$4,243	$310	$4,553
12.4 KV line	mile	$ 9,725	$1,032	$292	$1,324
Line capacitors	per KW demand	$ 1.60	$0.17	0	$0.17
Transmission SS	KVA	$13.83	$1.47	$0.30	$1.77
Distribution SS	KVA	$15.84	$1.68	$0.40	$2.08
Line transformer	KVA	$27.38	$2.90	$0.20	$3.10

Notes:

1. Line costs are weighted averages of overhead and underground, different conductor sizes, single and double circuit.
2. A typical transmission substation is 47 MVA. Typical distribution substations are 20 MVA (138/12.4 KV) and 12 MVA (69/12.4 KV) costing $1,250 and $16.67 per KVA respectively; the figure of $15.84 is a weighted average, as is that for line transformers.
3. Since 34.5 KV pole miles has decreased since 1971, it has been assumed that future load growth will not be met by any further extensions. To the extent that some of the increase of 69 KV line miles has been achieved by conversion of 34.5 KV line, the cost per mile of the 69 KV line should be an average of the cost of new construction and of conversion.
4. The annual equivalent over thirty years of $1 at 10 percent is $0.1061.

Source: Wisconsin Power and Light Company.

offset by our exclusion of low voltage distribution line, some of which is load-related, but the bulk of which is customer-related. Having no figures for line miles, we accept 4.21 as a compromise for total load-related distribution. This will do for illustration, but for other purposes, further inquiry may be necessary.

Again applying slope coefficients and the cost figures per mile and per KVA shown in Table 4–7:

$$\left[\begin{array}{l} (1.13 \times \$2.08 \text{ for distribution SS}) \\ + \ (0.00416 \times \$1324 \text{ for 12.4 KV line}) \\ + \ (\$0.17 \text{ for line capacitors}) \end{array}\right] = \$8.028 \text{ at primary voltage}$$

and,

$$(4.21 \times \$3.10 \text{ for line transformers}) = \$13.05 \text{ at secondary voltage.}$$

Using the demand loss multipliers and the marginal annual cost per KW at time of system peak at each supply voltage level, we can now obtain the marginal annual distribution and transmission cost of a KW demanded at time of system peak by existing secondary voltage consumers as:

$$\$13.05 + (1.044 \times 8.028) + (1.044 \times 1.049 \times \$7.62) = \$29.78$$

Similarly, for primary voltage consumers, the marginal cost is:

$$\$8.028 + (1.049 \times \$7.62) = \$16.02$$

For high voltage consumers it is simply $7.62.

Unavailable data and limitation on time precluded certain refinements that might have been made in the above analysis. The most important refinements relate to the separation of transmission and distribution cost from customer costs, and diversity between system peak demand and peaks on distribution radials. For 12.4 KV line, for line transformers and for (the unknown) low voltage line one would expect the coefficients to be much higher per KW of additional demand caused by new low voltage consumers than from increased demand caused by existing consumers. A procedure to allow for this and to bring in low voltage line costs would be as follows:

- From a random sample of work orders estimate the average 12.4 KV line length, low voltage line length, service line length and line transformer KVA installed per new low voltage consumer.

- Multiply by unit costs and add meter cost to obtain the average cost per new consumer.
- Multiply the average 12.4 KV line length and line transformer KVA per new consumer by the cumulative total number of new consumers in each year since 1968 and subtract these figures from the total line lengths and KVA given in Table 4–6.
- Estimate the average demand per new consumer in his first year, multiply by the cumulative total number of new consumers in each year since 1968 and subtract these figures from the total low voltage demands.
- Estimated 12.4 KV line and line transformer reinforcement can then be regressed upon the estimated growth in the load of existing consumers.

It is also desirable to recognize that reinforcement expenditure that consists of increasing capacity per pole per mile (i.e., of additional circuits or of replacing conductors with larger sizes) has been neglected. Allowance for this would lower marginal costs.

Further, to the extent that peak demands upon the local distribution system significantly exceed the corresponding demands at the time of total system peak (a matter which there has been no time to investigate) the above analysis of marginal costs is excessively simple. The total capacity of line transformers is related to the diversified maximum demand of the few consumers served by each. Hence, their costs, and consequently marginal line transformer cost, are related to the consumer's demand at the time a customer and his or her neighbors are consuming most heavily. A comparable point obviously applies to 12.4 KV lines and distribution transformers (and indeed to line capacitors).

The result of all this is that the single figure of marginal annual cost per KW ought in principle to be replaced by three:

- Marginal transmission cost per KW of demand at time of total system peak;
- Marginal distribution substation, capacitor and primary circuit cost per KW of demand at time of local distribution peak;
- Marginal line transformer cost per KW of demand of the low voltage consumer at time of after-diversity peak of him and his neighbors.

One final note is important in this regard. The magnitude of the last two items, though not the times to which they relate, can be ascertained by an alternative approach. For example, if, on average, line transformers' maximum demands amount to 60 percent of their rated capacities, if the power factor is 0.9, and if the secondary line loss multiplier is 1.02, then on average each extra KW of low voltage consumers' demand at time of their group peak will, over a period of years require $1.02 \times \frac{1}{0.9} \times \frac{1}{0.6} = 1.89$ extra KVA of line transformer capacity. This approach could also be applied in analyzing the second of the three marginal cost components listed above.

MARGINAL ENERGY COSTS

The time pattern of marginal energy costs as anticipated in 1975 is set out in Table 4–8. It is not possible at present to produce a similar table for the early 1980s. The main difference would probably be that gas will then be unavailable during the valley and summer months, making daytime costs differ less between seasons than at present.

Although the marginal energy cost may change from each hour to the next, it is possible to group the 8,760 hours of the year into the twenty-four more or less homogeneous subsets shown in Table 4–8. Each subset differs in respect to plant availability, load levels or gas availability from the other subsets. The particular grouping used reflects the experience of the dispatcher and is in fact a version of the grouping used in the simulation model of the WP&L system. The subsets with the highest costs are hours when turbines are running; in 1974 this was the case for around 2,000 hours.

Further examination of the figures shows that a consolidation into only four subsets of hours is also possible. This is shown in Table 4–9. The costs shown are hourly weighted averages of those on page 00, though KWH-weighted averages are preferable. If, in the future, gas becomes unavailable throughout the year, requiring the use of oil for peaking plant more frequently, the summer and valley weekdays might be combined with the winter weekdays to form a single subset.

As with the estimation of the extra fuel savings from bringing forward new units, so here too, the simulation model of the system could be used to produce forward estimates of these marginal costs in a more sophisticated way. But the broad pattern revealed by the present figures certainly holds good for the next year or two. However, spot purchases of coal have a fairly large effect on these costs when they become necessary, and the price paid in such purchases is difficult to foresee.

The marginal energy costs given in Table 4–9 must also be multiplied by the marginal loss multipliers for energy that are given in

Table 4–8. 1975 Production Energy Costs

	Daytime (8:00 A.M.–10:00 P.M.)		Nighttime (10:00 P.M.–8:00 A.M.)	
Period	*Number of Hours*	*Incremental Energy Cost (¢/KWH)*	*Number of Hours*	*Incremental Energy Cost (¢/KWH)*
Summer				
Monday	196	1.75	140	0.90
Weekday	826	1.70	590	0.90
Saturday	210	1.30	150	0.70
Sunday, Holiday	238	1.28	170	0.60
Winter				
Monday	294	2.70	210	0.90
Weekday	1,120	2.10	800	0.90
Saturday	308	1.30	220	0.70
Sunday, Holiday	406	1.15	290	0.60
Valley				
Monday	182	1.75	130	1.10
Weekday	896	1.70	640	1.10
Saturday	210	1.30	150	1.00
Sunday, Holiday	224	1.28	160	1.00
Total Hours	5,110		3,650	

Notes:

1. Assumes 1976 load and capacity conditions.
2. Use 1975 replacement fuel costs.
3. Assumes gas availability for summer period.
4. Definition of periods:
   Summer: June, July, August, first half September.
   Winter: November, December, January, February, March.
   Valley: April, May, October, second half September.
5. Costs represent total fuel and variable O & M costs for the generating unit most likely to serve an increment of additional energy during each of the twenty-four operating periods. Incremental hourly costs were not available.
6. The costs during the daytime valley period are similar to the costs in the daytime summer period due mainly to scheduled outages of baseload equipment. Thus the same gas turbine units would be used for peak shaving in both periods.
7. The high cost in the daytime winter period is due to the unavailability of gas, requiring the use of oil.

Table 4–9. 1975 Production Energy Costs *(Weighted for Selected Periods)*

Period	*Number of Hours*	*Cost (¢/KWH)*
Peak		
Winter weekdays from 8:00 A.M. to 10:00 P.M. from November to March	1,414	2.220
Summer and valley weekdays from 8:00 A.M. to 10:00 P.M. April to October	2,100	1.710
	3,514	
Off Peak		
Saturday, Sunday and Holiday from 8:00 A.M. to 10:00 P.M.	1,596	1.260
Nighttime from 10:00 P.M. to 8:00 A.M. throughout the year	3,650	0.894
	5,246	

Table 4–5 to obtain the marginal costs of energy delivered at the various voltage levels as follows:

Voltage Level	*Winter Weekdays*	*Summer and Valley Weekdays*	*Weekends and Holidays*	*Nighttime*
69/34.5	2.300	1.772	1.299	0.922
Primary	2.384	1.837	1.341	0.951
Secondary	2.464	1.898	1.380	0.979

The various components of marginal costs per KW and per KWH may now be summarized and summed; and these are shown in Table 4–10. This completes the first case study analysis of marginal cost.

Table 4–10. Summary of WP&L Marginal Costs *(1975 Dollars)*

Consumers	Capacity: KW at Annual System (Day) Peak		Capacity: KWH During Peak Period*	Energy: KWH Winter** Weekdays	Energy: KWH Summer and** Valley Weekdays	Energy: KWH Weekends and Holidays	Energy: KWH Nighttime
	$		¢	¢	¢	¢	¢
69/34.5 KV	25.68 gen. 7.62 dist. 33.28	OR	0.951	2.300 (3.251	1.772 (2.723)	1.299	0.926
Primary Voltage	26.92 gen. 16.02 dist. 42.94	OR	1.227	2.384 (3.611)	1.837 (3.164)	1.341	0.951
Low Voltage	28.12 gen. 29.78 57.90	OR	1.655	2.464 (4.118)	1.898 (3.552)	1.380	0.979

*As defined in Table 4–9.

**Numbers shown in parenthesis equal the marginal capacity costs shown in Column 2 plus the marginal energy costs shown above.

 *Chapter 5*

Case Study B: Sacramento Municipal Utility District

SMUD is a municipally owned generating system that serves the area around Sacramento, California, via its own transmission and distribution system. SMUD is interconnected with the Pacific Gas and Electric Company (PG&E) for joint dispatch. SMUD's 1974 energy sales were distributed as follows:

Residential	1,903,800	MW	46.1%
Small Commercial	317,100	MWH	7.7
Large Commercial	1,812,800	MWH	43.9
Agricultural	57,500	MWH	1.4
Net Resale	2,900	MWH	—
Street Lighting	36,700	MWH	0.9
Total	4,130,800	MWH	100.0%

This represents a decrease of 77,040 MWH over the previous year. The 1975 generation increased approximately 10 percent over 1974, and 1976 generation was expected to increase approximately 6 percent over 1975. The 1975 figures appear to represent a diminished propensity on the part of consumers to conserve energy as compared with the unusual circumstances of the previous year. The current longer run expectation for planning purposes is that energy sales will increase at an annual rate of about 6 percent.

Until 1974 SMUD's generating capacity was entirely hydro, with maximum capability of 650 MW. A 900 MW nuclear unit has recently been brought on line, and until recently a second 900 MW unit was planned to be brought on line by 1984. As a combined hydro-thermal system, with important interconnections to a much larger regional system, SMUD is a particularly interesting case for analysis of marginal costs.

MARGINAL GENERATION CAPACITY COST

At the time of the initial SMUD study, the generation expansion plan called for the construction of a second 900 MW nuclear unit, with a scheduled operation date in 1983. Plans for the second plant were subsequently cancelled, and a gas turbine unit was planned instead. We have revised the case study to take into account this change in plans, but we have retained parts of the earlier version. We have done so for two reasons. First, the former plan illustrated an interesting case; namely, one in which the utility expects to have considerable excess capacity for extended periods and which further involves nuclear plants. Nuclear plants are often difficult to reschedule, either to defer or to accelerate, which diminishes the usefulness of the approach used in the WP&L case. Second, it is interesting to compare the effect of a change in the expansion plan on marginal cost. *A priori*, we would not expect a particularly great effect on marginal cost unless the change in plans were occasioned by a significant change in the pattern of demand. (Here, cancellation of the nuclear plant was brought about by uncertainties concerning the cost and availability of nuclear fuel and by the prospect of Proposition 15 before the California electorate, which would virtually eliminate nuclear plants as a planning alternative for California utilities and would require the gradual derating of existing plants.) Utility system planners, like all economic decisionmakers, are continually making choices along a fine margin between alternatives. When actual events indicate that the choice was a close one, the marginal cost analysis should reflect it. If it does not, it may be that there is something wrong with the analysis. Below we will see that despite the change from a nuclear plant to a gas turbine, the effect on marginal costs is minimal. We will consider first the marginal generation capacity cost under the old plan.

As noted in Chapter 1, marginal cost is determined by what a utility actually plans to do to meet the demand for additional capacity. While it is frequently the case that marginal cost may be estimated by the effect on system costs of moving plants forward and/or back in the planning schedule, SMUD is not such a case. The nuclear plant was not "accelerable" and was deemed more likely to be replaced than postponed, as events proved. Purchased capacity was likewise out of the question, since there was no excess capacity within the region.

SMUD itself does have considerable excess capacity, due to lumpiness in its construction plan. The size of the nuclear plant brought on line in 1974 was quite large relative to the existing load within SMUD's service area. In order to minimize system costs, SMUD sold its excess capacity to PG&E, thereby achieving a very high utilization rate for its total plant. The selling price to PG&E is $3.47 per KW per month or $41.64 per KW per year. An increase in demand from SMUD's own customers would most likely have been met by reducing the capacity made available for purchase by PG&E. The marginal cost to SMUD of additional demand was, therefore, the revenue foregone in not selling that capacity, i.e., $41.64 per KW per year.

Since SMUD attempts to maintain a 19.5 percent reserve margin, the marginal annual cost per KW of generating capacity, including reserves, was $\$41.64 \times 1.195 = \$49.76$. Because of diversity between the maximum demand on the SMUD system and all or part of the PG&E system, this capacity is available for sale to PG&E throughout the year, without seasonal variation.*

There is, however, diurnal variation in the margin between SMUD's demand and its available capacity. SMUD could readily provide additional KW during nighttime hours throughout the year, either from its own plants or by purchasing the excess nighttime capacity that exists throughout the region. Hence, the marginal generating capacity cost of $49.76 applies only to additional KW drawn during daytime and evening hours.

For the foreseeable future, SMUD will have excess capacity during the hours of 10:30 P.M. to 6:30 A.M. on weekdays and Saturdays, and during all hours on Sundays and holidays. There are about 3,800 such nighttime, weekend and holiday hours during the year, and we shall refer to such hours as the off-peak period. All other hours, totaling 4,960, are designated on-peak. If the probability of actual peak** is equal over all these hours, then the expected marginal cost per KW of generating capacity is $49.76, times the probability of an additional KW demand during any one such hour. That is, $\$49.76 \times \frac{1}{4960 \text{ hours}} = \$0.0100$ per KW per peak period hour. Applying the demand loss multipliers from Table 5–1, the marginal generating capacity cost at the principle SMUD supply voltages was

*i.e., there are no periods, or seasons, during which PG&E finds itself in a position of excess capacity, and therefore, unwilling to purchase SMUD capacity.

**Peak being defined in terms of the *difference* between demand and available capacity, not merely maximum demand.

Table 5–1. Loss Multipliers

	*Average Multiplier for Demand at Time of System Peak***		*Marginal Multiplier for Energy****			
			*Peak Hours (6:30 A.M. to 10:30 P.M., weekdays and Saturdays)**		*Off-peak Hours (all other times, including holidays)*	
Stage	*Simple*	*Cumulative*	*Simple*	*Cumulative*	*Simple*	*Cumulative*
From generation to high voltage customers and high side of distribution substation transformers	1.049	1.049	1.029	1.029	1.006	1.006
From high side of distribution substation transformers to primary voltage customers and high side of line transformers	1.049	1.100	1.029	1.059	1.006	1.012
From high side of line transformers to low voltage customers	1.065	1.172	1.036	1.097	1.007	1.019

*From 6:30 A.M. to 10:30 P.M., or approximately 4,960 hours per year.

** $\frac{\text{KWH input}}{\text{KWH output}}$ at time of peak, or $\frac{1}{1-\frac{\text{loss}}{\text{load}}}$ at time of system peak.

*** $\frac{\text{d KWH input}}{\text{d KWH output}}$ during peak and off-peak periods.

High Voltage	\$52.21 per KW or 1.052¢ per peak KWH
Primary Distribution Voltage	\$54.79 per KW or 1.105¢ per peak KWH
Secondary Distribution Voltage	\$58.35 per KW or 1.176¢ per peak KWH

With more information about the pattern of demand and available supply, it may be useful to dispense with the assumption of constant loss of load probability for all hours (except late night) and designate various periods as "peak," "shoulder" and "off peak." SMUD would prefer this refinement, but time and information did not allow it during the course of this study. The effect, in any case, would be costs per KHW somewhat higher than those given above during peak periods and somewhat lower during shoulder periods.

In light of the aforementioned change in plans, it became appropriate during the course of the study to revise the estimate of SMUD's marginal generation capacity cost. The data for the gas turbine unit that replaced the nuclear plant are as follows:

Capital cost	\$ 24,900,000
Capacity	150,000 KW
Annual fixed operation and maintenance	\$300,000
Running cost	28 mills per KWH
Expected life	35 years*
Interest rate	7 percent

SMUD's joint dispatch agreement with PG&E provides that SMUD will operate the gas turbine at least 876 hours per year, which provision will add \$3,679,200 to the annual costs of the unit. Total annual costs of the unit are, therefore,

$$\frac{(0.07723 \times 24{,}900{,}000) + 3{,}979{,}200}{150{,}000} = \$37.348$$

Allowing for a reserve margin of 19.5 percent and for losses as set out in Table 4–1, the annual marginal costs of generating capacity at each voltage level are

*The expected life of the plant is somewhat extended since it is not expected to operate frequently but to be held in reserve most of the time. With different circumstances and frequent stop-start operation, life could decrease to as few as twenty-five years.

High Voltage	\$49.34 or 0.995¢ per peak KWH
Primary Distribution Voltage	51.77 or 1.044¢ per peak KWH
Secondary Distribution Voltage	55.14 or 1.112¢ per peak KWH

TRANSMISSION AND DISTRIBUTION CAPACITY COST

The planned additions to the SMUD transmission and distribution network through 1980 are shown in Table 5–2. The maximum demands at each voltage level to which this expansion relates can be estimated in the following manner. The cumulative average loss multipliers are 1.049, 1.100 and 1.172 for low, primary and high voltage, respectively. The relationship between system maximum demand in 1974 (given in Table 5–2) and maximum demand at high voltage is 1109 MW ÷ 1.049 for losses = 1057 MW. The contribution to this of HV customers is estimated at 160 MW, and the balance is consumer demand from downstream. Demand at primary voltage, therefore, is (1057 – 50) ÷ 1.049 = 855 MW, of which the contribution of primary voltage consumers is estimated to be 50 MW. Low voltage demand then is (855 – 50) ÷ 1.065 = 756 MW.

Assuming the loss and coincidence factors hold constant, and 1980 system maximum demand is, as projected, 1756 MW, then with the same ratios of low, primary and high voltage demands, the equivalent 1980 figures are

1756 MW ÷ 1.049 = 1674 MW at high voltage
(1674 – 253) ÷ 1.049 = 1355 MW at primary voltage
1355 – 79) ÷ 1.065 = 1198 MW at low voltage

The change in demand at each voltage level between 1974 and 1980 is

617 MW at HV
500 MW at PV
442 MW at LV

These are the changes in load to which the changes in transmission and distribution capacity (the right column of Table 5–2) are to be related. The computation is done at the foot of Table 5–4, based

Table 5–2. Expansion Plan for Transmission and Distribution Facilities

	1975	1976	1977	1978	1979	1980	Total Change
	(1974=1109)						
System Maximum Demand (MW)	1263	1351	1452	1556	1653	1756	647
230 KV line (miles)				13 (urban)		19 (rural)	32
115 KV line (miles		4		1.5			5.5
230/69 KV substations (MVA)	224			224			448
115/21 KV substations (MVA)	75 (Type 2)			75 (Type 1)		75 (Type 1)	225
69 KV line (miles)	0.6 (rural) 13.8 (urban)	4.5 (rural) 10.9 (urban)		13 (urban)	8.0 (urban)		60.7
21 KV and 12 KV line (trench miles)	74.4	68.8	71.2	68.8	70.4	68.0	421.6
69/12 KV substations (MVA)	120	120	60	120	140	140	700
line transformers (KVA)	200,000	200,000	200,000	200,000	200,000	200,000	1,200,000

Source: SMUD

upon the information in Table 5–3. Allowing for losses, marginal costs of transmission and distribution capacity are

$$\$2.17 + (\$11.45 \times 1.065) + (\$1.02 \times 1.049 \times 1.049) = \$15.49 \text{ per KW at LV}$$

$$\$11.45 + (\$1.02 \times 1.049) = \$12.52 \text{ per KW at PV}$$

At HV, the figure is simply $1.02

The marked difference in the marginal costs at each level is due to the differences in the transmission and distribution facilities that demands originating at different points require. Few facilities are needed to serve high voltage demands, whereas low voltage demands require reinforcement of the network at each stage. One explanation for the sharp increase in marginal costs between primary and high voltage is the high cost and quantity of buried 21 and 12 KV cable.

In SMUD's case, the marginal transmission and distribution capacity costs can readily be converted into a KWH cost in the same manner as generating capacity costs. This is not always the case, since in larger systems, various segments of the transmission and distribution system may peak at different times, and not coincidently with the generation peak. In the present case, there is very little diversity between peak generation times and peak transmission and distribution times. Assuming 4,960 peak hours, the resultant marginal costs are

high voltage	0.0002¢ per KWH
primary voltage	0.2524¢ per KWH
low voltage	0.3123¢ per KWH

Here, as in the WP&L case, it would have been desirable, were more information available, to distinguish line transformers added to meet growth in load from line transformers added to meet growth in the number of customers. The former are capacity costs; the latter are properly treated as customer costs.

ENERGY COMPONENTS

In a predominantly thermal generating system, marginal running costs vary continually throughout the year because of the varying heat rates (the ratio of BTU input to KWH output) of the units that make up the generating system. A hydro system, however, is characterized by running costs that are both very low in comparison to other conventional forms of generation and nearly constant for any

Table 5–3. Cost of Additional Transmission and Distribution Facilities *(1975 Dollars)*

Item	*Unit*	*Capital Cost*	*Annual Equivalent*[a] *CRF = 0.07723*	*Annual Operation*[f] *and Maintenance*	*Total Annual Cost*
230 KV line	mile	$122,812[b]	$9,485	$ 610	$10,095
115 KV line	mile	113,182[c]	8,741	597	9,338
69 KV line	mile	46,795	3,614	597	4,211
230/69 substations	MVA	4,464	345	14	359
115/21 substations	MVA	17,422[d]	1,346	54	1,400
69/12 substations	MVA	14,175[e]	1,095	44	1,139
21 and 12 KV line	trench mile	105,600	8,156	2,283	10,439
Line Transformers	KVA	10	0.77	0.03	0.80

[a] For simplicity, all facilities are assumed to have an expected life of thirty-five years. Actual lives range from thirty to forty-five years. The interest used is 7 percent, which reflects borrowing cost, in lieu of taxes payments, insurance, etc.

[b] Weighted average of single circuit urban lines @ $105,000/mile and double circuit rural lines @ $135,000/mile.

[c] Weighted average of 1.5 miles @ 135,000
4.0 miles @ 105,000.

[d] Weighted average.

[e] Including cost of line capacitors.

[f] Estimated from accounting data.

Table 5–4. Calculation of Marginal Transmission and Distribution Capacity Cost Per KW Demand at Each Voltage

(1) Item	(2) Unit	(3) Annual Cost	(4) 1975 – 1980 Facilities Additions	(5) 1975–1980 Demand Increase (MW)	Serving
230 KV line	Mile	$10,095	32	685.3	HV, PV, LV
115 KV line	Mile	9,338	5.5	685.3	HV, PV, LV
69 KV line	Mile	4,211	60.7	685.3	HV, PV, LV
21 and 21 KV Cable	Mile	10,439	421.6	598.3	PV, LV
230/69 KV SS	MVA	359	448	598.3	PV, LV
115/21 KV SS	MVA	1,400	225	598.3	PV, LV
69/21 KV SS	MVA	1,139	700	598.3	PV, LV
Distributor Transformers	KVA	0.8	1,200,000	564.9	LV

1. Marginal T&D capacity cost without losses at high voltage:

$$\frac{1}{1000} \times \frac{(32 \times 10095) + (5.5 \times 9338) + (60.7 \times 4211)}{617} = \$1,0211$$

2. Marginal T&D capacity cost without losses at primary voltage:

$$\frac{1}{1000} \times \frac{(421.6 \times 10439) + (448 \times 359) + (225 \times 1400) + (700 \times 1139)}{500} = \$11.4502$$

3. Marginal T&D capacity cost without losses at low voltage*:

$$\frac{1}{1000} \times \frac{0.8 \times 1200000}{442} = \$2.1719$$

*Power factor of 0.9 and average transformer loading of 10 percent were assumed in estimating transformer additions between 1975 and 1980. Had these considerations not previously be taken account of, the right term in brackets below would be multiplied by 0.9 and divided by 1.1.

level of load. Similarly, the running costs of nuclear plants are both relatively low and nearly constant. SMUD is a combined hydro-nuclear system.

In the case of a mixed hydro-thermal system, hydro power is usually conserved for use during periods of highest demand, when otherwise it would be necessary to run the highest cost thermal generating units.* Thus, it may appear that a mixed hydro-thermal system has low running costs during periods of high demand and higher running costs during periods of lower demand. This, of course, is the opposite of what one expects in an efficiently dispatched all thermal system.

In fact, however, the effect of the availability of hydro power is to even out marginal running costs at all hours of the year. With enough hydro power available, marginal running costs become constant at the level of the highest cost thermal unit in use. The reason for this is that over the course of the annual hydro cycle, all available water power will be used up. If because of an increase in maximum demand, more hydro is used during peak periods than was previously the case, then less will be available during other hours. Therefore, the marginal running cost of an additional KW of demand at time of system peak is the marginal opportunity cost, which results from the hydro not being available at other times—i.e., the cost of the thermal power that replaces the hydro during an off-peak period. In the case of SMUD, running costs are constant throughout the year at 2.95 mills per kilowatt hour at generation.

There is, however, another factor that needs to be taken into account. The SMUD system is jointly dispatched with PG&E. Since demand within SMUD's own service area is always less than SMUD's available capacity, and since the SMUD system has very low operating costs, there is a continuous flow of energy from SMUD to PG&E. The price paid by PG&E for this energy is, according to a formula common in the industry, equal to the seller's marginal running cost plus one-half the difference between the buyer's and the seller's respective marginal running costs. For almost all hours of the year, this amounts to a selling price of 10 mills per KWH.

As with capacity, PG&E absorbs all of SMUD's excess energy. The marginal cost of energy within the SMUD system, therefore, is the additional cost to SMUD of not being able to sell additional KWH to PG&E, or conversely, the savings to SMUD from having more KWH

*Actually, scheduling hydro generation is a very complex problem in dynamic programming, taking into account such variables as seasonal variation in water supply, reservoir storage capacity, permissible reservoir drawdown, competing demands for water and so forth. The scenario contemplated here is exceedingly simple.

available to sell to PG&E. So while the marginal running cost of the SMUD system is 2.95 mills, the marginal energy cost is 10 mills. Applying the loss multipliers of Table 5–1 yields the following marginal energy costs:

	Peak Hours (6:30 A.M. to 10:30 P.M., weekdays and Saturdays)	*Off-peak Hours (All other times, including holidays)*
High Voltage	1.029 mills per KWH	1.006
Primary Voltage	1.060	1.011
Secondary Voltage	1.098	1.018

Table 5–5 summarizes the components of marginal cost for the SMUD system.

Table 5–5. Summary of Marginal Costs *(¢/KWH)*

		Peak Hours (6:30 A.M. to 10:30 P.M., weekdays and Saturdays)	Off-peak Hours (All other times, including holidays)
High Voltage	generation	0.9950	—
	transmission and distribution	0.0002	—
	energy	1.0290	1.006
		2.0242¢ per KWH	1.006 per KWH
Primary Voltages	generation	1.0440	—
	transmission and distribution	0.2524	—
	energy	1.0600	1.011
		2.3564 per KWH	1.011 per KWH
Low Voltage	generation	1.1120	—
	transmission and distribution	0.3123	—
		1.0980	1.018
		2.5223 per KWH	1.018 per KWH

Chapter 6

Case Study C: Los Angeles Department of Water and Power

The department is the largest municipally owned electricity supplier in the U.S., with annual sales in excess of 20 million MWH to over a million consumers. Oil is the largest single energy source as shown in Table 6–1.

Table 6–1. Energy Source by Prime Mover, 1975 *(percent)*

Oil	39.7
Hydro	25.7
Coal	16.3
Gas	13.9
Sewer Gas	0.1
Interchanges	4.2

For the future, gas will be almost entirely unavailable and, for the near term, it will be replaced largely by oil. For the longer term, coal and perhaps nuclear generation will become more important.

Present capacity is 5,300 megawatts, including four oil and gas steam plants in the Los Angeles Basin, 550 MW of capacity (and no energy) via the 800 KV DC intertie to the Bonneville Power Administration, and run of the river, storage and pumped storage hydro. The next plant to be constructed is a coal-fired unit being built jointly with Nevada and Utah utilities.

The most interesting feature of the LADWP system is that it is expected to have substantial excess reserves (more spare capacity than is needed to meet reliability criteria) at least through 1983. At the same time, the system will be rather short in total energy availability, principally because gas will not be available.

MARGINAL GENERATING CAPACITY

In the typical case, marginal generating capacity cost is calculated by evaluating the additional costs of having capacity earlier than planned, which as we saw in the WP&L case is basically the annuitized cost of the plant, less fuel savings. In other cases, such as an extended period of excess capacity caused by lumpiness in the construction schedule, marginal generating capacity cost is the price at which the extra capacity is being sold to other utilities; that is the SMUD case. Excess capacity, however, means more than merely idle physical plant. To be "excess," capacity must not only be there, it must be available; there must be fuel or water to run it.

LADWP is an example of a system that has idle capacity, some of which is excess and some not. It has, for example, the Scattergood #3 unit, which is one of the most efficient gas-fired generators in the U.S., but there is no gas to run it. There may, similarly, be hydro capacity without the water to run it all out. In treating a system with limited total energy availability, therefore, more needs to be done than simply to compare installed capacity and maximum demand. Until recently, a significant share of LADWP's idle capacity was not available, could not be sold, and hence was no guide to marginal cost.

With the recent addition of the Castaic pumped storage plant, LADWP does have capacity that it can sell. It also has plans to bring on line a second 125 MW coal-fired unit at the Warner plant in 1982.* The question is, which is the appropriate measure of marginal cost: the potential selling price of existing excess capacity, or the added cost of accelerating Warner #2 (or a weighted average of the two, much as if two plants were being accelerated, as in the WP&L case)?

The costs associated with the Warner #2 unit are

Plant	$ 51,900,000
Stepup transformation	1,830,000
Transmission	46,370,000
	$100,100,000
Annual O & M	1,767,700
Fuel	5 mills

With a plant life of thirty-five years, interest at 7.5 percent and an availability factor of 0.8, the fully amortized cost of the unit is somewhat in excess of 16 mills per KWH. Because of the high cost of oil,

*The department's share of a 250 MW unit built jointly with Nevada and Utah utilities.

which without Warner #2 is the source of incremental energy, Warner #2 should be built for the sake of fuel savings alone. The unit is not needed to expand capacity, although it will also do that. The effect is that the marginal *production* cost of added capacity is zero, which means simply that the reduction in fuel costs exceeds the addition in capacity costs. This is a special case due to the new optimality associated with unexpected changes in fuel availability and prices. It appears that adding capacity to an idle capacity system does not have any marginal capacity cost. This is because LADWP is in a period of reoptimizing. Accordingly, a more appropriate measure of marginal capacity cost may be the revenue LADWP could receive from selling its extra capacity.

At present, LADWP is not selling its extra capacity, but it is investigating the possibility. Of course, the opportunity costs are there whether the department sells or not; the difficulty is in determining what the market is in the meantime. A fairly strong market is believed to exist for LADWP's excess capacity during the summer daytime hours and a weaker market at other times. In the absence of more information, we shall suppose that LADWP's excess capacity could be sold during the former period only, and at a price equal to that at which SMUD sells to PG&E, viz., $41.64 per KW. With a reserve margin of 26.2 percent (which seems inordinately high), the annual cost per KW is $52.55.

Summer daytime is defined for the region as 7 A.M. to 10 P.M., Monday through Saturday, June through September. There being 1,620 such hours, the value of an extra KW of demand during any one hour is $(\frac{1}{1620} \times \$52.55) = \$0.0324$. Allowing for losses, then, the cost of an extra KW demand is

3.40¢ per KWH at HV

3.58¢ per KWH at PV

3.72¢ per KWH at LV

MARGINAL TRANSMISSION AND DISTRIBUTION CAPACITY COSTS

The loss multipliers for the LADWP case study are shown in Table 6–2.

The LADWP transmission and distribution network serves consumers at these principle voltage levels: 34.5 KV (high voltage), 4.8 KV (primary) and low (secondary) voltage. There are no consumers

Table 6–2. Loss Multipliers

Stage	*Average Multiplier for Demand at Time of System Peak*		*Marginal Multiplier for Energy*			
			Summer Daytime		*Other Times*	
	Simple	*Cumulative*	*Simple*	*Cumulative*	*Simple*	*Cumulative*
From generation to HV consumers and high side of distribution SS	1.049	1.049	1.044	1.044	1.040	1.040
From high side of distribution SS to primary voltage consumers and high side of line transformers	1.052	1.104	1.037	1.083	1.027	1.068
From high side of line transformers to low voltage consumers	1.040	1.148	1.030	1.115	1.021	1.091

served directly off HV transmission above the receiving stations. Most HV consumers are provided, singly or in small groups, from what are called customer stations. These stations serve no one else, and should be treated separately as customer costs.

The remaining components of the system are shown in Table 6–3, with historic data for each type of facility. Table 6–3 also shows historical data for maximum consumer demand at each level. As the note to Table 6–5 indicates, these latter data are little more than guesses. Nonetheless, those are the data points that are relevant, even if the precise numbers are in error.* Accordingly, we proceed to relate the demand at each level to MVA or miles of line installed, the assumption being that it is "better to be roughly right than precisely wrong." The resultant regression equations are

KVA Transmission SS = −1075000 + 2.39 (HV demand)
$R^2 = 0.95$

Miles 34.5 KV line = 746.4 + 0.00028 (HV demand)
$R^2 = 0.98$

KVA Distribution SS = 1032 + 1.228 (PV demand)
$R^2 = 0.97$

Miles 4.8 KV line = 5124 + 0.001 (PV demand)
$R^2 = 0.98$

KVA line Transmission = 1118 + 1.471 (LV demand)
$R^2 = 0.98$

Miles secondary line = 4049 + 0.00027 (LV demand)
$R^2 = 0.91$

Note that secondary line miles are included in this case study, whereas in the preceding case studies these lines have been treated as customer related. The different treatment reflects the judgment of the department.

Applying these coefficients to the annual cost figures in Table 6–4, we obtain the following estimates of additional transmission and distribution capacity costs per additional KW of demand:

*The Department of Water and Power advises that in view of the uncertainty of the estimated demands at each voltage level it would, as a practical matter, relate changes in line miles and transformer capacity only to receiving station demand. For illustrative purposes we have chosen the conceptually more appropriate (but more uncertain) approach above.

Table 6–3. Transmission and Distribution Capacity and Demand at Time of System Peak

		1965	*1966*	*1967*	*1968*	*1969*	*1970*	*1971*	*1972*	*1973*
Transmission SS	(MVA)	3838	3962	4542	4478	5382	6107	6427	6882	6944
34.5 KV line	(miles)	1327	1362	1410	1435	1471	1555	1623	1684	1727
Distribution SS	(MVA)	2615	2784	2855	2929	3139	3330	3475	3598	3789
4.8 KV line	(miles)	6432	6553	6660	6758	6851	7052	7191	7286	7369
Line transformers	(MVA)	2789	2951	3079	3218	3377	3561	3718	3869	4040
Secondary line	(miles)	4312	4387	4439	4463	4469	4509	4527	4551	4570
Demand at generation (net)	(MW)	2123	2303	2407	2679	2772	2974	3107	3439	3679
Demand at receiving station	(MW)	2038	2228	2320	2580	2674	2891	3062	3435	3456
Demand at high voltage	(MW)	2016	2204	2295	2552	2645	2860	3029	3398	3418
Demand at primary voltage	(MW)	1303	1424	1483	1650	1710	1848	1959	2196	2210
Demand at secondary voltage	(MW)	1153	1260	1312	1459	1512	1635	1732	1943	1955

Table 6–4. Cost of Transmission and Distribution Facilities *(1975 dollars)*

	Unit	*Capital Cost*	*Annual Equivalent*	*Operation & Maintenance*	*Annual Cost*
Transmission	KVA	$ 34.00	$ 2.77	$ 0.67	$ 3.44
34.5 KV line	Circuit miles	76,000.00	6,193.00	1,660.00	7,853.00
Distribution SS	KVA	50.00	4.07	1.20	5.27
4.8 KV line	Circuit miles	47,000.00	3,830.00	750.00	4,580.00
Line transformers	KVA	25.00	2.04	0.46	2.50
Secondary line	Circuit miles	49,000.00	3,993.00	940.00	4,933.00

Notes:

1. Transmission lines of voltages higher than 34.5 KV are omitted. Such lines serve no customers and are generation related.
2. The annual equivalent over thirty-five years of $1 at 7.5 percent is $0.08148.

Table 6–5. Estimating Demand at High, Primary and Low Voltage

	1965	*1966*	*1967*	*1968*	*1969*	*1970*	*1971*	*1972*	*1973*
Demand at Receiving Station	2038	2228	2320	2580	2674	2891	3062	3435	3456
÷ 1.011 for losses from RS									
= High voltage demand	2016	2204	2295	2552	2645	2860	3029	3398	3418
÷ 1.052 for HV losses									
− 32 percent for HV customers	613	670	698	776	805	870	921	1033	1040
= Primary voltage demand	1303	1424	1483	1650	1710	1848	1958	2196	2210
÷ 1.040 for PV losses	1253	1370	1426	1586	1644	1777	1882	2112	2125
− 8 percent for PV customers	100	110	114	127	132	142	151	169	170
= LV demand	1153	1260	1312	1459	1512	1635	1732	1943	1955

Note:

The above table provides a very rough estimate of demand at three voltage levels. The receiving station demands, 1965–1973, are accurate, and the loss multipliers and proportional contributions to receiving station demand are reasonably accurate for 1973. The remaining data are backward extrapolations.

Diversity between demand at each level and maximum RS demand is virtually zero. The implied diversity factor, therefore, is 1.0.

$$[(2.39 \times \$3.44) + (0.00028 \times \$7852)] = \$10.42 \text{ per KW at HV}$$
$$[(1.228 \times \$5.27) + (0.001 \times \$4580)] = \$11.05 \text{ per KW at PV}$$
$$[(1.471 \times \$2.50) + (0.00027 \times \$4933)] = \$5.01 \text{ per KW at LV}$$

Allowing for losses, we have $10.42 as HV, and

$$\$11.05 + (1.052 \times \$10.42) = \$22.01 \text{ at PV;}$$
$$\$5.01 + (1.04 \times \$11.05)$$
$$+ (1.04 \times 1.052 \times \$10.42) = \$27.90 \text{ at LV.}$$

It is demand during the summer weekday hours that determines the transmission and distribution capacity required. The summer peak period being defined as 7 A.M. to 10 P.M., Monday through Saturday, from June through September, the above costs per KW may be converted to an hourly equivalent by dividing by 1,620 such hours; yielding

6.43 mills per KWH at HV
13.59 mills per KWH at PV
17.22 mills per KWH at LV

MARGINAL ENERGY COSTS

A significant portion of LADWP's annual energy production is from hydro sources, which tends to reduce, but not to eliminate, seasonal and diurnal variation in system running costs. Table 6–6 reflects this fact. Low cost hydro power is seldom available to meet all the demand on the LADWP system, thus requiring that some oil be burned nearly every day. This accounts for the relatively high level of system λ at all times. By taking an hourly weighted average (KWH weights would have been preferred but were not available) of system running costs and regrouping the hours into a manageable number of periods, we derive the value of λ during summer days, the spring hydro season and all other hours (Table 6–7).

Applying the energy loss multipliers of Table 6–2 yields the following estimate of costs per KWH during the three periods* at each service voltage.

	Summer Daytime	*Spring Hydro*	*Other Times*
High Voltage	3.258	2.424	2.708
Primary Voltage	3.380	2.490	2.781
Low Voltage	3.480	2.543	2.841

*The periods are defined in Table 6–7.

Table 6–6. Production Energy Costs *(November 1974–October 1975)*

Period	*Daytime (7 A.M.–10 P.M.)*		*Nighttime (10 P.M.–7 A.M.)*	
Summer (June–September)	*Number Hours*	*Incremental Energy Cost (mills/KWH)*	*Number Hours*	*Incremental Energy Cost (mills/KWH)*
Sunday	210	23.96	126	23.96
Monday		27.83		24.56
Tuesday		31.70		26.28
Wednesday	1620	33.38	972	25.64
Thursday		35.53		26.43
Friday		29.05		26.31
Saturday		29.75		
	1830		1098	
Winter (October–March)				
Sunday		26.41		26.41
Monday		27.71		25.73
Tuesday		27.35		25.67
Wednesday		26.80		25.24
Thursday		26.77		25.44
Friday		26.88		25.72
Saturday		25.02		25.08
	2730		1638	
Spring Hydro Season (April–May)				
Sunday	120	22.19	72	22.19
Monday		24.83		22.28
Tuesday		24.33		22.32
Wednesday	795	23.92	477	22.38
Thursday		24.09		21.58
Friday		26.36		22.64
Saturday		24.61		22.64
	915		549	
	5475		3285	

These estimates, although based on the past year's experience, are believed reasonably accurate for the coming year. If expectations about fuel cost change, the figures should, of course be revised accordingly.

All the above estimates of marginal cost are summed and summarized in Table 6–8.

Table 6–7. Production Energy Costs *(Weighted for Selected Periods)*

Period	*Number of Hours*	*Cost (mills/KWH)*
Summer daytime, Monday-Saturday, June-September, 7 A.M.–10 P.M.	1620	31.21
Spring hydro season, April-May, all hours	1464	23.31
Other times	5676	26.04
	8760	

Table 6–8. Summary of Marginal Costs of LADWP System *(¢/KWH)*

	Summer Daytime	*Spring Hydro*	*All Other Times*
High Voltage			
Generation	3.400	—	—
Transmission and Distribution	0.643	—	—
Energy	3.258	2.424	2.708
Total	7.301	2.424	2.708
Primary Voltage			
Generation	3.580	—	—
Transmission and Distribution	1.359	—	—
Energy	3.380	2.490	2.781
Total	8.319	2.490	2.781
Low Voltage			
Generation	3.720	—	—
Transmission and Distribution	1.722	—	—
Energy	3.480	2.543	2.841
Total	8.922	2.543	2.841

Chapter 7

Marginal Cost and Tariffs

Thus far we have conscientiously avoided any more than fleeting reference to the subject of tariff design. We had hoped to keep the swirling controversy about the merits of designing tariffs on the basis of marginal cost structure from obscuring the question of what that structure is, primarily because we believe that in a given case there is precious little one can say about the proper design of tariffs without an inquiry into the characteristics of a particular utility system. In large measure the case studies confirm this conclusion.

Nonetheless, an inquiry of the sort that this study represents requires at least some consideration of the reasons the analysis is suggested in the first place. Accordingly, we present here a discussion of the tradition of tariff design in the United States; the principles that suggest the use of marginal cost for the design of the electrical utility tariffs; and some comments on a few areas where we believe there has been a regrettable failure of communication and/or understanding about what the difficulties actually are with respect to implementation of marginal cost pricing in the United States. While there are certain real difficulties, we are not persuaded that they are the same as those that have surfaced in the public debate that has surrounded the subject of marginal cost pricing for electricity.

The basic forms for pricing electric power in the United States emerged at about the turn of the century. While increases in electricity consumption, coupled with improvements in electricity usage-metering technology, have led to some modifications in tariffs, the vast bulk of electricity consumed in the United States is still priced according to formulas devised by Dr. John Hopkinson in 1892 and Arthur Wright in 1896. In essence, these tariffs provided for

1. A "customer" component, based (more or less) on the cost of connecting a single customer to the utility network, including service drops, meters, meter reading, etc.;
2. A "demand" component, based on the maximum kilowatt demand of the customer during the billing period (usually one month); and
3. An "energy" component based on the total kilowatt hours during the billing period.

The customer component consists of a fixed monthly charge. The demand and energy components usually consist of a number of declining steps in which prices for KW or KWH, respectively, decrease in succeeding blocks. Since these tariffs require separate metering of demand and energy, simplified variations of the tariffs are applied to smaller (primarily residential) customers by compressing the demand and energy components into a single rate that also consists of a number of declining blocks. For these consumers, the customer component as well is sometimes included in a single rate and expressed as a relatively high charge with the first few KWH of consumption.

Interestingly, the rationale offered for these tariff designs at their inception is quite similar to the argument now being advanced to abandon them, at least as they are presently applied. In the early days of the electric power industry, the primary use of electricity was for lighting. To price such usage, a simple flat charge per KWH was adequate. Since all consumers used electricity at essentially the same time, peak and off-peak distinctions simply did not exist. As power usage expanded to other services, however, it was recognized that to the extent such additional uses could be served by plants that would otherwise be idle, such "off-peak" use could be promoted by selling larger volumes of electricity at lower prices. That is, nonlighting uses, to the extent they did not occur simultaneously with lighting uses, could be furnished at, basically, the cost of the additional fuel consumed. Since utilities served relatively small, homogenous territories, it was not difficult to discern typical or "average" usage patterns. Few consumers used electricity in any pattern significantly different from normal patterns. As service territories and usage patterns expanded, however, it became far less useful to speak in terms of "normal" or "average" patterns of electricity use.

Concurrently, industrial use of electricity expanded to the point that it became feasible to increase the sophistication of usage metering beyond the single dimension of total KWH consumption. It became equally important to know how much electricity was consumed at one time as how much was consumed over a longer period of time since the size of the utility's generating plant was a function of its maximum demand. Hence, the emergence of maximum demand metering developed in addition to energy metering. The fact that industrial consumers' maximum demand did not all occur at precisely the same time was a limitation on the usefulness of the technique, but one that did not matter all that much since, again, usage patterns tended to be similar among the relatively small number of consumers. In addition, metering to measure the coincidence of consumer demands was impracticable. What stands out, however, in these early developments in electricity tariff design is the extent of the effort to have prices reflect as systematically as possible the structure of costs to the utility.

Before long, two circumstances combined to diminish concern for the relationship between patterns of cost to the utility and tariff design. First, because of the monopolistic structure of the electric power industry, greater attention was paid to the overall level of profitability to the companies and relatively less concern was accorded to design of particular tariffs. Second, technological progress in power supply was very rapid, so that the price of electricity relative to other goods and services declined quite rapidly. Both of these factors tended to make tariff design a subject of lesser importance. As recently as 1973, regulatory commissions were *regularly* advised that the price of electricity was still such a small item in the budget of firms and households that tariff structure did not significantly influence consumer demands. Such assertions are now as rare as they once were commonplace.

During the ascendancy of concern with overall profitability and "revenue requirements," the principal consideration in tariff design became the allocation or apportionment of the total revenue requirement among various classes of customers. The structure of tariffs remained essentially unchanged. What mattered more was the level of the tariff—that is, how much of the total revenue requirement was to be apportioned to each class of consumer. Given the resolution of that question, previous tariffs would be raised or lowered, often across the board, but sometimes with modifications in the size of the various "blocks".

Overall profitability, revenue requirements and the apportionment of these among consumers remains an important aspect of utility regulation. But by the early 1970s, concern with the design and structure of tariffs reemerged as a parallel consideration. The reasons are, first, that electricity costs increased dramatically as fuel costs increased and technological progress tapered off. Second, there was a heightened perception of the need for conservation of scarce resources of all types. Questions then arose about

1. Who should bear the increased costs of electricity, and
2. What incentives were built into ages-old tariff structures that promoted or thwarted efforts to conserve energy?

Much of the public debate centered around the existing structure of tariffs. Attempts were made to prove the virtue of consumers in one "block" and the profligacy of users in other blocks. What emerged most clearly from this debate was the awkwardness of the framework within which this discussion was set. Simple empirical distinctions were exceedingly difficult to make between consumers in various tariff blocks on the one hand and their relative rate of increase in consumption, their income and their propensity to conserve energy on the other. Logical distinctions were no less elusive. The convenient correlations of an earlier part of the century were no longer useful. They could not be pushed or stretched or scaled to fit present circumstances.

The confused state of the debate and the complex nature of the problem require a return to first principles. Broadly stated, there is a dual objective in the design of tariffs for electricity, viz., equity and efficiency. One objective is that the costs of producing electricity be equitably apportioned among consumers. Rates must be just, reasonable and sufficient. This objective derives from fundamental notions of fairness and is explicit in the law of the various states. The specific means by which this objective is met is via the determination by regulatory authorities in individual cases of a total revenue target designed to generate a level of profit that is equitable to the utility and to the ratepayers. (Usually this is expressed as the "revenue requirement." This is an unfortunate misstatement of the true objective criterion, which is profitability or rate of return. It is not revenues, per se, that are important, but earnings. Despite the misnomer, the point is generally understood and deserves mention only because of occasional ill-considered statements such as those to the effect that stability of revenues is a desirable end. *Stable earnings*, which may indeed be desirable, might be completely inconsistent with *stable revenues*.) Having determined a total revenue target, regulatory agencies must then apportion the total sum among the various classes of consumers to arrive at their respective contributions. The latter step, incidentally, is required only if *a priori* there is some condition that makes it necessary to have class distinctions in the first place. As discussed below, it may be more appropriate to distinguish consumers according to the voltage at which they receive service rather than by the character of the consumer. In any case, the determination of the aggregate revenue target and its distribution among consumer classes is the principal means by which the equity objective is met.

A second, equally important, objective is the efficient allocation of society's scarce resources among alternative uses. Conceptually, the allocation of resources among alternative uses is said to be "efficient" when no other combination of resources and uses would produce a greater benefit to society. Before an attempt is made to give practical meaning to the rather abstract definition just articulated, let it be clear that the twin objectives of equity and efficiency do not necessarily yield the same result. They might or they might not. In practice, the role of efficiency in the use of resources must be tempered by requirements of fairness; that is, by equity.

While the definition and objective of efficiency in the use of resources *can* be stated abstractly, rigorously and with mathematical precision, it is not obvious that the task of regulatory commissions is much facilitated by doing so. Indeed, the idea is basically a simple one. To wit:

- We (society) have limited resources to satisfy a multiplicity of needs; and
- Resources ought to be channeled to various uses in a way that maximizes the benefits society receives from the use of those resources.

The primary means by which resources are channeled from one use to another is by means of pricing signals. If the price that a resource will attract in one use is higher than what that resource will attract in some other use, resources will tend to flow toward the higher valued use. This is as true of fossil fuels and generating capacity as it is of land, human labor and other resources.

For the most part, the prices attached to resources reflect the value society attaches to those various uses, and these prices are determined in the marketplace. In the case of some commodities and services, however, unfettered market transactions would *not* yield prices that could be expected to reflect accurately the value of those resources to society. Two important causes of such distortions are

1. The absence of competition in certain markets, and
2. The existence of societal concerns that, for any number of reasons, may not be appropriately weighted by individuals acting independently.

Both of these conditions prevail in the case of electricity. In any given service territory there is only one supplier of electricity; thus, there is no competition. In addition, while all of us (i.e., society at large) have an interest in energy conservation, there is no way for us individually to reflect the full benefits or costs of energy usage in independent consumer decisions. We will bear the cost of abrupt energy shortages, for example, not individually but jointly, regardless of whether as individuals our behavior contributed to the onset of such shortages or helped to avert them. A critical function of regulatory agencies, therefore, is to operate where the free market fails.

One task (among many) of regulatory agencies is to see to it that prices perform the signaling function discussed above. Consumers should have some way of knowing whether it is relatively cheap or relatively expensive to satisfy their demands for electricity and other things. As Justice Jackson observed: "I must admit that I possess no instinct by which to know the 'reasonable' from the 'unreasonable' in prices and must seek some conscious design for decisions."* The crux of the task before the price-regulating agencies, then, is to see to it that as consumers make decisions to increase or decrease their consumption of electricity, or to alter the pattern of their consumption, those consumers are faced with a tariff structure that reflects the structure of costs to the utility and to society of meeting those demands. This, essentially, is what is encompassed in the economists' concept of marginal cost. Marginal cost is simply the cost (or savings) incurred by the utility in providing more (or less) electricity.

The concept of marginal cost itself is a fairly simple one. The process of supplying electricity, however, is rather complicated. Accordingly, the structure of marginal cost of electricity is also rather complicated. Inevitably, electricity tariffs must be modified and simplified from actual marginal costs if tariffs are to perform the function of being price signals. At the same time, a serious effort must be made to reflect the essential characteristics of marginal cost structure in tariffs.

Marginal cost pricing is, as Professor Alfred Kahn, current chairman of the New York Public Service Commission, puts it, the "benchmark" for efficient pricing in the regulated sector. The theoretical objective from which this principle flows, the maximization of total social welfare, can be reduced to somewhat less grand terms and recast for present purposes as an objective either to minimize the investment necessary to meet consumer demands for electricity or to

*FPC v. Hope Natural Gas Company, 320 U.S. 591, 645 (1944), Jackson, J., dissenting.

maximize the output of electricity given a fixed level of plant investment.

What, then, are the principle features of a tariff that reflects the basic structure of marginal costs? Three characteristics of electricity production dominate the structure of marginal costs. One is heat losses in transmission and distribution. Such losses vary primarily with distance and voltage changes between the points of generation and consumption. Consequently, the voltage at which a consumer receives power is one of the determinants of marginal cost. Second, the size of the physical plant is determined mainly by the expected demand on the system during peak periods (allowance being made for forced outage, maintenance, and reserve requirements). It follows that there are considerable periods (nights, weekends, and sometimes entire seasons) during which excess capacity is available and during which additional energy can be supplied without expanding existing facilities. Time, therefore, becomes a significant determinant of cost structure in the sense that there are times when additional consumer demand requires the expansion of facilities and times when additional consumer demand requires little more than an expenditure for fuel (and some maintenance). Finally, electricity production plants vary in the efficiency with which fuel is converted to electrical energy. Efficient operation of the system requires that the relatively more expensive units run as infrequently as possible. This, too, imposes a time dimension on marginal costs.

A tariff that conforms to marginal cost structure, therefore, will have the following characteristics. First, different tariffs will be established for each of the principal voltages at which consumers receive service. This will reflect both the difference in transmission and distribution losses at each voltage level and the fact that some consumers use only a portion of the transmission and distribution network. Second, for service at a particular voltage level, different prices will be established for electricity consumption at various hours, days and seasons of the year. For example, there may be one price for winter weekdays between 9:00 A.M. and 7:00 P.M., a second price for summer weekday afternoons and a third price for all other times. These price differentials will reflect the effects of transmission and distribution losses, as well as variations in system operating or fuel costs and system capacity costs for generation, transmission and distribution. (Additional tariff provisions may be appropriate for larger volume consumers—for high or low power factor, for example.) It cannot be stressed too much, however, that a particular set of marginal costs and tariffs are relevant only to a given set of expectations about the amount and pattern of additional consumer demand. The development of data pertaining to marginal costs and consumer response is perforce a continuing process.

The tendency of marginal costs to vary according to time of day and according to peaks and valleys in the demand for electricity leads often to the description of these tariffs as "time of day pricing" or "peak load pricing." Both descriptions obviously convey more information than the technically more correct and more precise term "marginal cost pricing." Two reasons suggest that the expression "peak load pricing" may have been a particularly unfortunate simplification. First, marginal costs merely *tend* to vary with peaks and valleys in utility loads. There are many exceptions. Second, it has sometimes been suggested that even if marginal costs do not correspond to peaks and valleys in loads, prices nonetheless ought to. This, it appears, reflects a greater commitment to nomenclature than to good sense.

Turning from that skeletal description of what marginal cost pricing is about, there are several areas in which questions have arisen that warrant specific attention here.

The area in which there has been the greatest misapprehension of marginal cost pricing has been with respect to the relationship between revenues derived from marginal-cost-based tariffs and administratively determined total revenue requirements. There is, apparently, a very widespread belief that pricing at marginal cost will yield more revenue than will be required to provide an adequate return on utility investment. Since this unwarranted assumption is the premise upon which certain public policy decisions are being made, it is appropriate here to set the record straight—even at pain of somewhat more technical detail than would be preferred if matters were not already so confused.

The argument usually has been that since the electric power industry is one of increasing costs, marginal costs exceed average costs and, therefore, pricing at marginal costs will yield excess revenues. That is the proposition to be examined, and it requires reference to a standard paradigm of economics and to the recent history of the industry.

There are two senses in which electric power costs might be said to be increasing. The first is a classic textbook sense in which a marginal cost curve is drawn for various quantities of output. Typically, such curves are "U-shaped." For smaller volumes of output, the cost function is decreasing. As output increases, the curve flattens or bottoms out, and finally starts an upswing as greater volumes of output are reached. (The particular marginal cost curve may be of the short-run variety or the long-run sort; at this point it does not matter, and neither does the point at which the upswing begins. Thus far, all that matters is the classical textbook presentation of the general principle.) For every marginal cost curve, there is one and only one corresponding average cost curve. By drawing horizontal and vertical lines out from a point on the upward sloping segment of the marginal cost curve, as economists are wont to do, it can be "proved" that marginal cost pricing yields revenues in excess of average costs, and thus, there are excess revenues. Since electric power is an "increasing cost" industry, so the argument goes, there will be excess revenues. That much is probably familiar to most students of elementary economics. Unfortunately, that is mere curve drawing and does not remotely represent a *useful* picture of the electric power production process—certainly not one useful in a regulatory context.

First, the curves are static, i.e., timeless. They might be a reasonably good representation of a utility system built instantaneously from scratch. Real utility systems, however, are a composite of facilities of various vintages. Utility systems planners take account both of the fact that they have very large existing stocks of facilities (the fruit of yesterday's decisions) and of the fact that they are continually expanding their stock of equipment. In addition, those hypothetical cost curves are, in fact, continually shifting in time. They shift up or down with each change in fuel prices, with each change in technology and, indeed, with each change in the policies of regulatory agencies.

Second, it is not at all clear that electric utilities do operate on the upward sloping segment of a static marginal cost curve even if one could be drawn. While particular plants may exhibit cost characteristics that increase as output increases, utilities are not mere aggregates of individual plants. They are *systems*, complex and interrelated. Generating plants are only part of the system. Enormous parts of the system are comprised of distribution facilities, the costs of which, in large part, are not marginal at all (in the sense that they do not vary with the load on the system). In isolation, this aspect of utility operation would suggest *decreasing*, not increasing, marginal costs. While simple, two dimensional cost curves may be suitable fare for freshmen students in economics, they do not do much to inform the decisions of regulatory authorities.

There is a second sense in which the electric power industry may be said to be one of increasing costs and from which the conclusion is drawn that marginal cost pricing will produce excess revenues. In recent years, the costs of generating plants and fuel have increased rapidly. Since marginal costs are measured, in part, by the costs of expanding utility capacity, and since new facilities cost more to provide than facilities previously constructed, the conclusion is drawn that pricing at marginal cost will produce greater revenues than pricing at average costs. Note that "average" here refers to something quite different than the "average cost" curves discussed in the previous paragraphs. There, the reference is to an average of historical costs. Care should be taken not to confuse the two, since the mathematical relationship between marginal costs and average costs, both taken on a current basis, simply does not hold between marginal costs and average historical costs.

It is indeed correct that the costs of constructing generation, transmission and distribution capacity are higher now than before. However, this does *not* support the contention that marginal cost pricing will yield greater revenues than present tariffs. The reason that the contention is thought to be true derives from a mistaken conception of the nature of marginal costs, whereby *capital* costs are identified with *capacity* costs. In addition, excessive attention is directed to the costs of generating capacity and less to transmission and distribution capacity costs. Take, first, the distinction between capital costs and the capacity costs. Capital cost is, basically, the construction cost of a plant. It is usually expressed in dollars per kilowatt, and new baseload plants may cost upwards of $1,000 per kilowatt. Capacity cost, on the other hand, is the change in system costs that results from increasing system capacity by 1 KW. It is *not* $1,000 per kilowatt or anything like it. The plants which do cost $1,000 per kilowatt also produce significant fuel savings to a utility by displacing other, less efficient generating plants in the system dispatching schedule. These fuel savings are measured by the difference in system fuel costs with and without the new plant. They must be deducted from capital costs to arrive at a net cost of additional capacity. These fuel savings may be so high that utilities that burn large quantities of oil will sometimes find that the new baseload plants, despite higher initial capital costs, will pay for themselves in fuel cost savings over a period of years. The extra capacity, in effect, is something one gets for free. Indeed, it may be the need for additional energy, not additional capacity, that necessitates the capital expenditure in the first place.* There is no simple identity between capital and capacity costs or between operating and energy costs. It cannot, therefore, be said that because the capital costs of new plants are higher than was previously the case, that basing tariffs on the marginal generating capacity costs of new plants will produce excess revenues. Perhaps; perhaps not. It will depend on the particular case.

*A capital expenditure to increase the storage area of a reservoir, for example, may increase the energy available from it, but not the capacity.

There is also the point about undue attention to generation capacity costs. It is often the case that a utility's investment in generation capacity is considerably less than its investment in transmission and distribution capacity. Note that it is total investment that, among other things, determines the size of the rate base and, thus, the size of the "revenue requirement." However, a utility may be able to increase its capacity to serve peak demands with a relatively modest additional investment in transmission and distribution capacity. That is, the marginal cost of transmission and distribution capacity may be quite small relative to the marginal cost of generation capacity, or relative to the investment historically required to serve similar increases in demand. Again, this is true notwithstanding that, per unit of capacity, transmission and distribution does cost more than it used to. The point, in short, is that concentration on the capital costs of new generating plants (1) focuses only on part of a system, and (2) misconstrues the nature of marginal costs in any case.

Given that tariffs based on marginal cost may produce more, less or (by happy and unlikely coincidence) precisely the same revenue as present tariffs, the question becomes how best to adjust for the discrepancy. Among the suggestions made in various regulatory proceedings has been the application of what is referred to in economics as "the inverse elasticity rule." In brief, this rule requires that the percentage deviation of prices from marginal costs be inversely related to the price elasticity of demand.* It should be no wonder that such a rule, invoked not in a discussion among economic theoreticians but in an electric utility rate case, should cause some considerable discontent—probably because few understood what it meant, much less why it was asserted to be a good idea.**

Nor is it necessary here to resort to the esoterica of welfare economics to prescribe a useful standard for adjustments to marginal costs in order to meet revenue requirements. Common sense suggests a solution: when revenue requirements require a departure from marginal costs as the basis for tariff design, customer charges (fixed monthly charges) should be adjusted up or down as required to meet the revenue constraint. Additional adjustments, if necessary, should be made depending on the particularities of each case. The rationale

*W. Baumol and Bradford D., "Optimal Departures from Marginal Cost Pricing," *American Economic Review* 60 (June 1970).

**A co-author of one version of the rule was himself reluctant to bring it up in congressional hearings since he had recently been "driven to some rather horrifying mathematics" in discussing it before the Federal Communications Commissions. *See*, Testimony of William J. Baumol, Hearings before the Subcommittee on Activities of Regulatory Agencies, Select Committee on Small Business, House of Representatives, Feb. 1, 1968, p. 638.

for this fairly simple rule is that consumer decisions on when or how much electricity to consume are not affected by the size of the fixed monthly charge. If the premise is that pricing at marginal costs will generate a rational set of price signals to guide consumer decisions, it follows that departures from marginal costs to meet other objectives ought to do the minimum possible violence to the basic structure of marginal cost. Adjusting customer charges to meet revenue requirements serves that end.

Finally, a word is in order about a pricing proposal that has generated at least as much controversy as marginal cost pricing, viz., "lifeline" rates. "Lifeline" is a term once applied to minimal telephone service that furnished a critical communications link for certain consumers. Applied to electricity, the term suggests some minimal quantity of low cost electric power for needy consumers. In essence, the proposal is an effort to relieve certain consumers of some part of the burden of increasing electricity prices. Relief is achieved by transferring some of the cost of serving low volume consumers to others. It is an argument grounded in perceptions of what is equitable. Regrettably, the argument has also been cast in economic terms, which clouds a straightforward consideration of the merits of the proposal.

By now it should be clear that electricity costs vary according to the time, place and voltage at which consumption takes place; these costs are not a function of how much or little electricity consumers have previously taken. Lifeline rates, and indeed most conventional tariffs, make price a function of volume. Marginal cost tariffs do not. There may be many reasons why it is socially desirable to transfer income from one group of consumers to another, but it is not obvious that the best way to do so is to give consumers signals that imply that the cost to society of providing electricity is more or less than it actually is. Nor is it clear why regulatory agencies should supposedly be in a better position than, say, legislators either to identify the proper beneficiaries of lifeline rates or the amount of the subsidy.

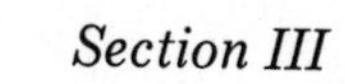

Section III

A Generalized Computer Methodology for Analyzing Marginal Cost and Related Matters

Introduction

As the case studies in Section II demonstrate, the determination of the marginal costs of electricity usually depends on estimates—sometimes rather rough estimates—of certain variables such as the annual operation and maintenance expenses associated with high voltage transmission line. Other variables, like reserve margin, have no preordained value, but can assume any value the analyst wishes to prescribe. A reserve margin is, in effect, insurance against brownouts and one buys as much or as little insurance as one likes. Still, the computational process itself is, at least for the vast majority of cases, essentially similar for all utilities.

Any serious study of marginal costs is a process of continually revising and updating the estimates that form the basis of the analysis. Often the need for improved estimates is not apparent until the preliminary results are considered. At that point it may be clear that, for example, estimated marginal generation capacity costs are too high, and some backtracking is required to find out why (perhaps fuel savings were underestimated, or average loss multipliers were exaggerated). In short, the analyst may wish (or have) to work with more than a simple fixed set of data inputs.

MARGINALCOST is a computer program that permits the user to begin with a fixed set of inputs and then, for most of the variables, to change one or several of those inputs to alternative levels, or to specify a range of values for the inputs. For example, an initial specification of loss multipliers may be replaced by several alternative specifications, perhaps high, medium and low estimates. Likewise, a discount rate of 10 percent may be respecified as all values between

7 percent and 20 percent in increments of 2 percent. The user, therefore, can call for an infinite number of marginal cost estimates—although if the number called for exceeds ten iterations, MARGINALCOST will count up the possibilities and inquire whether the user really wants that many or would prefer to moderate his or her demands. In any case, MARGINALCOST will provide a separate listing of marginal costs for each combination of input values.

Moreover, if there are alternative ways of estimating certain values, MARGINALCOST will inquire at the start which procedure is to be used—for example, whether or not future plants are to be considered interdependent. Additionally, the relation of transmission capacity to load can be estimated either from future or historical data. MARGINALCOST uses whichever procedure the user prefers.

WHAT DOES IT COST AND HOW LONG DOES IT TAKE?

The cost of computer time is trivial. If long distance telephone lines are the link between the user and the computer, the cost of the phone call will inevitably exceed the cost of computer time.

A complete printout of marginal cost structure takes about two minutes on a thirty character per second teletype and runs to less than twice the length of this page. Thus, a command for marginal cost structure at all interest rates from 8 percent to 20 percent in increments of 2 percent will take about fourteen minutes and produce fourteen pages of copy.

WHAT ELSE DOES THE PROGRAM PACKAGE DO?

Four additional programs are available: REVENUE, TYPICAL-BILL, METER-COST and LOAD. These are described more fully below, but briefly, REVENUE imposes a total revenue constraint on a set of prices and permits the user to see the effect of satisfying the constraint in various ways. TYPICAL-BILL prints out consumer bills for a number of consumption levels with varying proportions of total consumption on and off peak. METER-COST computes the break-even cost of installing new metering equipment for assumed changes in consumption patterns. LOAD is simply a program that draws load and load duration curves.

Most users will have their own means of performing the functions of these additional programs. They are included here as a convenience to the user who does not.

Chapter 8

An Algebraic Summary of MARGINALCOST

The MARGINALCOST computer program calculates the cost to an electrical utility of providing an additional KWH at various times of the year and for various voltage levels. This calculation may be viewed as consisting of six processes to be performed in series by the computer:

1. Calculation of loss multipliers,
2. Calculation of the marginal annual cost of generating capacity,
3. Calculation of the marginal annual cost of transmission and distribution capacity,
4. Calculation of the number of hours in each period,
5. Calculation of the marginal cost of energy, and
6. Calculation of the total marginal cost (¢/KWH).

CALCULATION OF LOSS MULTIPLIERS

The user has two options. A and B refer to the data inputs of each option.

A. Load during a peak period when loss overloads are known *[LK]*, load during a peak period when loss over loads are unknown *[LU]*, loss overloads during a peak period for each voltage level *j [KLOL(j)]*, and an indicator of whether the peak period to which *KLOL(j)* refers is "on peak" or "off peak" *[KPEAK]*.
B. Loss overloads on peak for each voltage level *j [LOLP(j)]*, the derivative of loss with respect to load on peak for each voltage

level j *[DLDLP(j)]*, the derivative of loss with respect to load off peak for each voltage level j *[DLDLO(j)]*.

If the set of inputs specified in (A) above are used, then the set of variables specified in (B) above are computed from them as follows:

- If *KPEAK* indicates "on peak" then, for each voltage level j, compute the following:

  $LOLP(j)$ is computed as $KLOL(j)$

  $DLDLP(j)$ is computed as $2 \cdot KLOL(j)$

  $DLDLO(j)$ is computed as $2 \cdot KLOL(j) \cdot \frac{LU}{LK}$

- If *KPEAK* indicates "off peak" then, for each voltage level j, compute the following:

  $LOLP(j)$ is computed as $KLOL(j) \cdot \frac{LU}{LK}$

  $DLDLP(j)$ is computed as $2 \cdot KLOL(j) \cdot \frac{LU}{LK}$

  $DLDLO(j)$ is computed as $2 \cdot KLOL(j)$

The following three loss multipliers are calculated for each voltage level j:

- Average loss multiplier for demand at peak *[ALMDP(j)]*:

$$\frac{1}{1 - LOLP(j)}$$

- Marginal loss multiplier for energy at peak *[MLMEP(j)]*:

$$\frac{1}{1 - DLDLP(j)}$$

- Marginal loss multiplier for energy off peak *[MLMEO(j)]*:

$$\frac{1}{1 - DLDLO(j)}$$

These are the "simple" loss multipliers, since they reflect losses occurring at a particular voltage level. In order to get "cumulative" loss multipliers, which will reflect full losses occurring at a particular voltage level of service, including those losses occurring "up stream" from the point of consumption, the computation is as follows for each voltage level j:

- Cumulative average loss multiplier for demand at peak *[CALMDP(j)]*:

  CALMDP(1) is set equal to *ALMDP*(1)

  CALMDP(j) is computed as *ASMDP(j)* · *CALMDP(j*−1), where *j* ranges from 2 to the number of voltage levels *[NVL]*.

- Cumulative marginal loss multiplier for energy on peak *[CMLMEP(j)]*:

  CMLMEP(1) is set equal to *MLMEP*(1)

  CMLMEP(j) is computed as *MLMEP(j)* · *CMLMEP(j*−1), where *j* ranges from 2 to *NVL*.

- Cumulative marginal loss multiplier for energy off peak *(CMLMEO(j)]*;

  CMLMEO(1) is set equal to *MLMEO*(1)

  CMLMEO(j) is computed as *MLMEO(j)* · *CMLMEO(j*−1*)*, where *j* ranges from 2 to *NVL*.

CALCULATION OF THE MARGINAL ANNUAL COST OF GENERATING CAPACITY

The user is allowed to set an interest rate *[IR]*. Two forms may be used:

As a percent (e.g., 10);
As a decimal (e.g., .10).

If *IR* is greater than 1, then it is assumed to have been expressed as a percent and is divided by 100 in order to have it expressed in decimal form.

For each voltage level *j*, where *j* ranges from 1 to *NVL*, the marginal cost per kilowatt of generating capacity *[MCKWGC(j)]* is initialized to zero.

When each power plant *[noplnt]* comes on line in a different year *FY(noplant)*, where *noplnt* ranges from 1 to the number of power plants being considered *[NPLNTS]*, a series of sequential calculations are performed:

$$CRF = \frac{IR}{1 - (1 + IR)^{-NYA\,(noplnt)}} \tag{8.1}$$

where *NYA(noplnt)* is the number of years over which the particular power plant *noplnt* with which we are dealing is annuitized.

- Initialize the present value of fuel savings for each power plant to zero.
- The variable *NYNPL* is set equal to tne value of *NY(noplnt)*, which is the number of years of fuel savings for power plant *noplnt*.
- *PVFS*, present value of fuel savings in the first year of the plant's fuel savings, is calculated as follows:

$$PVFS = \sum_{j=1}^{NYNPL} \frac{FS(noplnt, j)}{(1 + IR)^{j-1}} \quad , \tag{8.2}$$

where *FS(noplnt, j)* is the fuel savings for power plant *noplnt* in the *j*th year.

- The annuitized capital cost *[ACC]* is calculated as follows:

$$CRF \cdot CGP(noplnt), \tag{8.3}$$

where *CGP(noplnt)* is the cost of the generating plant *noplnt*, which is input.

- The cost of increased generating capacity *[CIGC]* for a particular power plant *noplnt* is calculated as follows:

$$CIGC = \frac{ACC + AFOM(noplnt) - PVFS}{(1 + IR)^{FY(noplnt) - FY(1)}} \tag{8.4}$$

where *FY(noplnt)* is the first year in which there are fuel savings for plant *noplnt*.

- The user is allowed the option of inputting the reserve margin *[RM]* as either a percent or a decimal. If *RM* is greater than 1, then it is assumed to have been expressed as a percent and is divided by 100 in order to have it expressed in decimal form.

- The annual cost of increasing generating capacity per kilowatt *[ACGCKW]* adjusted for reserve margin for this power plant *noplnt* is calculated as follows:

$$ACGCKW = \frac{CICG}{NEKWGC(noplnt)} \cdot (1 + RM) \qquad (8.5)$$

where *NEKWGC(noplnt)* is the number of extra kilowatts of generating capacity provided by power plant *noplnt.*

- For each voltage level j, where j ranges from 1 to NVL,
- The marginal cost per kilowatt of generating capacity for power plant *noplnt* at voltage level *j [MCKWG(noplnt, j)]* is calculated as follows:

$$MCKWG(noplnt, j) = CALMPD(j) \cdot ACGCKW \qquad (8.6)$$

The previous nine steps outline the calculations for a single plant in what may be a multiple plant analysis. (The contributions *MCKWG (noplnt j)* from the plants *noplnt* = 1,2, . . . , *NPLNTS* are summed to get the total marginal cost per KW of generating capacity *MCKWGC(j)*, for voltage level *j*.) As the discussion in the previous two sections indicates, there is more than one way to interpret and, therefore, to analyze the multiple plant futures. First, they may be considered as a single addition to supply because of their closeness in time and the interdependent nature in which they may fit into the long-term planning of the system. This is the usual case, and the calculations performed in MARGINALCOST presume this to be so.

Second, the basis for calculating marginal cost may for some special cases be to estimate the effect of changes in demand relative to the long-run expansion plan of the system rather than with respect to a specific time, e.g., the current year. This option, corresponding to the nine step computation described above, is also included in MARGINALCOST as a "nonstandard case" and is brought into play by requesting it explicitly when asked. The incremental costs of all future plants are calculated independently in this case and discounted to the year in which the initial plant is being computed.

Finally, in order to make the program completely general, a combination of the first two cases, with some plants interdependent and some independent, is possible. This is again the "nonstandard case," with some plants being brought on line during the same year and treated as one unit. The marginal (annual) cost per KW of generating capacity at voltage level v is computed as

$$MCKWGC(v) = \frac{\sum_{units\ u} CALMDP(v)*(1+RM)* \sum_{\substack{plants\ p \\ in\ units\ u}} \frac{\frac{IR}{(1+IR)^{-NY(p)}}*CGP(p) + AFOM(p) - \sum_{year\ y=1}^{NYA(p)} \frac{FS(p,y)}{(1+IR)^{y-1}}}{(1+IR)^{FY(p)-FY(1)}}}{\sum_{\substack{plants\ p \\ in\ units\ u}} NEKWGC(p)} \qquad (8.7)$$

where a "unit" is a set of plants that come on line in the same year (have the same value of FY). In order to help programmers a flow diagram and example are presented in Figure 8–1. (See page 110.)

CALCULATION OF THE MARGINAL ANNUAL COST OF TRANSMISSION AND DISTRIBUTION CAPACITY

For each voltage level i, where k ranges from 1 to NYL, the annual cost per unit of the jth facility, $ACUF(i,j)$ is calculated as follows:

$$ACUF(i,j) = (CCUF(i,j) \cdot CRF) + AOMCF(i,j), \qquad (8.8)$$

where: $CCUF(i,j)$ is the capital cost per unit for the jth facility;

CRF is the capital recovery factor;

$AOMCF(i,j)$ is the annual fixed operation and maintenance cost per unit for the jth facility.

The annual cost per KW of transmission and distribution costs for each plant i, is calculated by one of two alternative methods, A or B:

Method A: Using Historical Data.

For each observation k, where k ranges from 1 to $NOBS$, the load $[L(i,h)]$ is segregated as follows:

$CL(NVL,k)$, which is the customer load for the lowest voltage level, NVL;

$CL(i,k)$, which is the customer load for the other voltage levels upstream, $i = 1, \ldots, (NVL-1)$.

For each voltage level i, where i ranges from 1 to NVL, the annual cost per kilowatt for transmission and distribution without losses $[CKWTDL(i)]$ is calculated as follows:

$$CKWTDL(i) = \begin{cases} \sum_{j=i}^{NFI} ACUF(i,j) \cdot ENUFKW(i,j) & \text{(for } i=1\text{)} \\ \sum_{j=1}^{NFI} [ACUF(i,j) \cdot ENUFKW(i,j)] + CKWTDL(i-1), & \text{(for } i=2,\ldots,NVL \end{cases} \quad (i=1,NVL) \tag{8.9}$$

where: $NFI = NF(i)$;

$ENUFKW(i,j)$ is the number of additional units of facility j at the ith voltage level needed per additional KW of total load (l) at that part of the system. It can be estimated by the following regression coefficient (b) from historical data:

$$b = \frac{(NOBS \cdot SUMLF) - (SUML \cdot SUMF)}{(NOBS \cdot SUML2) - (SUML \cdot SUML)} \tag{8.10}$$

where

$$SUMLF = \sum_{k=1}^{NOBS} L(i,k) \cdot F(i,j,k)$$

$$SUML = \sum_{k=1}^{NOBS} L(i,k)$$

$$SUMF = \sum_{k=1}^{NOBS} F(i,j,k)$$

$$SUML2 = \sum_{k=1}^{NOBS} L(i,k)^2$$

Method B: Using Estimated Future Data

If the relationship between additions to transmission and distribution capacity and future changes in demand are known, an alternative computational method may be used.

For each voltage level i, where i ranges from 1 to NVL, the annual

Figure 8–1. Flow Diagram and Example for MARGINALCOST

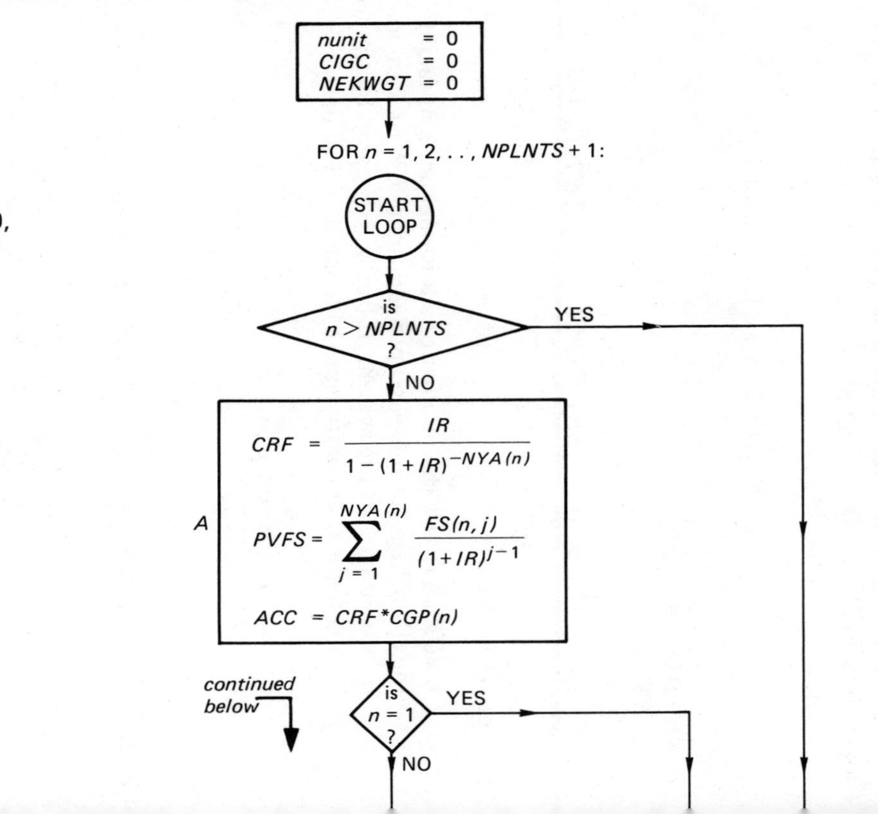

Example: Four plants at 1980, 1980, 1985, 1985:

n = 1: A,C,D (nunit = 1)
n = 2: A,D
n = 3: A,B,C,D (nunit = 2)
n = 4: A,D
n = 5: B

B finishes off a unit
C starts off a unit
A&D add a plant's contribution

Key:

nunit: # of current unit
CIGC: cost of increasing generating capacity (net) for the current unit
NEKWGT: total # extra KW-generating capacity provided by current unit
NPLNTS: # of plants
CRF: capital recovery factor
IR: annual interest rate
NYA(n): # years of annuitization of capital cost of plant *n*
PVFS: present value of fuel savings for current plant
ACC: annuitized capital cost of current plant
CGP(n): cost of generating plant *n*
FY(n): first year of fuel savings of plant *n*
ACGCKW: annual cost of generation capacity per KW for current unit
MCKWG(nunit, j): marginal cost per KW of generation capacity for unit nunit and voltage level *j*
MCKWGC(j): marginal cost per KW of generation capacity for unit nunit and voltage level *j* (total: summed over all units)

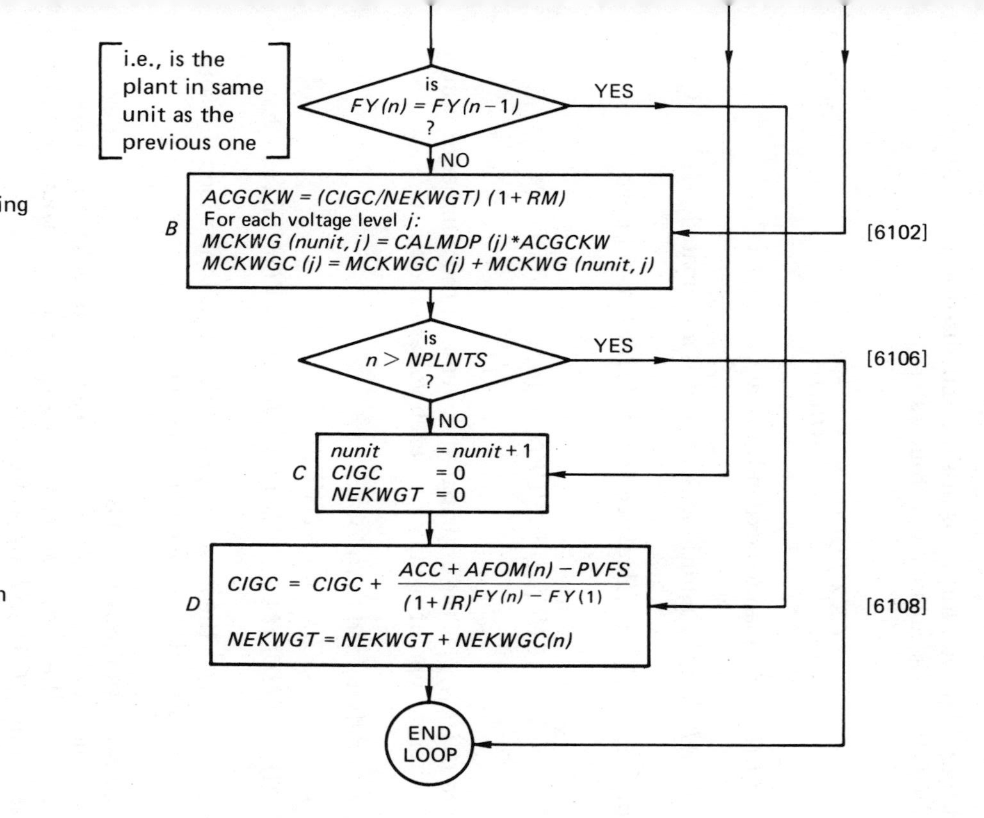

cost per kilowatt for transmission and distribution without losses [$CKWTDL(i)$] is calculated as follows:

$$CKWTDL(i) = \frac{E(i)}{AL(i)} \tag{8.11}$$

where $E(i)$ is the planned expenditure at voltage level i;

$AL(i)$ is the additional load that is anticipated.

Additionally, $E(i)$ is calculated for $i = 1, NVL$ as follows:

$$E(i) = \sum_{j=1}^{NFI} ACUF(i,j) \cdot INUF(i,j), \text{ for } i = 1, NVL \tag{8.12}$$

where $INUF(i, j)$ is the anticipated increase in the number of units of each type of facility j, at each voltage stage i.

$AL(i)$ is determined as follows:

$$ACL(NVL), \text{ for } i = NVL, \tag{8.13}$$

$$ACL(i) + ALMDP(i+1)*AL(i+1), \text{ for } i = (NVL-1), \ldots, 1.$$

where $ACL(i)$ is the anticipated additional customer load (by some future date) at each voltage level.

For Both Methods A and B

It is necessary to calculate, for each voltage level i, where $i = 1, \ldots, NVL$, the total capacity costs (generation + transmission and distribution) [$CAPCST(i)$] as follows:

$$CAPCST(i) = MCKWGC(i) + MCKWTD(i) \tag{8.14}$$

where $MCKWTD(i)$ is the marginal annual cost of transmission and distribution capacity.

$$MCKWTD(i) = CKWTDL(1), \text{ for } i = 1 \tag{8.15}$$

$$\underset{(\text{for } i=2,\ldots,NVL)}{MCKWTD(i),} = CKWTDL(i) + \sum_{m=1}^{i-1} CKWTDL(m) \prod_{n=m+1}^{i} ALMDP(n)$$

$$= CKWTDL(i) + ALMDP(i) \cdot MCKWTD(i-1)$$

CALCULATION OF THE NUMBER OF HOURS IN EACH PERIOD

The number of periods, each being designated as peak or off peak, must also be defined. It is possible to group the hours of the year, taking particular account of holiday hours.

CALCULATION OF THE MARGINAL COST OF ENERGY

For each voltage level i, where i ranges from 1 to NVL, the marginal cost in cents per kilowatt hour for peak generation $[MCKWHG(i)]$ is calculated as follows:

$$MCKWHG(i) = 100* \frac{MCKWGC(i)}{HRSPK} \tag{8.16}$$

and the marginal cost in cents per kilowatt hour for peak transmission $[MCKWHT(i)]$ is calculated as follows:

$$MCKWHT(i) = 100* \frac{MCKWTD(i)}{HRSPK} \tag{8.17}$$

where $HRSPK$ is the number of peak hours. One hundred converts dollars to cents.

For each voltage level i, where $i = 1, \ldots, NVL$, and each period j, where $j = i, \ldots, NPER$, calculate the marginal cost of energy per $KWH\ [MCEKWH(i,j)]$ as follows:

$$MCEKWH(i,j) = \frac{IFCKWH(j)}{CMLMEP(i)} \text{ for peak periods} \tag{8.18}$$

$$\frac{IFCKWH(j)}{CMLMEO(i)} \text{ for off-peak periods}$$

where $IFCKWH(j)$ is the incremental fuel cost per KWH for period j and the denominators are the respective cumulative marginal loss multipliers for voltage level i.

CALCULATION OF TOTAL MARGINAL COST IN CENTS PER KWH

Total marginal costs for peak and off peak are calculated as follows:

For voltage levels $i = 1, \ldots, NVL$

For peak periods:

$$\underset{\text{(total)}}{TOTMC(i)} = \underset{\text{(generation)}}{MCKWHG(i)} + \underset{\text{(transmission \& distribution)}}{MCKWHT(i)} + \underset{\text{(energy)}}{MCEKWH(i, \text{peak periods})} \tag{8.19}$$

For off-peak periods:

$$TOTMC(i) = MCEKWH(i, \text{off-peak periods}) \tag{8.20}$$

Chapter 9

User's Guide to MARGINALCOST

This user's guide consists of two parts: (1) a description of how to create the input file, and (2) a description of how to run the program from an interactive terminal. While reading this guide, the reader is urged to follow illustrative aids for each of the two parts: (1) a sample MARGINALCOST data input questionnaire and its corresponding data file, and (2) a sample interactive run of the MARGINALCOST program, which follow this user's guide.

CREATING THE INPUT FILE

This part of the user's guide to the MARGINALCOST program explains how to place the information from a completed marginal cost data input questionnaire onto a data file (the storage medium may be magnetic tape, magnetic disk, punched cards, etc.) that can be readily accessed by the particular computer being used. The description in this part of the guide will be both machine-independent and medium-independent.

The data file consists of a set of sequential records, where each record contains pieces of data. Each piece of data is expected to be of a particular type, where there are three allowable types:

1. An alphanumeric string—e.g., "YES" or "PEAK".
2. An integer—e.g., "7200" or "-83".
3. A real number—e.g., "25.74" or "3.48E4" [$3.48.10^4$] or "17E5" [17.10^5] or an integer.

The maximum usable length of a record is seventy-two characters.

Some of the pieces of data are to be expressed in free format fashion. This means two things:

1. A particular set of pieces of data can be continued from one record to another, provided each particular piece of data is contained totally on only one record.
2. On a particular record the pieces of data are separated by one or more spaces and/or commas.

The sequence of data in the data file will parallel the sequence of data on the marginal cost data input questionnaire (see page 000). The following description of the records in the data file will proceed through the records sequentially. Since the number of records is variable, we will not be able to refer to them by number, but must simply proceed by continually referring to the next records or next set of records, showing where each piece of data originates on the questionnaire (see the sample questionnaire and corresponding data file).

Data for Loss Multipliers

I. The first record in the data file consists of an integer that represents the number of voltage levels [NVL].

II. The next record consists of an alphanumeric string that can take on either the value "YES" or the value "NO" and represents the answer to the question "Do we have all the loss overloads as inputs?" [KALL]. If the answer is "YES" then the next set of records is as specified in (a), below; otherwise they are as specified in (b):

   a. The next set of records is free formatted and contains 3 · NVL pieces of real number data. The data consists, for each voltage level, of (1) loss overload on peak, (2) the derivative of loss with respect to load on peak, and (3) the derivative of loss with respect to load off peak. Thus we have the following sequence of pieces of data: [LOLP (1), DLDLP (1), DLDLO (1), LOLP (2), DLDLP (2), DLDLO (2), . . . , LOLP (NVL), DLDLP (NVL), DLDLO (NVL)].
   b. The next record consists of an alphanumeric string that can take on either the value "PEAK" or the value "OFF PEAK" and represents the answer to the question, "What is the peak of the known loss overloads?" [KPEAK]. The next record(s) is free formatted and contains NVL + 2 pieces of integer data. The data consist of load at peak, load off peak, and known loss overload for each voltage level. Thus we have the following sequence of pieces of data: [LP, LO, KLOL (1), KLOL (2), . . . , KLOL (NVL)].

Data for Generation Cost

III. a. The next record consists of three pieces of data in free format form in the following sequence: the interest rate [IR] expressed as a real number (note: 8 percent may be expressed either as "0.08" or as "8."), the reserve margin [RM] expressed as real number (note: 21 percent may be expressed either as "0.21" or as "21."), and the number of plants brought forward or back [NPLANTS] expressed as an integer.

b. The next NPLNTS sets of records, $i = 1, 2, \ldots,$ NPLNTS, are each in free format form, where each set consists of the following sequence of data: the number of extra kilowatts of generating capacity [NEKWGC (i)] expressed as a real number, the cost of the generating plant [CGP (i)] expressed as a real number, the annual fixed operation and maintenance [AFOM (i)] expressed as a real number, the number of years over which to annuitize the cost [NYA (i)] expressed as a real number, the number of years of fuel savings [NY (i)] expressed as an integer, and the fuel savings for each of those years [FS (i, 1), FS (i, 2), . . . , FS (i, NY (i))] expressed as real numbers.

Data for Transmission and Distribution Cost

IV. a. The next set of records, $i = 1, 2, \ldots,$ NVL, are each in free format form, where each set consists of the following sequence of data: the number of types of transmission and distribution facilities needed [NF (i)] expressed as an integer, and the corresponding set of capital costs per unit and annual fixed operation and maintenance costs per unit [CCUF (i, 1), AOMCF (i, 1), CCUF (i, 2), AOMCF (i, 2), . . . , CCUF (i, NF (i)), AOMCF (i, NF (i))] expressed as real numbers.

V. The next record consists of an alphanumeric string that can take on either the value "YES" or the value "NO" and represents the answer to the question "Do we have future, as opposed to historical, data on the relationship of the physical transmission and distribution facilities associated with changes in demand at various voltage levels?" [FUTDAT]. If the answer is "YES" then the next set of records is as specified in (a) below; if the answer is "NO", then they are as specified in (b):

a. This record(s) contains NVL pieces of real number data in free format form representing the anticipated additional customer load, by some future date, at each voltage level [ACL (1), ACL (2), . . . , ACL (NVL)]. The next NVL sets of records, $i = 1, 2, \ldots$, NVL, are each in free format form, where each set consists of the anticipated increase in the number of each type of facility: [INUF (i, 1), INUF (i, 2), . . . , INUF (i, NF (i))] expressed in real numbers.

b. This record consists of the number of historical observations [NOBS] expressed as an integer. The next NVL sets of records, $i = 1, 2, \ldots$, NVL, are each in free format form, where each set consists of the number of units of each facility for each of the NOBS observations: [F (i, l, l), F (i, 1, 2), . . . , F(i, l, NOBS), F (i, 2, 1), F (i, 2, 2), . . . , F (i, 2, NOBS), . . . , F (i, NF (i), 1), F (i, NF (i), 2), . . . , F(i, NF (i), NOBS)] expressed as real numbers. The next record(s) is free formatted and contains NVL · NOBS pieces of real number data representing the customer load in kilowatts at each voltage level for each observation [CL (1, 1), CL (1, 2), . . . , CL (1, NOBS), CL (2, 1), CL (2, 2), . . . , CL (2, NOBS), . . . , CL (NVL, 1), CL (NVL, 2), . . . , CL (NVL, NOBS)].

Data for KWH Charges

VI. a. The next record consists of an integer that represents the number of periods [NPER].

b. The next two records contain alphanumeric data that represent the names (they are simply for use as column headings on the output) of the NPER periods, where each period has associated with it twelve alphanumeric characters (two variables of six characters each) on the first record (for the top line of the heading), and twelve alphanumeric characters similarly on the second record (for the bottom line of the heading). Thus the first record here consists of 2 · NPER pieces of data representing the top line of the period names [PERNAM(1,1), PERNAM(1,2), PERNAM(2,1), PERNAM (2, 2), . . . , PERNAM(NPER, 1), PERNAM(NPER, 2)], and the second record here consists of 2 · NPER pieces of data representing the bottom line of the period names [PERNAM (1, 3), PERNAM(1, 4), PERNAM(2, 3), PERNAM(2, 4), . . . , PERNAM(NPER, 3), PERNAM(NPER, 4)].

c. The next NPER records, $i = 1, 2, \ldots$, NPER, each contain a string of seventy-two alphanumeric characters. For input purposes only, these seventy-two characters are broken up in into twelve pieces of data, each six characters in length, representing the period description [PRDSCR(i, 1), PRDSCR (i, 2), . . . , PRDSCR(i, 12)]. These seventy-two characters define the hours of the days of the year that are to be grouped into a period. The string of characters that define a particular period are divided into at most four continguous substrings:

1. The first substring determines the data specifications. It may begin with any number of spaces, commas, and/or dashes. It then contains a sequence consisting of an even number of dates (i.e., a set of "from" and "to" dates). Each date consists of a string unambiguously specifying the month; followed by a set of spaces, commas, and/or dashes; followed by the number of the day of the month; followed by a set of spaces, commas and/or dashes.
2. The second substring determines the day specifications. It contains a sequence of individual days and grouped days separated by spaces and commas. For example, "T" for Tuesday, "R" for Thursday, and "W-SAT" for Wednesday through Saturday.
3. The third substring determines the holiday specifications. There are three options here, followed by spaces, commas, and/or dashes:

   "I(NCLUDE HOLIDAYS)"
   "E(XCLUDE HOLIDAYS)"
   "O(NLY HOLIDAYS)"

4. The fourth substring determines the hour specifications. Here we have two numbers (i.e., "from" and "to" hour numbers) separated by spaces, commas, and/or dashes.

d. The next record(s) consists of the following sequence of free-formatted pieces of data: the number of peak periods [NPPS] expressed as an integer, and the number of each of the peak periods [NPP(1), NPP(2), . . . , NPP(NPPS)] expressed as integers.

e. The next record(s) consists of the following sequence of free-formatted pieces of data: the number of holidays in the year [NHOLS] expressed as an integer, and the year [YEAR] expressed as an integer.

f. The next NPPS records specify one holiday per record. The date of the holiday is specified as the month of the year and the day of the month separated by a comma.

g. The final record(s) consists of the following sequence of free-formatted pieces of data: the incremental fuel cost per KWH for each period [IFCKWH(1), IFCKWH(2), . . . , IFCKWH (PER)] expressed in ¢/KWH as real numbers.

RUNNING THE PROGRAM FROM AN INTERACTIVE TERMINAL

This part of the user's guide for the MARGINALCOST program explains how to run the program from an interactive terminal (while a few of the instructions to the computer are machine-dependent with respect to the Univac 1110, they are sufficiently straightforward that they should present no real problem). At each step in the description of the interactive process, the set of options with which the user is confronted is given along with a description of the resulting computer actions corresponding to each of the options.

After the preliminary sign on procedure to get on line to the particular computer from a terminal, there are only two fundamental control language statements that are needed: a statement commanding the computer to begin execution of the program (this would consist of "@XQT P*S.MARGINALCOST" for the UNIVAC 1110 in Madison, Wisconsin) and, after that program responds with "HELLO. PLEASE FURNISH INITIAL DATA", a statement giving the program the input data set to be used (e.g., this could consist of "@ADD W*G.WISDATA2" for the UNIVAC 1110 in Madison, Wisconsin). From this point forward the user will be interacting not with the computer's control system, but with the MARGINALCOST program itself.

After receiving the input data, the program responds with the message "DO YOU WANT THE INPUTS PRINTED? (THEY'RE LONG)". The user may then respond with either "YES" or "NO". If the user responds with "YES", then the input data will be displayed in six groupings (data for loss multipliers, data for generation cost, data for transmission and distribution cost, data for KWH charges, numbers of the days of the year that are holidays, and incremental fuel costs); otherwise it will not be displayed.

The program then computes and prints out the loss multipliers. Then, in the event that there is more than one plant being brought forward or backward, it will respond by asking "DO YOU WANT THE NONSTANDARD CASE, WHEREBY FUTURE PLANTS ARE TREATED AS DISTINCT UNITS AND DISCOUNTED?", to which the user must then respond with a "YES" or "NO". The program then proceeds to compute and print out the following information: marginal annual cost of generating capacity ($/KWH), marginal annual cost of transmission and distribution capacity ($/KWH), length of periods (hours), marginal cost of energy (¢/KWH), and total marginal cost (¢/KWH).

After the computer finishes these computations, the user is confronted with the option of changing the data as the program asks "ARE THERE ANY CHANGES YOU WISH TO MAKE IN THE DATA?" If the user responds with "NO", then the program signs with "AU REVOIR" and the computer's control system removes control from the program. If the user responds with "YES", then the user is instructed by the program as to how to specify the changes. The user, following those instructions, then specifies the variables to be changed and their new values. If variables are desired to be ranged (i.e., to take on a set of values, implying that a corresponding set of computations are to be performed), then they should be set to the value "−1". If there is an error in the specification of the changed variables, then the program will respond with the message "THERE WAS AN ERROR IN THOSE CHANGES; PLEASE TRY AGAIN", at which point the user may retype the changes. The program will then ask the user "DO YOU WANT THE INPUTS PRINTED? (THEY'RE LONG)", to which the user responds either "YES" or "NO" with the results as described previously.

If there are variables that have been assigned the value "−1", then the program will respond with "PLEASE SUPPLY THE VALUES OF THE CHANGING VARIABLES". It will then list, successively, each variable number. After each variable number the user must respond by specifying the set of values that the ranged variable is to assume (this specification can take the form of either a string of numbers separated by commas or a beginning number followed by a dash followed by an ending number followed by a comma followed by an increment value that specifies the additive "leaps" in value to be used in getting from the beginning number to the ending number). The program then responds by telling the user how many runs are dictated by the set of ranged variables. It then asks "DO YOU WISH TO RESUPPLY THE VALUES OF THE CHANGING VARIABLES?" If the user responds with "YES", then the process of specifying the ranged variables is repeated, otherwise not.

The computation and display of the loss multipliers (as well as later computations, as described previously) then proceeds, utilizing the new input variables' values, and is again followed by asking the user for changed values and proceeds as described previously.

Figure 9–1. MARGINALCOST Data Input Questionnaire

Variable Description	Computer Symbol	Variable Number
DATA FOR LOSS MULTIPLIERS:		
I Number of Voltage Levels:	NVL*[≤5]	1
II a do you know:	KALL*[='YES' or 'NO']	2
[if KALL='YES':] for each voltage level:	voltage level ↓	
(1) $\frac{\text{loss}}{\text{load}}$ on peak, $\frac{\text{d loss}}{\text{d load}}$ on peak, $\frac{\text{d loss}}{\text{d load}}$ off peak:	LOLP(1),DLDLP(1),DLDLO(1)	3,8,13
(2)	LOLP(2),DLDLP(2),DLDLO(2)	4,9,14
(3)	LOLP(3),DLDLP(3),DLDLO(3)	5,10,15
(4)	LOLP(4),DLDLP(4),DLDLO(4)	6,11,16
(5)	LOLP(5),DLDLP(5),DLDLO(5)	7,12,17
[otherwise; if KALL='NO'] which do you know,		
II b (1) the peak or off-peak $\frac{\text{loss}}{\text{load}}$?	KPEAK*[='PEAK' or 'OFF-PEAK']	18
(2) Load on Peak, Load Off peak (both loads in same units), known $\frac{\text{loss}}{\text{load}}$ for each voltage level:	LP,LO,KLOL(1),KLOL(2),...KLOL(NVL)	19,20,21,22,...(25)
III DATA FOR GENERATION COST:		
a annual Interest Rate, Reserve Margin, Number of Plants brought forward or back:	IR,RM,NPLNTS[≤5]	33,34,32

I 3

II a YES

(1) .0485 .0347 .0300

(2) .0467 .0357 .0310

(3) .0421 .0323 .0281

(4) ______ ______ ______

(5) ______ ______ ______

II b (1) ______

(2) ______ ______ ______ ______ ______ ______ ______

III a .10 .15 2

	Variable Description (cont.)	Computer Symbol (cont.)	Variable Number (cont.)
III b(1)	for each plant (1,2,...,NPLNTS): Number of Extra KW of Generating Capacity provided, Cost of the Generating Plant, Annual Fixed Operation and Maintenance, Number of Years over which to Annuitize the cost (usually=lifetime of plant), Number of Years of fuel savings, Fuel Savings for each year (1,2,...NY)	NEKWGC(1),CGP(1),AFOM(1),NYA(1), NY(1)*[≤ 25] FS(1,1),FS(1,2),...FS(1,NY(1))	35,40,45,185,55,60,65,...(180)
(2)		Repeat Subscript 2	36,41,46,186,56,61,66,...(181)
(3)		Repeat Subscript 3	37,42,47,187,57,62,67,...(182)
(4)		Repeat Subscript 4	38,43,48,188,58,63,68,...(183)
(5)		Repeat Subscript 5	39,44,49,189,59,64,69,...(184)

III b(1) 400000 159200000 680000 30 1
7505000

(2) 172000 83690000 258000 30 1
7050000

(3)

(4)

(5)

		Variable Description (cont.)	Computer Symbol (cont.)	Variable Number (cont.)
IV		DATA FOR TRANSMISSION & DISTRIBUTION COST:		
	a (1)	For each voltage stage (1,2,...,NVL): Number of types of T.&D. facilities needed, for each type of facility (1,2,...,NF) (NF≤5): Capital Cost per unit, Annual Fixed O.&M. per unit	(voltage stage; facility) NF(1)*[≤5],CCUF(1,1),AOMCF(1,1),CCUF(1,2), AOMCF(1,2),...,CCUF(1,NF(1)),AOMCF(1,NF(1))	196,701,726,706,731,...,721,746
	(2)		Repeat Subscript 2	197,702,727,707,732,...,722,747
	(3)		Repeat Subscript 3	198,703,728,708,733,...,723,748
	(4)		Repeat Subscript 4	199,704,729,709,734,...,724,749
	(5)		Repeat Subscript 5	200,705,730,710,735,...,725,750
V		do you know:	FUTDAT*[='YES' or 'NO']	751
	a	[If FUTDAT = 'YES':] (future data) anticipated Additional Customer Load (by some future date) at each voltage level	ACL(1),...ACL(NVL)	852,853,...(856)
	b (1)	anticipated Increase in the Number of Units of each type of Facility, at each voltage stage	(voltage stage; facility) INUF(1,1),INUF(1,2),...,INUF(1,NF(1))	857,862,...(877)
	(2)		INUF(2,1),INUF(2,2),...,INUF(2,NF(2))	858,863,...(878)
	(3)		Repeat Subscript 3	859,864,...(879)
	(4)		Repeat Subscript 4	860,865,...(880)
	(5)		Repeat Subscript 5	861,866,...(881)

IV a (1) 3 60000 225 40000 310 13.83 .30

(2) 3 9725 292 15.84 .40 1.51 .01

(3) 1 27.38 .20

(4)

(5)

V NO

a

b(1)

(2)

(3)

(4)

(5)

		Variable Description (cont.)	Computer Symbol (cont.)	Variable Number (cont.)
V	c	[otherwise, if FUTDAT = 'NO':] (historical data:) Number of Observations;	NOBS*[≤20]	195
			voltage stage facility observation	
	d (1)	number of units of each facility at each voltage level for each of the NOBS observations	F(1,1,1),F(1,1,2),F(1,1,3)...F(1,1,NOBS)	201,226,251,...(676)
			F(1,2,1),F(1,2,2),F(1,2,3)...F(1,2,NOBS)	206,231,256,...(681)
			Repeat for up to 5 facilities at each voltage stage	
			F(1,5,1),F(1,5,2),F(1,5,3)...F((1,5,NOBS)	221,246,271,...(696)
	d (2)		F(2,1,1),F(2,1,2),F(2,1,3)...F(2,1,NOBS)	202,227,252,...(677)
			Repeat as in voltage 1 for up to 5 facilities and continue to repeat for up to five voltage stages (d(2),...d(5))	207,232,257,...(682)
	d (3)			
	d (4)			
	d (5)(5)		F(NVL,NF(NVL),1)...F(NVL,NF(NVL),NOBS)	225,250,275,...(700)

v c 9

d(1)(1)	644	720	740	766	766	773	800	800	857
(2)	1388	1219	1356	1359	1408	1466	1519	1549	1600
(3)	1213E3	1246E3	1361E3	1528E3	1415E3	1640E3	2000E3	2000E3	2000E3
(4)									
(5)									
d(2)(1)	14776	14997	15233	15474	15721	15932	16100	16300	16500
(2)	935E3	1254E3	1313E3	1246E3	1313E3	1338E3	1385E3	1485E3	1577E3
(3)	203.1E3	193.1E3	223.1E3	254.1E3	282.1E3	276.2E3	268.2E3	283.3E3	326.3E3
(4)									
(5)									
d(3)(1)	1338E3	1437E3	1547E3	1666E3	1821E3	1995E3	2160E3	2325E3	2590E3
(2)									
(3)									
(4)									
(5)									
d(4)(1)									
(2)									
(3)									
(4)									
(5)									

Variable Description (cont.)	Computer Symbol (cont.)	Variable Number (cont.)
V e(1) Customer Load at each voltage stage for each observation (KW)	CL(1,1),CL(1,2),...,CL(1,NOBS)	752,757,...(847)
(2)	CL(2,1),CL(2,2),...,CL(2,NOBS)	753,778,...(848)
(3)	Repeat Subscript 3	
(4)	Repeat Subscript 4	
(5)	Repeat Subscript 5	756,781,...(851)
VI DATA FOR KWH CHARGES:		
a Number of periods:	NPER*[≤6]	882
b Period names: (one character per "-", these names will be printed exactly as entered here, with the first twelve characters of both lines as the name of the first period, etc.)	PERNAM*	Separate Common Block: no variable number

```
V d    (5)(1) ____ ____ ____ ____ ____ ____ ____ ____ ____ ____ ____ ____ ____ ____ ____ ____ ____ ____ ____ ____
          (2) ____ ____ ____ ____ ____ ____ ____ ____ ____ ____ ____ ____ ____ ____ ____ ____ ____ ____ ____ ____
          (3) ____ ____ ____ ____ ____ ____ ____ ____ ____ ____ ____ ____ ____ ____ ____ ____ ____ ____ ____ ____
          (4) ____ ____ ____ ____ ____ ____ ____ ____ ____ ____ ____ ____ ____ ____ ____ ____ ____ ____ ____ ____
          (5) ____ ____ ____ ____ ____ ____ ____ ____ ____ ____ ____ ____ ____ ____ ____ ____ ____ ____ ____ ____

  e       (1) 113E3 121E3 130E3 142E3 162E3 173E3 182E3 195E3 211E3 ____ ____ ____ ____ ____ ____ ____ ____ ____ ____ ____
          (2) 187E3 175E3 204E3 234E3 260E3 255E3 244E3 256E3 297E3 ____ ____ ____ ____ ____ ____ ____ ____ ____ ____ ____
          (3) 366E3 401E3 427E3 457E3 500E3 480E3 547E3 610E3 670E3 ____ ____ ____ ____ ____ ____ ____ ____ ____ ____ ____
          (4) ____ ____ ____ ____ ____ ____ ____ ____ ____ ____ ____ ____ ____ ____ ____ ____ ____ ____ ____ ____
          (5) ____ ____ ____ ____ ____ ____ ____ ____ ____ ____ ____ ____ ____ ____ ____ ____ ____ ____ ____ ____

VI a          4

  b       (1) WINTER   (2) SUMMER &     (3) SAT., SUN    (4) NIGHTTIME     (5) ______   (6) ______
              WEEKDAY      VALLEY WKDY      & HOL. DAY       THRUOUT YR.       ______       ______
```

	Variable Description (cont.)	Computer Symbol (cont.)	Variable Number (cont.)
VI c(1)	Period descriptions (dates, days of the week, holidays, hours; [below "x(y)" means that y is optional] dates - in form: "DEC. 25-FEB. 13, OCT. 1-NOV. 15" with each month abbreviated unambiguously and separated from the number by at least one blank (up to 5 pairs of dates per period may be specified. If no dates are given "JAN. 1-DEC. 31" is assumed.) days - in form: "M,W-SAT" with each day abbreviated unambiguously, or "WE(EKEND)" for "SAT,SUN" or "R" for "TH(URSDAY)", or "T" for "TU(ESDAY)" Do not "-" over Sunday (e.g., don't enter "SAT-M"). If no days are given, "M-SUN" is assumed. holidays - "I(NCLUDE HOLIDAYS)" "E(XCLUDE HOLIDAYS)" or "ONLY H(OLIDAYS)" only and all holidays in the dates of the period are considered, regardless of the days of the week. hours - in form: "22-7", with only two hours specified: The 22nd through 7th hours, inclusive, are specified. If no hrs. specified, "1-24" is assumed.)	[≤72 characters] PRDSCR*	
(2)		Repeat for each period c(2),...c(6)	
(3)			
(4)			
(5)			
(6)			

VI c(1) NOV. 1 - MARCH 31, M-F, EXCL. HOLS., 8-12

(2) APRIL 1 - OCT. 31, M-F, EXCL. HOLS, 8-21

(3) WEEKENDS, HOLIDAYS, 8-21

(4) 22-7

(5) ______

(6) ______

	Variable Description (cont.)	Computer Symbol (cont.)	Variable Number (cont.)
VI d	Number of Peak Periods, Number of each of the Peak Periods (1,2,...NPPS)	NPPS*[≤6],NPP(1)*,...,NPP(NPPS)*	907,908,...(913)
e	Number of holidays in the year, Year (e.g., 1975)	NHOLS*[≤15], YEAR*	
f (1)	Dates of holidays in the indicated year (1,2,...,NHOLS)(dates in same form as VI, c(1), above).	Converted to number of the day of the year: HOLDYR(1)*	Separate Common Block: no variable number
(2)			
(3)			
(4)			
(5)			
(6)			
(7)			
(8)			
(9)			
(10)			
(11)			
(12)			
(13)			
(14)			
(15)		HOLDYR(NHOLS)*	
g	Incremental Fuel Cost per KWH for each period (1,2,...,NPER)(¢/kwh)	IFCKWH(1),...IFCKWH(NPER)	944,...(949)

*Integer variable

VI	(d)	2	1	2				
	(e)	10	1975					
	(f) (1)	JAN 1						
	(2)	FEB 17						
	(3)	MAR 28						
	(4)	MAY 26						
	(5)	JULY 4						
	(6)	SEPT 1						
	(7)	OCT 13						
	(8)	OCT 27						
	(9)	NOV 27						
	(10)	DEC 25						
	(11)							
	(12)							
	(13)							
	(14)							
	(15)							
	(g)	2.22	1.17	1.26	.894			

Figure 9–2. MARGINALCOST Data List

```
@PRT,S W*G.WISDATA2
FURPUR-MACC  2.04-01/07-14:21

W*G.WISDATA2
     1       3
     2       YES
     3       .0485,.0347,.0300,.0467,.0357,.0310,.0421,.0323,.0281
     4       .10,.15,2
     5       4E5 159200E3 680E3 30 1 7505000
     6       172000 8369E4 258000 30 1 7050000
     7       3 60000 225 40000 310 13.83 .30
     8       3 9725 292 15.84 .40 1.51 .01
     9       1 27.38 .20
    10       NO
    11       9
    12       644 720 740 766 766 773 800 800 857
    13       1388 1219 1356 1359 1408 1466 1519 1549 1600
    14       1213E3 1246E3 1361E3 1528E3 1415E3 1640E3 2000E3 2000E3 2000
E3
    15       14776 14997 15233 15474 15721 15932 16100 16300 16500
    16       935E3 1254E3 1313E3 1246E3 1313E3 1338E3 1385E3 1485E3 1577E
3
    17       203.1E3 193.1E3 223.1E3 254.1E3 282.1E3 276.2E3 268.2E3 283.
3E3 326.3E3
    18       1338E3 1437E3 1547E3 1666E3 1821E3 1995E3 2160E3 2325E3 2590
E3
    19       113E3 121E3 130E3 142E3 162E3 173E3 182E3 195E3 211E3
    20       187E3 175E3 204E3 234E3 260E3 255E3 244E3 256E3 297E3
    21       366E3 401E3 427E3 457E3 500E3 480E3 547E3 610E3 670E3
    22       4
    23          WINTER      SUMMER &    SAT., SUN.   NIGHTTIME
    24         WEEKDAY   VALLEY WKDY  & HOL. DAY  THRUOUT YR.
    25       NOV. 1 - MARCH 31, M-F, EXCL. HOLS, 8-21
    26       APRIL 1 - OCT. 31, M-F, EXCL, 8-21
    27       WEEKENDS, HOLIDAYS, 8-21
    28       22-7
    29       2 1,2
    30       10 1975
    31       JAN 1
    32       FEB 17
    33       MAR 28
    34       MAY 26
    35       JULY 4
    36       SEPT 1
    37       OCT 13
    38       OCT 27
    39       NOV 27
    40       DEC 25
    41       2.22,1.71,1.26,.894
 PRT    COMPLETED..
```

Figure 9–3. A Sample Interactive Run of the MARGINALCOST Program

INPUT DATA

```
@XQT P*S.MARGINALCOST


 HELLO.  PLEASE FURNISH INITIAL DATA
@ADD W*G.WISDATA2

 DO YOU WANT THE INPUTS PRINTED? (THEY'RE LONG)
YES

 DATA FOR LOSS MULTIPLIERS:
             3
           YES
    4.8500E-02      3.4700E-02      3.0000E-02      4.6700E-02      3.5700E
-02      3.1000E-02      4.2100E-02      3.2300E-02
    2.8100E-02

 DATA FOR GENERATION COST:
    1.0000E-01      1.5000E-01               2
    4.0000E+05      1.5920E+08      6.8000E+05      30.0000
  1      7.5050E+06
    1.7200E+05      8.3690E+07      2.5800E+05      30.0000
  1       .0500E+06

 DATA FOR TRANSM. & DISTR. COST:
             3      6.0000E+04    225.0000          4.0000E+04    310.0000
      13.8300          3.0000E-01
             3   9725.0000      292.0000          15.8400          4.0000E
-01       1.5100          1.0000E-02
             1      27.3800         2.0000E-01
           NO
             9
   644.0000        720.0000        740.0000        766.0000        766.0000
      773.0000        800.0000        800.0000
   857.0000       1388.0000       1219.0000       1356.0000       1359.0000
     1408.0000       1466.0000       1519.0000
  1549.0000       1600.0000        1.2130E+06      1.2460E+06      1.3610E
+06      1.5280E+06      1.4150E+06      1.6400E+06
    2.0000E+06      2.0000E+06      2.0000E+06
    1.4776E+04      1.4997E+04      1.5233E+04      1.5474E+04      1.5721E
+04      1.5932E+04      1.6100E+04      1.6300E+04
    1.6500E+04      9.3500E+05      1.2540E+06      1.3130E+06      1.2460E
+06      1.3130E+06      1.3380E+06      1.3850E+06
    1.4850E+06      1.5770E+06      2.0310E+05      1.9310E+05      2.2310E
+05      2.5410E+05      2.8210E+05      2.7620E+05
    2.6820E+05      2.8330E+05      3.2630E+05
    1.3380E+06      1.4370E+06      1.5470E+06      1.6660E+06      1.8210E
+06      1.9950E+06      2.1600E+06      2.3250E+06
    2.5900E+06
    1.1300E+05      1.2100E+05      1.3000E+05      1.4200E+05      1.6200E
+05      1.7300E+05      1.8200E+05      1.9500E+05
    2.1100E+05      1.8700E+05      1.7500E+05      2.0400E+05      2.3400E
+05      2.6000E+05      2.5500E+05      2.4400E+05
    2.5600E+05      2.9700E+05      3.6600E+05      4.0100E+05      4.2700E
+05      4.5700E+05      5.0000E+05      4.8000E+05
    5.4700E+05      6.1000E+05      6.7000E+05
```

```
DATA FOR KWH CHARGES:
            4
    WINTER      SUMMER &    SAT., SUN.    NIGHTTIME
   WEEKDAY    VALLEY WKDY  & HOL. DAY   THRUOUT YR.
  NOV. 1 - MARCH 31, M-F, EXCL. HOLS, 8-21
  APRIL 1 - OCT. 31, M-F, EXCL, 8-21
  WEEKENDS, HOLIDAYS, 8-21
  22-7
            2                1                 2
           10              1975
NUMBERS OF THE DAYS OF THE YEAR WHICH ARE HOLIDAYS:   1  48  87 146 185
244 286 300 331 359
INCREMENTAL FUEL COSTS:
    2.2200          1.7100          1.2600          8.9400E-01
```

OUTPUT

LOSS MULTIPLIERS

VOLTAGE STAGE	FOR DEMAND ON PEAK SIMPLE	FOR DEMAND ON PEAK CUMULATIVE	FOR ENERGY ON PEAK SIMPLE	FOR ENERGY ON PEAK CUMUL.	FOR ENERGY OFF PEAK SIMPLE	FOR ENERGY OFF PEAK CUMUL.
FROM GENERATION TO HIGH VOLTAGE CUSTOMERS AND HIGH SIDE OF STAGE ONE TRANSFORMERS	1.0510	1.0510	1.0359	1.0359	1.0309	1.0309
FROM HIGH SIDE OF STAGE ONE TRANSFORMERS TO STAGE TWO CUSTOMERS AND HIGH SIDE OF STAGE TWO TRANSFORMERS	1.0490	1.1025	1.0370	1.0743	1.0320	1.0639
FROM HIGH SIDE OF STAGE TWO TRANSFORMERS TO STAGE THREE CUSTOMERS AND HIGH SIDE OF STAGE THREE TRANSFORMERS	1.0440	1.1509	1.0334	1.1102	1.0289	1.0947

DO YOU WANT THE NONSTANDARD CASE, WHEREBY FUTURE PLANTS ARE TREATED AS DISTINCT UNITS AND DISCOUNTED?

NO

MARGINAL ANNUAL COST OF GENERATING CAPACITY ($/KW)

VOLTAGE LEVEL (1=HI VOLTAGE)	MARGINAL COST
1	25.670
2	26.927
3	28.111

MARGINAL ANNUAL COST OF TRANSMISSION AND DISTRIBUTION CAPACITY ($/KW)

VOLTAGE LEVEL (1=HI VOLTAGE)	MARGINAL COST	GEN. + TRANSM. & DISTR.
1	7.577	33.247
2	15.836	42.763
3	29.620	57.731

LENGTH OF PERIODS (HOURS)

WINTER WEEKDAY	SUMMER & VALLEY WKDY	SAT., SUN. & HOL. DAY	NIGHTTIME THRUOUT YR.
1428	2086	1596	3650

MARGINAL COST OF ENERGY (CENTS/KWH)

VOLTAGE STAGE (1= HI)	PERIOD WINTER WEEKDAY	SUMMER & VALLEY WKDY	SAT., SUN. & HOL. DAY	NIGHTTIME THRUOUT YR.
1	2.300	1.771	1.299	.922
2	2.385	1.837	1.341	.951
3	2.465	1.898	1.379	.979

TOTAL MARGINAL COST (CENTS/KWH)

ON-PEAK PERIODS

VOLT. LEVEL	GENER.	TRANS. & DIS.	ENERGY/TOTAL WINTER WEEKDAY	SUMMER & VALLEY WKDY
1	.730	.216	2.300	1.771
			3.246	2.718
2	.766	.451	2.385	1.837
			3.602	3.054
3	.800	.843	2.465	1.898
			4.107	3.541

OFF-PEAK PERIODS: TOTAL MARGINAL COST (= ENERGY COST)

VOLTAGE LEVEL	SAT., SUN. & HOL. DAY	NIGHTTIME THRUOUT YR.
1	1.299	.922
2	1.341	.951
3	1.379	.979

```
 ARE THERE ANY CHANGES YOU WISH TO MAKE IN THE DATA?
YES

 ENTER THE NEW VALUE(S) AS IN THIS EXAMPLE:
 (NEVER TYPE IN COLUMN ONE - IT IS IGNORED - AND END LINES AT COMMAS)
 $NEW NEKWGC = 5E5,  AFOM = 75E6,
 CGP = 200E6, V(33) = 2 * .05
 $END


 $NEQ   IR = -1,RM = -1,
    NPLNTS=1
 $END


 THERE WAS AN ERROR IN THOSE CHANGES;  PLEASE TRY AGAIN


 $NEW   IR = -1,RM = -1,
    NPLNTS=1
 $END

 DO YOU WANT THE INPUTS PRINTED? (THEY'RE LONG)
YES
                               INPUT
 DATA FOR LOSS MULTIPLIERS:
              3
             YES
    4.8500E-02      3.4700E-02      3.0000E-02      4.6700E-02      3.5700E
-02      3.1000E-02      4.2100E-02      3.2300E-02
    2.8100E-02

 DATA FOR GENERATION COST:
   -1.0000         -1.0000                    1
    4.0000E+05      1.5920E+08      6.8000E+05    30.6000
 1      7.5050E+06

 DATA FOR TRANSM. & DISTR. COST:
              3      6.0000E+04    225.0000         4.0000E+04    310.0000
      13.8300          3.0000E-01
              3  9725.0000        292.0000         15.8400          4.0000E
-01      1.5100          1.0000E-02
              1     27.3800          2.0000E-01
             NO
              9
```

```
   644.0000        720.0000        740.0000        766.0000        766.0000
      773.0000        800.0000        800.0000
   857.0000       1388.0000       1219.0000       1356.0000       1359.0000
     1408.0000       1466.0000       1519.0000
  1549.0000       1600.0000          1.2130E+06      1.2460E+06      1.3610E
+06      1.5280E+06      1.4150E+06      1.6400E+06
     2.0000E+06      2.0000E+06      2.0000E+06
     1.4776E+04      1.4997E+04      1.5233E+04      1.5474E+04      1.5721E
+04      1.5932E+04      1.6100E+04      1.6300E+04
     1.6500E+04      9.3500E+05      1.2540E+06      1.3130E+06      1.2460E
+06      1.3130E+06      1.3380E+06      1.3850E+06
     1.4850E+06      1.5770E+06      2.0310E+05      1.9310E+05      2.2310E
+05      2.5410E+05      2.8210E+05      2.7620E+05
     2.6820E+05      2.8330E+05      3.2630E+05
     1.3380E+06      1.4370E+06      1.5470E+06      1.6660E+06      1.8210E
+06      1.9950E+06      2.1600E+06      2.3250E+06
     2.5900E+06
     1.1300E+05      1.2100E+05      1.3000E+05      1.4200E+05      1.6200E
+05      1.7300E+05      1.8200E+05      1.9500E+05
     2.1100E+05      1.8700E+05      1.7500E+05      2.0400E+05      2.3400E
+05      2.6000E+05      2.5500E+05      2.4400E+05
     2.5600E+05      2.9700E+05      3.6600E+05      4.0100E+05      4.2700E
+05      4.5700E+05      5.0000E+05      4.8000E+05
     5.4700E+05      6.1000E+05      6.7000E+05

 DATA FOR KWH CHARGES:
              4
      WINTER     SUMMER &    SAT., SUN.   NIGHTTIME
     WEEKDAY   VALLEY WKDY  & HOL. DAY  THRUOUT YR.
   NOV. 1 - MARCH 31, M-F, EXCL.. HOLS, 8-21
   APRIL 1 - OCT. 31, M-F, EXCL, 8-21
   WEEKENDS, HOLIDAYS, 8-21
   22-7
              2                1                 2
             10             1975
 NUMBERS OF THE DAYS OF THE YEAR WHICH ARE HOLIDAYS:   1  48  87 146 185
 244 286 300 331 359
 INCREMENTAL FUEL COSTS:
     2.2200          1.7100          1.2600          8.9400E-01

 PLEASE SUPPLY THE VALUES OF THE CHANGING VARIABLES
   (VARIABLE NUMBER   33:)
.07 -.10, .003
   (VARIABLE NUMBER   34:)
10,15

 YOU HAVE ASKED FOR       22 RUNS;
 DO YOU WISH TO RESUPPLY THE VALUES OF THE CHANGING VARIABLES?
YES
 THEN PLEASE DO SO, EXACTLY AS BEFORE

 PLEASE SUPPLY THE VALUES OF THE CHANGING VARIABLES
   (VARIABLE NUMBER   33:)
.07 -.10, .03
   (VARIABLE NUMBER   34:)
10,15
```

OUTPUT

*** RUN NUMBER 1 - VALUES OF CHANGING VARIABLES:

CHANGING VARIABLE NO.	VARIABLE NO.	VALUE
1	33	.0700
2	34	10.0000

LOSS MULTIPLIERS

VOLTAGE STAGE	FOR DEMAND ON PEAK SIMPLE	CUMULATIVE	FOR ENERGY ON PEAK SIMPLE	CUMUL.	OFF PEAK SIMPLE	CUMUL.
FROM GENERATION TO HIGH VOLTAGE CUSTOMERS AND HIGH SIDE OF STAGE ONE TRANSFORMERS	1.0510	1.0510	1.0359	1.0359	1.0309	1.0309
FROM HIGH SIDE OF STAGE ONE TRANSFORMERS TO STAGE TWO CUSTOMERS AND HIGH SIDE OF STAGE TWO TRANSFORMERS	1.0490	1.1025	1.0370	1.0743	1.0320	1.0639
FROM HIGH SIDE OF STAGE TWO TRANSFORMERS TO STAGE THREE CUSTOMERS AND HIGH SIDE OF STAGE THREE TRANSFORMERS	1.0440	1.1509	1.0334	1.1102	1.0289	1.0947

MARGINAL ANNUAL COST OF GENERATING CAPACITY ($/KW)

VOLTAGE LEVEL (1=HI VOLTAGE)	MARGINAL COST
1	17.354
2	18.204
3	19.004

MARGINAL ANNUAL COST OF TRANSMISSION AND DISTRIBUTION CAPACITY ($/KW)

VOLTAGE LEVEL (1=HI VOLTAGE)	MARGINAL COST	GEN. + TRANSM. & DISTR.
1	5.935	23.289
2	12.618	30.822
3	23.318	42.322

LENGTH OF PERIODS (HOURS)

WINTER WEEKDAY	SUMMER & VALLEY WKDY	SAT., SUN. & HOL. DAY	NIGHTTIME THRUOUT YR.
1428	2086	1596	3650

MARGINAL COST OF ENERGY (CENTS/KWH)

VOLTAGE STAGE (1= HI)	PERIOD WINTER WEEKDAY	SUMMER & VALLEY WKDY	SAT., SUN. & HOL. DAY	NIGHTTIME THRUOUT YR.
1	2.300	1.771	1.299	.922
2	2.385	1.837	1.341	.951
3	2.465	1.898	1.379	.979

TOTAL MARGINAL COST (CENTS/KWH)

ON-PEAK PERIODS

VOLT. LEVEL	GENER.	TRANS. & DIS.	ENERGY/TOTAL WINTER WEEKDAY	SUMMER & VALLEY WKDY
1	.494	.169	2.300	1.771
			2.963	2.434
2	.518	.359	2.385	1.837
			3.262	2.714
3	.541	.664	2.465	1.898
			3.669	3.103

OFF-PEAK PERIODS: TOTAL MARGINAL COST (= ENERGY COST)

VOLTAGE LEVEL	SAT., SUN. & HOL. DAY	NIGHTTIME THRUOUT YR.
1	1.299	.922
2	1.341	.951
3	1.379	.979

*** RUN NUMBER 2 - VALUES OF CHANGING VARIABLES:

CHANGING VARIABLE NO.	VARIABLE NO.	VALUE
1	33	.1000
2	34	10.0000

LOSS MULTIPLIERS

VOLTAGE STAGE	FOR DEMAND ON PEAK SIMPLE	FOR DEMAND ON PEAK CUMULATIVE	FOR ENERGY ON PEAK SIMPLE	FOR ENERGY ON PEAK CUMUL.	FOR ENERGY OFF PEAK SIMPLE	FOR ENERGY OFF PEAK CUMUL.
FROM GENERATION TO HIGH VOLTAGE CUSTOMERS AND HIGH SIDE OF STAGE ONE TRANSFORMERS	1.0510	1.0510	1.0359	1.0359	1.0309	1.0309
FROM HIGH SIDE OF STAGE ONE TRANSFORMERS TO STAGE TWO CUSTOMERS AND HIGH SIDE OF STAGE TWO TRANSFORMERS	1.0490	1.1025	1.0370	1.0743	1.0320	1.0639
FROM HIGH SIDE OF STAGE TWO TRANSFORMERS TO STAGE THREE CUSTOMERS AND HIGH SIDE OF STAGE THREE TRANSFORMERS	1.0440	1.1509	1.0334	1.1102	1.0289	1.0947

MARGINAL ANNUAL COST OF GENERATING CAPACITY ($/KW)

VOLTAGE LEVEL (1=HI VOLTAGE)	MARGINAL COST
1	29.083
2	30.508
3	31.849

MARGINAL ANNUAL COST OF TRANSMISSION AND DISTRIBUTION CAPACITY ($/KW)

VOLTAGE LEVEL (1=HI VOLTAGE)	MARGINAL COST	GEN. + TRANSM. & DISTR.
1	7.577	36.660
2	15.836	46.344
3	29.620	61.469

LENGTH OF PERIODS (HOURS)

WINTER WEEKDAY	SUMMER & VALLEY WKDY	SAT., SUN. & HOL. DAY	NIGHTTIME THRUOUT YR.
1428	2086	1596	3650

MARGINAL COST OF ENERGY (CENTS/KWH)

VOLTAGE	PERIOD			
STAGE (1= HI)	WINTER WEEKDAY	SUMMER & VALLEY WKDY	SAT., SUN. & HOL. DAY	NIGHTTIME THRUOUT YR.
1	2.300	1.771	1.299	.922
2	2.385	1.837	1.341	.951
3	2.465	1.898	1.379	.979

TOTAL MARGINAL COST (CENTS/KWH)

ON-PEAK PERIODS

VOLT. LEVEL	GENER.	TRANS. & DIS.	ENERGY/TOTAL WINTER WEEKDAY	SUMMER & VALLEY WKDY
1	.828	.216	2.300	1.771
			3.343	2.815
2	.868	.451	2.385	1.837
			3.704	3.156
3	.906	.843	2.465	1.898
			4.214	3.648

OFF-PEAK PERIODS: TOTAL MARGINAL COST (= ENERGY COST)

VOLTAGE LEVEL	SAT., SUN. & HOL. DAY	NIGHTTIME THRUOUT YR.
1	1.299	.922
2	1.341	.951
3	1.379	.979

*** RUN NUMBER 3 - VALUES OF CHANGING VARIABLES:

CHANGING VARIABLE NO.	VARIABLE NO.	VALUE
1	33	.0700
2	34	15.0000

LOSS MULTIPLIERS

VOLTAGE STAGE	FOR DEMAND ON PEAK SIMPLE	FOR DEMAND ON PEAK CUMULATIVE	FOR ENERGY ON PEAK SIMPLE	FOR ENERGY ON PEAK CUMUL.	FOR ENERGY OFF PEAK SIMPLE	FOR ENERGY OFF PEAK CUMUL.
FROM GENERATION TO HIGH VOLTAGE CUSTOMERS AND HIGH SIDE OF STAGE ONE TRANSFORMERS	1.0510	1.0510	1.0359	1.0359	1.0309	1.0309
FROM HIGH SIDE OF STAGE ONE TRANSFORMERS TO STAGE TWO CUSTOMERS AND HIGH SIDE OF STAGE TWO TRANSFORMERS	1.0490	1.1025	1.0370	1.0743	1.0320	1.0639
FROM HIGH SIDE OF STAGE TWO TRANSFORMERS TO STAGE THREE CUSTOMERS AND HIGH SIDE OF STAGE THREE TRANSFORMERS	1.0440	1.1509	1.0334	1.1102	1.0289	1.0947

MARGINAL ANNUAL COST OF GENERATING CAPACITY ($/KW)

VOLTAGE LEVEL (1=HI VOLTAGE)	MARGINAL COST
1	18.142
2	19.031
3	19.868

MARGINAL ANNUAL COST OF TRANSMISSION AND DISTRIBUTION CAPACITY ($/KW)

VOLTAGE LEVEL (1=HI VOLTAGE)	MARGINAL COST	GEN. + TRANSM. & DISTR.
1	5.935	24.078
2	12.618	31.649
3	23.318	43.186

LENGTH OF PERIODS (HOURS)

WINTER WEEKDAY	SUMMER & VALLEY WKDY	SAT., SUN. & HOL. DAY	NIGHTTIME THRUOUT YR.
1428	2086	1596	3650

MARGINAL COST OF ENERGY (CENTS/KWH)

VOLTAGE STAGE (1= HI)	PERIOD WINTER WEEKDAY	SUMMER & VALLEY WKDY	SAT., SUN. & HOL. DAY	NIGHTTIME THRUOUT YR.
1	2.300	1.771	1.299	.922
2	2.385	1.837	1.341	.951
3	2.465	1.898	1.379	.979

TOTAL MARGINAL COST (CENTS/KWH)

ON-PEAK PERIODS

VOLT. LEVEL	GENER.	TRANS. & DIS.	ENERGY/TOTAL WINTER WEEKDAY	SUMMER & VALLEY WKDY
1	.516	.169	2.300	1.771
			2.985	2.457
2	.542	.359	2.385	1.837
			3.286	2.738
3	.565	.664	2.465	1.898
			3.694	3.127

OFF-PEAK PERIODS: TOTAL MARGINAL COST (= ENERGY COST)

VOLTAGE LEVEL	SAT., SUN. & HOL. DAY	NIGHTTIME THRUOUT YR.
1	1.299	.922
2	1.341	.951
3	1.379	.979

*** RUN NUMBER 4 - VALUES OF CHANGING VARIABLES:

CHANGING VARIABLE NO.	VARIABLE NO.	VALUE
1	33	.1000
2	34	15.0000

LOSS MULTIPLIERS

VOLTAGE STAGE	FOR DEMAND ON PEAK SIMPLE	FOR DEMAND ON PEAK CUMULATIVE	FOR ENERGY ON PEAK SIMPLE	FOR ENERGY ON PEAK CUMUL.	FOR ENERGY OFF PEAK SIMPLE	FOR ENERGY OFF PEAK CUMUL.
FROM GENERATION TO HIGH VOLTAGE CUSTOMERS AND HIGH SIDE OF STAGE ONE TRANSFORMERS	1.0510	1.0510	1.0359	1.0359	1.0309	1.0309
FROM HIGH SIDE OF STAGE ONE TRANSFORMERS TO STAGE TWO CUSTOMERS AND HIGH SIDE OF STAGE TWO TRANSFORMERS	1.0490	1.1025	1.0370	1.0743	1.0320	1.0639
FROM HIGH SIDE OF STAGE TWO TRANSFORMERS TO STAGE THREE CUSTOMERS AND HIGH SIDE OF STAGE THREE TRANSFORMERS	1.0440	1.1509	1.0334	1.1102	1.0289	1.0947

MARGINAL ANNUAL COST OF GENERATING CAPACITY ($/KW)

VOLTAGE LEVEL (1=HI VOLTAGE)	MARGINAL COST
1	30.405
2	31.895
3	33.297

MARGINAL ANNUAL COST OF TRANSMISSION AND DISTRIBUTION CAPACITY ($/KW)

VOLTAGE LEVEL (1=HI VOLTAGE)	MARGINAL COST	GEN. + TRANSM. & DISTR.
1	7.577	37.982
2	15.836	47.730
3	29.620	62.917

LENGTH OF PERIODS (HOURS)

WINTER WEEKDAY	SUMMER & VALLEY WKDY	SAT., SUN. & HOL. DAY	NIGHTTIME THRUOUT YR.
1428	2086	1596	3650

MARGINAL COST OF ENERGY (CENTS/KWH)

VOLTAGE STAGE (1= HI)	PERIOD WINTER WEEKDAY	SUMMER & VALLEY WKDY	SAT., SUN. & HOL. DAY	NIGHTTIME THRUOUT YR.
1	2.300	1.771	1.299	.922
2	2.385	1.837	1.341	.951
3	2.465	1.898	1.379	.979

TOTAL MARGINAL COST (CENTS/KWH)

ON-PEAK PERIODS

VOLT. LEVEL	GENER.	TRANS. & DIS.	ENERGY/TOTAL WINTER WEEKDAY	SUMMER & VALLEY WKDY
1	.865	.216	2.300	1.771
			3.381	2.852
2	.908	.451	2.385	1.837
			3.743	3.195
3	.948	.843	2.465	1.898
			4.255	3.689

OFF-PEAK PERIODS: TOTAL MARGINAL COST (= ENERGY COST)

VOLTAGE LEVEL	SAT., SUN. & HOL. DAY	NIGHTTIME THRUOUT YR.
1	1.299	.922
2	1.341	.951
3	1.379	.979

SENSITIVITY II

```
 ARE THERE ANY CHANGES YOU WISH TO MAKE IN THE DATA?
YES

 ENTER THE NEW VALUE(S) AS BEFORE (PRECEDING CHANGES REMAIN IN EFFECT)


 $NEW NPLNTS = 2, IR=10,RM = .15
 $END

 DO YOU WANT THE INPUTS PRINTED? (THEY'RE LONG)
NO
```

LOSS MULTIPLIERS

VOLTAGE STAGE	FOR DEMAND ON PEAK		FOR ENERGY ON PEAK		FOR ENERGY OFF PEAK	
	SIMPLE	CUMULATIVE	SIMPLE	CUMUL.	SIMPLE	CUMUL.
FROM GENERATION TO HIGH VOLTAGE CUSTOMERS AND HIGH SIDE OF STAGE ONE TRANSFORMERS	1.0510	1.0510	1.0359	1.0359	1.0309	1.0309
FROM HIGH SIDE OF STAGE ONE TRANSFORMERS TO STAGE TWO CUSTOMERS AND HIGH SIDE OF STAGE TWO TRANSFORMERS	1.0490	1.1025	1.0370	1.0743	1.0320	1.0639
FROM HIGH SIDE OF STAGE TWO TRANSFORMERS TO STAGE THREE CUSTOMERS AND HIGH SIDE OF STAGE THREE TRANSFORMERS	1.0440	1.1509	1.0334	1.1102	1.0289	1.0947

MARGINAL ANNUAL COST OF GENERATING CAPACITY ($/KW)

VOLTAGE LEVEL (1=HI VOLTAGE)	MARGINAL COST
1	25.670
2	26.927
3	28.111

MARGINAL ANNUAL COST OF TRANSMISSION AND DISTRIBUTION CAPACITY ($/KW)

VOLTAGE LEVEL (1=HI VOLTAGE)	MARGINAL COST	GEN. + TRANSM. & DISTR.
1	7.577	33.247
2	15.836	42.763
3	29.620	57.731

LENGTH OF PERIODS (HOURS)

WINTER WEEKDAY	SUMMER & VALLEY WKDY	SAT., SUN. & HOL. DAY	NIGHTTIME THRUOUT YR.
1428	2086	1596	3650

MARGINAL COST OF ENERGY (CENTS/KWH)

VOLTAGE	PERIOD			
STAGE (1= HI)	WINTER WEEKDAY	SUMMER & VALLEY WKDY	SAT., SUN. & HOL. DAY	NIGHTTIME THRUOUT YR.
1	2.300	1.771	1.299	.922
2	2.385	1.837	1.341	.951
3	2.465	1.898	1.379	.979

TOTAL MARGINAL COST (CENTS/KWH)

ON-PEAK PERIODS

VOLT. LEVEL	GENER.	TRANS. & DIS.	ENERGY/TOTAL WINTER WEEKDAY	SUMMER & VALLEY WKDY
1	.730	.216	2.300	1.771
			3.246	2.718
2	.766	.451	2.385	1.837
			3.602	3.054
3	.800	.843	2.465	1.898
			4.107	3.541

OFF-PEAK PERIODS: TOTAL MARGINAL COST (= ENERGY COST)

VOLTAGE LEVEL	SAT., SUN. & HOL. DAY	NIGHTTIME THRUOUT YR.
1	1.299	.922
2	1.341	.951
3	1.379	.979

ARE THERE ANY CHANGES YOU WISH TO MAKE IN THE DATA?
NO

AU REVOIR

❋ *Chapter 10*

User's Guide to REVENUE

This user's guide consists of two parts: (1) a description of how to create the input file, and (2) a description of how to run the program from an interactive terminal. While reading this guide, the reader is urged to follow illustrative aids for each of the two parts, (1) a sample REVENUE data file (Figure 10–1), and (2) a sample interactive run of the REVENUE program (Figure 10–2), which follow this user's guide.

CREATING THE INPUT FILE

This part of the user's guide to the REVENUE program explains how to put the input data on a data file (the storage medium may be magnetic tape, magnetic disk, punched cards, etc.) that can be readily accessed by the particular computer being used. The discription in this part of the guide will be both machine-independent and medium-independent.

The data file consists of a set of sequential records, where each record contains pieces of data. Each particular piece of data is expected to be of a particular type, where there are three allowable types:

1. An alphanumeric string—e.g., "YES" or "PEAK"
2. An integer—e.g., "7200" or "–83"
3. A real number—e.g., "25.74" or "3.48E4" [$3.48 \cdot 10^4$] or "17E5" [$17 \cdot 10^5$] or an integer

The maximum usable length of a record is eighty characters.

Some of the pieces of data are to be expressed in free format fashion. This means two things:

1. A particular set of pieces of data can be continued from one record to another, provided each particular piece of data is contained totally on only one record.
2. On a particular record, the pieces of data are separated by one or more spaces and/or commas.

The following description of the records in the data file will proceed through the records sequentially, showing where each piece of data goes on the data file.

The first record(s) in the data file consists of two integers in free-format fashion: the number of periods [NPER] and the number of customer classes [NCSCLS].

The next record(s) in the data file consists of the following five sets of data in free format fashion in the following sequence:

1. For each period and for each customer class, the price in dollars per kilowatt [P(1,1), P(2, 1), . . . , P(NPER, 1), P(1, 2), P(2, 2), . . . , P(NPER, 2), . . . , P(1, NCSCLS), P (2, NCSCLS), . . . , P(NPER, NCSCLS)] expressed as real numbers.
2. For each period and for each customer class, the sales in KWH [SALES (1, 1), SALES (2, 1), . . . , SALES (NPER, 1), SALES (1, 2), SALES (2, 2), . . . , SALES (NPER, 2), . . . , SALES (1, NCSCLS), SALES (2, NCSCLS), . . . , SALES (NPER, NCSCLS)] expressed as real numbers.
3. For each customer class, the number of customers [NCUST (1), NCUST (2), . . . , NCUST (NCSCLS)] expressed as real numbers.
4. For each customer class, the desired revenue in dollars [DESREV (1), DESREV (2), . . . , DESREV (NCSCLS)] expressed as real numbers.
5. For each customer class, the customer charges in dollars per month [CSCHRG (1), CSCHRG (2), . . . , CSCHRG (NCSCLS)] expressed as real numbers.

RUNNING THE PROGRAM FROM AN INTERACTIVE TERMINAL

This part of the user's guide for the REVENUE program will explain how to run the program from an interactive terminal. At each step in the description of the interactive process the set of options with which the user is confronted is given along with a description of the resulting computer actions corresponding to each of the options.

After the preliminary sign on procedure to get on line to the particular computer from a terminal there are only two fundamental control-language statements that are needed: a statement commanding the computer to begin execution of the program (this would consist of "@XQT P*S.REVENUE" for the Univac 1110 in Madison, Wisconsin) and, after that program responds with "PLEASE FURNISH INITIAL DATA", a statement giving the program the input data set (e.g., this could consist of "@ADD P*S.REVDATA" for the Univac 1110 in Madison, Wisconsin). From this point forward the user will be interacting not with the computer's control system, but with the REVENUE program itself.

After receiving the input data, the program displays the initial input data.

The program then asks "DO YOU WANT TO CHANGE THE DATA?", (and adds "(PRECEDING CHANGES REMAIN IN EFFECT)" if previous results were calculated with changes to the initial data), to which the user may respond "YES" or "NO". If the user specifies "NO", then the program calculates and prints the results. If this is the first time that results are calculated in this run, then the results will be followed by a key explaining the results.

If the user specifies "YES", then the user is instructed by the program as to how to specify the changes. The user, following those instructions, then specifies the variables to be changed and their new values. If there is an error in the specification of the changed variables, then the program will respond with the message "THERE WAS AN ERROR IN THOSE CHANGES—PLEASE TRY AGAIN", at which point the user may retype the changes. The program will then print the revised data, followed by the results. The process will then be repeated, beginning with the program asking if there are any changes. If the user responds with "NO", then the program will sign off with "GOOD BYE THEN", and the computer's control system removes control from the program.

Figure 10–1. A Sample REVENUE Data File

```
@PRT,S P*S.REVDATA
FURPUR-MACC  2.03-09/19-13:07

P*S.REVDATA
     1        3, 3
     2       .05 .03 .01
     3       .06 .02 .005
     4       .07 .01 .001
     5       4E9 7E9 10E9
     6       3E9 1E9 5E9
     7       2E9 2E9 5E9
     8       2E3 1E5 1.5E6
     9       5E8 2E8 4E8
    10       200 10 2
PRT    COMPLETED..
```

Figure 10–2. A Sample Interactive Run of the REVENUE Program

```
@XQT P*S.REVENUE

 PLEASE FURNISH INITIAL DATA
@ADD P*S.REVDATA


 INITIAL DATA:



 NUMBER OF PERIODS:                   3               NPER
 NUMBER OF CUSTOMER CLASSES:          3               NCSCLS

                        CUSTOMER CLASS (J)
      PERIOD (I)      1: IND.  2: COM.  3: RES.

 PRICES (CENTS/KWH):                                  P(I,J)
      1: ON PEAK       5.00     6.00     7.00
      2: INTERM.       3.00     2.00     1.00
      3: OFF PEAK      1.00      .50      .10

 SALES (BILLION KWH):                                 SALES(I,J)
      1: ON PEAK       4.00     3.00     2.00
      2: INTERM.       7.00     1.00     2.00
      3: OFF PEAK     10.00     5.00     5.00

 NUMBER OF CUSTOMERS:                                 NCUST(J)
                      2000.  100000. 1500000.

 DESIRED REVENUE (MILLIOM DOLLARS):                   DESREV(J)
                     500.00   200.00   400.00

 CUSTOMER CHARGES ($/MONTH):                          CSCHRG(J)
                     200.00    10.00     2.00


 DO YOU WANT TO CHANGE THE DATA?
NO
```

```
RESULTS:

ACTUAL REVENUE (MILLION DOLLARS):
                      510.40   226.00   168.00

ADJUSTED        CUSTOMER                 PRICE                         PRICE
  CHARGE:        CHARGE               OFF  PEAK                       ON PEAK

C  PRICE(CTS/KWH)  CUST. (%)  PRICE(CTS/KWH) (%)  CUST. PRICE(CTS/KWH)
U   ON   INT.  OFF CHARGE RED-  ON   INT.  OFF    CHARGE  ON   INT.  OFF
S  PEAK        PEAK ($/MO) UC.) PEAK        PEAK   ($/MO) PEAK       PEAK


1
 A 5.00 3.00 1.00-416.67       5.00 3.00  .85      200.00 4.63 3.00 1.00
 B 4.90 2.94  .98     .00  2.
 C 5.00 3.00  .90     .00 10.

2
 A 6.00 2.00  .50 -20.83       6.00 2.00 -.24       10.00 4.77 2.00  .50
 B 5.33 1.78  .44     .00 11.  5.64 1.88  .00  6.
 C 6.00 2.00  .00     .00100.  6.00  .80  .00 60.
 D 5.63 1.88  .25     .00  6.

3
 A 7.00 1.00  .10  13.06       7.00 1.00 4.08        2.0016.95 1.00  .10
```

KEY:

A: THE FIRST LINE OF EACH CUSTOMER CLASS ('A') SHOWS WHAT THE TARIFF WOULD BE IF THE 'ADJUSTED CHARGE' WERE SET TO YIELD THE DESIRED REVENUE FOR THAT CUSTOMER CLASS

B: THE SECOND LINE ('B') APPEARS WHEN THE ADJUSTED CHARGE IN 'A' BECOMES NEGATIVE. IT SHOWS A TARIFF WITH THE ADJUSTED CHARGE SET EQUAL TO ZERO AND THE OTHER CHARGES REDUCED BY A COMMON PERCENTAGE

C: LINE 'C' IS LIKE 'B' EXCEPT THAT ONLY THE PRICE DURING THE PERIOD WITH LEAST DEMAND IS REDUCED

D: IF IN 'C' THE PERCENT REDUCTION OF THE OFF-PEAK PRICE IS GREATER THAN 50%, A FOURTH LINE ('D') APPEARS, IN WHICH THE CUSTOMER CHARGE IS SET EQUAL TO ZERO, THE OFF-PEAK PRICE IS REDUCED BY 50% AND THE OTHER PRICES ARE REDUCED BY A COMMON PERCENTAGE

```
 DO YOU WANT TO CHANGE THE DATA?
YES

 ENTER THE NEW VALUE(S) AS IN THIS EXAMPLE:
 (END LINES AT COMMAS AND NEVER TYPE IN COLUMN ONE - IT IS IGNORED)
 $NEW DESREV(2) = 800E6, P(1,2) = .02,
  .01, .005
 $END

 $NEQ      P(1,2) = .055,.025,
     CSCHRG(2) = 9
 $END

 THERE WAS AN ERROR IN THOSE CHANGES - PLEASE TRY AGAIN
 $NEW      P(1,2) = .055,.025,
     CSCHRG(2) = 9
 $END


 REVISED DATA:


 NUMBER OF PERIODS:                  3                    NPEP
 NUMBER OF CUSTOMER CLASSES:         3                    NCSCLS

                          CUSTOMER CLASS (J)
      PERIOD (I)      1: IND.   2: COM.   3: RES.

 PRICES (CENTS/KWH):                                      P(I,J)
      1: ON PEAK       5.00      5.50      7.00
      2: INTERM.       3.00      2.50      1.00
      3: OFF PEAK      1.00       .50       .10

 SALES (BILLION KWH):                                     SALES(I,J)
      1: ON PEAK       4.00      3.00      2.00
      2: INTERM.       7.00      1.00      2.00
      3: OFF PEAK     10.00      5.00      5.00

 NUMBER OF CUSTOMERS:                                     NCUST(J)
                      2000.   100000.  1500000.

 DESIRED REVENUE (MILLION DOLLARS):                       DESREV(J)
                     500.00    200.00    400.00

 CUSTOMER CHARGES ($/MONTH):                              CSCHRG(J)
                     200.00      9.00      2.00
```

```
RESULTS:

ACTUAL REVENUE (MILLION DOLLARS):
                       510.40   215.90   168.00

ADJUSTED        CUSTOMER                PRICE                          PRICE
  CHARGE:        CHARGE              OFF  PEAK                       ON PEAK

C  PRICE(CTS/KWH)  CUST. (%    PRICE(CTS/KWH) (%)  CUST. PRICE(CTS/KWH)
U   ON   INT.   OFF CHARGE RED-  ON   INT.  OFF     CHARGE  ON   INT.  OFF
S  PEAK         PEAK ($/MO) UC.) PEAK        PEAK    ($/MO) PEAK        PEAK


1
 A 5.00 3.00 1.00-416.67       5.00 3.00  .85      200.00 4.63 3.00 1.00
 B 4.90 2.94  .98     .00  2.
 C 5.00 3.00  .90     .00 10.

2
 A 5.50 2.50  .50 -12.50       5.50 2.50 -.02        9.00 4.64 2.50  .50
 B 5.12 2.33  .47     .00  7.  5.48 2.49  .00  0.
 C 5.50 2.50  .20     .00 60.  5.50 2.42  .00  3.
 D 5.43 2.47  .25     .00  1.

3
 A 7.00 1.00  .10  13.06       7.00 1.00 4.08        2.0016.95 1.00  .10


DO YOU WANT TO CHANGE THE DATA?
(PRECEEDING CHANGES REMAIN IN EFFECT)
NO


GOOD BYE THEN
```

❋ *Chapter 11*

User's Guide to TYPICAL-BILL

This user's guide consists of two parts: (1) a description of how to create the input file, and (2) a description of how to run the program from an interactive terminal. While reading this guide, the reader is urged to follow the illustrative aids for each of the two parts: (1) a sample TYPICAL-BILL data input questionnaire (Figure 11–1) and its corresponding data file (Figure 11–2), and (2) a sample interactive run of the TYPICAL-BILL program (Figure 11–3), which follow this user's guide.

CREATING THE INPUT FILE

This part of the user's guide to the TYPICAL-BILL program will show the user how to place the data from a completed TYPICAL-BILL data input questionnaire on a data file (the storage medium may be magnetic tape, magnetic disk, punched cards, etc.) that can be readily accessed by the particular computer being used. The description in this part of the guide will be both machine-independent and medium-independent.

The data file consists of a set of sequential records, where each record contains pieces of data. Each particular piece of data is expected to be of a particular type, where there are three allowable types:

1. An alphanumeric string—e.g., "YES" or "PEAK".
2. An integer—e.g., "7200" or "-83".
3. A real number—e.g., "25.74" or "3.48E4" [$3.48 \cdot 10^4$] or "17E5" [$17 \cdot 10^5$] or an integer.

The maximum usable length of a record is eighty characters.

Some of the pieces of data are to be expressed in free format fashion. This means two things:

1. A particular set of pieces of data can be continued from one record to another, provided each particular piece of data is contained totally on only one record.
2. On a particular record, the pieces of data are separated by one or more spaces and/or commas.

The following description of the records in the data file will proceed through the records sequentially, showing where each piece of data originates on the questionnaire (see the sample questionnaire and its corresponding data file at the end of this user's guide).

The records consist of the following pieces of data in free format fashion in the following sequence:

I. The number of combinations of KW and KWH under which the various tariffs are to be analyzed, where none of the tariffs is a peak tariff [NROWS] expressed as an integer.
II. For each combination $i = 1, 2, \ldots,$ NROWS, the level of KWH [KWHA (i)] and the level of KW [KWA(i)] expressed as integers.
III. The number of combinations of KW, KWH and percent peak under which the various tariffs are to be analyzed, where at least one of the tariffs is a peak tariff [NPROWS] expressed as an integer.
IV. For each combination $i = 1, 2, \ldots,$ NPROWS, the level of KWH [KWHPA (i)] expressed as an integer, the level of KW [KWPA (i)] expressed as an integer, and the percent peak [PCPKA (i)] expressed as a real number.

RUNNING THE PROGRAM FROM AN INTERACTIVE TERMINAL

This part of the user's guide for the TYPICAL-BILL program will show the user how to run the program from an interactive terminal. At each step in the description of the interactive process, the set of options with which the user is confronted is given, along with a description of the resulting computer actions corresponding to each of the options.

After the preliminary sign on procedure to get on line to the particular computer from a terminal, only two fundamental control language statements are needed: a statement commanding the computer to begin execution of the program (this would consist of "@XQT P*S.TYPICAL-BILL" for the Univac 1110 in Madison, Wisconsin) and, after that program responds with "PLEASE SUPPLY THE CONSUMPTION LEVELS", a statement giving the program the input data set to be used (e.g., this could consist of "@ADD P*S. TYP-BILLNOS" for the Univac 1110 in Madison, Wisconsin). From this point forward the user will be interacting not with the computer's control system, but with the TYPICAL-BILL program itself.

After receiving the input data the program responds with "HOW MANY TARIFFS ARE THERE?" The user must then respond with an integer that is less than or equal to 9 and represents the number of different tariffs to be analyzed [NTARIF]. The program will then proceed through the tariffs, $i = 1, 2, \ldots,$ NTARIF, performing the following steps in conjunction with the user:

1. For the first tariff the program will begin by asking "WHAT TYPE IS THE FIRST TARIFF? (TYPE '?' FOR A LIST OF CHOICES)." If the user chooses to respond with "?", the program will respond with the following:

   "YOUR CHOICES ARE:
   FIXED BLOCK
   HOPKINSON
   PEAK
   EXPANDER BLOCK
   (YOU NEED ONLY ENTER THE FIRST LETTER
   OF THE NAME)
   NOW WHAT TYPE IS THE FIRST TARIFF?"

   For later tariffs, say the fourth one, it will ask "WHAT TYPE IS THE NEXT TARIFF (NUMBER 4)?" The user must then respond with the type of the tariff.
2. The program will then ask "WHAT IS THE (6 CHARACTER) NAME OF THE TARIFF?". The user must then respond with no more than six characters that represent the name that will be used to identify this tariff.
3. At this point the interactive process will follow one of the following four (a–d) procedures, depending on the type of the tariff:
   a. For a fixed block tariff the program will respond with "PLEASE ENTER THE UPPER LIMITS OF THE BLOCKS, STARTING WITH THE LOWEST (FOR A FLAT TARIFF ENTER A BLANK LINE)." The user must then enter as real numbers in free format fashion the upper limits in KWH of the blocks (if the tariff is just a flat KWH rate then enter a blank

line). If the user does specify a flat rate, then the program will respond with "PLEASE ENTER THE PRICE", to which the user must respond with the flat rate expressed as a real number. If the user does not specify a flat tariff, then the program will respond with "PLEASE ENTER THE PRICES OF THE BLOCKS (IN THE SAME ORDER)", to which the user must respond by entering as real numbers in free format fashion the prices of the blocks. (There will be one more price than the number of upper limits of the blocks.)

b. For a peak tariff the program will respond with "PLEASE ENTER THE ON- AND OFF-PEAK PRICES", to which the user must respond with the two desired real numbers in free format fashion.

c. For an expander block tariff the program will respond with "PLEASE ENTER THE SIZES OF THE BLOCKS, ADDING A MINUS SIGN ('−') TO EXPANDER BLOCKS", to which the user must respond by entering as real numbers in free format fashion the desired sizes of the blocks adding a minus sign in front of expander blocks. The program will then respond with "PLEASE ENTER THE PRICES OF THE BLOCKS", to which the user must respond by entering as real numbers in free format fashion the prices of the blocks. (There will be one more price than the number of sizes of blocks.)

d. For a Hopkinson tariff the procedure can be split into two parts (specifying the KWH charge and specifying the KW charge):

   (1) The program first states "FIRST CONSIDER THE KWH CHARGE." It then responds with "PLEASE ENTER THE UPPER LIMITS OF THE BLOCKS, STARTING WITH THE LOWEST (FOR A FLAT TARIFF ENTER A BLANK LINE)." The user must then enter as real numbers in free format fashion the upper limits in KWH of the blocks (if the KWH part of the tariff is just a flat KWH rate then enter a blank line). If the user does specify a flat rate, then the program will respond with "PLEASE ENTER THE PRICE", to which the user must respond with the flat rate expressed as a real number. If the user doesn't specify a flat tariff, then the program will respond with "PLEASE ENTER THE PRICES OF THE BLOCKS (IN THE SAME ORDER)", to which the user must respond by entering as real numbers in free format fashion the prices of the blocks (there will be one more price than the number of upper limits on the blocks).

(2) This part is identical to (1) with two exceptions:
   (a) Instead of beginning with "FIRST CONSIDER THE KWH CHARGE" it begins with "NOW CONSIDER THE KW CHARGE".
   (b) All references to KWH are changed to become references to KW.

4. The program will then calculate and print out the typical electric bills and sign off with "AUF WIEDERSEHEN" returning control to the computer's control system.

Figure 11–1. TYPICAL-BILL Data Input Questionnaire

	Variable Description	Computer Symbol
I.	The number of combinations of KW and KWH under which the various tariffs are to be analyzed.	NROWS
II.	For each combination i = 1,2,..., NROWS = the level of KWH and the level of KW.	KWHA(1), KWA(1), KWHA(2), KWA(2), ..., KWHA(NROWS), KWA(NROWS)
III.	The number of combinations of KW, KWH and percent peak under which the various tariffs are to be analyzed.	NPROWS
IV.	For each combination i = 1,2,..., NPROWS: the level of KWH, the level of KW, and the percent peak.	KWHPA(1), KWPA(1), PCPKA(1), KWHPA(2), KWPA(2), PCPKA(2),..., KWHPA(NPROWS), KWPA(NPROWS), PCPKA (NPROWS)

I. 4

II.					
50	5	100	5	100	10
3000	300				

III. 5

IV.								
50	5	5	50	5	.8	100	5	5
100	10	.8	3000	300	1			

Figure 11–2. TYPICAL-BILL Sample Data File

```
@PRT,S P*S.TYP-BILLNOS
FURPUR-MACC  2.03-09/19-14:03

P*S.TYP-BILLNOS
     1       4
     2       50 5, 100 5, 100 10, 3000 300
     3       5
     4       50 5 .5, 50 5 .3, 100 5 .5, 100 10 .3, 3000 300 1
PRT    COMPLETED..
```

Figure 11–3. Sample Interactive Runs of the TYPICAL-BILL Program

```
@XQT P*S.TYPICAL-BILL


 PLEASE SUPPLY THE CONSUMPTION LEVELS
@ADD P*S.TYP-BILLNOS

 HOW MANY TARIFFS ARE THERE?
4

 WHAT TYPE IS THE FIRST TARIFF? (TYPE '?' FOR A LIST OF CHOICES)
?

 YOUR CHOICES ARE:
 FIXED BLOCK
 HOPKINSON
 PEAK
 EXPANDER BLOCK
 (YOU NEED ONLY ENTER THE FIRST LETTER OF THE NAME)
 NOW WHAT TYPE IS THE FIRST TARIFF?
F

 WHAT IS THE (6 CHARACTER) NAME OF THE TARIFF?
 FLAT

 PLEASE ENTER THE UPPER LIMITS OF THE BLOCKS, STARTING WITH THE LOWEST
 (FOR A FLAT TARIFF ENTER A BLANK LINE)


 PLEASE ENTER THE PRICE
.02

 WHAT TYPE IS THE NEXT TARIFF (NUMBER 2)?
FIXED BLOCK

 WHAT IS THE (6 CHARACTER) NAME OF THE TARIFF?
DECLBL

 PLEASE ENTER THE UPPER LIMITS OF THE BLOCKS, STARTING WITH THE LOWEST
 (FOR A FLAT TARIFF ENTER A BLANK LINE)
50,100

 PLEASE ENTER THE PRICES OF THE BLOCKS (IN THE SAME ORDER)
.03,.02,.01
```

```
 WHAT TYPE IS THE NEXT TARIFF (NUMBER 3)?
FIXED BLOCK

 WHAT IS THE (6 CHARACTER) NAME OF THE TARIFF?
LIFELM

 PLEASE ENTER THE UPPER LIMITS OF THE BLOCKS, STARTING WITH THE LOWEST
 (FOR A FLAT TARIFF ENTER A BLANK LINE)
50

 PLEASE ENTER THE PRICES OF THE BLOCKS (IN THE SAME ORDER)
.01
.05

 WHAT TYPE IS THE NEXT TARIFF (NUMBER 4)?
HOPKINSON

 WHAT IS THE (6 CHARACTER) NAME OF THE TARIFF?
HOPKIN

 FIRST CONSIDER THE KWH CHARGE

 PLEASE ENTER THE UPPER LIMITS OF THE BLOCKS, STARTING WITH THE LOWEST
 (FOR A FLAT TARIFF ENTER A BLANK LINE)
75,300,2000.

 PLEASE ENTER THE PRICES OF THE BLOCKS (IN THE SAME ORDER)
.02,.01,.005,.001

 NOW CONSIDER THE KW CHARGE

 PLEASE ENTER THE UPPER LIMITS OF THE BLOCKS, STARTING WITH THE LOWEST
 (FOR A FLAT TARIFF ENTER A BLANK LINE)
10

 PLEASE ENTER THE PRICES OF THE BLOCKS (IN THE SAME ORDER)
.2,.1


           TYPICAL ELECTRIC BILLS


  KWH  KW                BILL
           FLAT  DECLBL LIFELN HOPKIN
   50   5  1.00   1.50    .50   2.00
  100   5  2.00   2.50   3.00   2.75
  100  10  2.00   2.50   3.00   3.75
 3000 300 60.00  31.50 148.00  44.25


AUF WIEDERSEHEN
```

```
@XQT P*S.TYPICAL-BILL


 PLEASE SUPPLY THE CONSUMPTION LEVELS
@ADD P*S.TYP-BILLNOS

 HOW MANY TARIFFS ARE THERE?
2

 WHAT TYPE IS THE FIRST TARIFF? (TYPE '?' FOR A LIST OF CHOICES)
?

 YOUR CHOICES ARE:
 FIXED BLOCK
 HOPKINSON
 PEAK
 EXPANDER BLOCK
 (YOU NEED ONLY ENTER THE FIRST LETTER OF THE NAME)
 NOW WHAT TYPE IS THE FIRST TARIFF?
P

 WHAT IS THE (6 CHARACTER) NAME OF THE TARIFF?
PEAK

 PLEASE ENTER THE ON- AND OFF-PEAK PRICES
.05 .01

 WHAT TYPE IS THE NEXT TARIFF (NUMBER 2)?
EXPANDER BLOCK

 WHAT IS THE (6 CHARACTER) NAME OF THE TARIFF?
EXPAND

 PLEASE ENTER THE SIZES OF THE BLOCKS, ADDING A MINUS SIGN ('-')
 TO EXPANDER BLOCKS
40 -2 -4, 200

 PLEASE ENTER THE PRICES OF THE BLOCKS
.05,.04 .03
.02 .01


          TYPICAL ELECTRIC BILLS


  KWH  KW  % ON          BILL
           PEAK  PEAK   EXPAND
   50   5   50    1.50   2.40
   50   5   30    2.10   2.40
  100   5   50    3.00   3.60
  100  10   30    4.20   4.00
 3000 300  100  150.00  75.60


 AUF WIEDERSEHEN
```

 *Chapter 12*

User's Guide to METER-COST

This user's guide explains how to run the METER-COST program from an interactive terminal. While reading this guide, the reader is urged to follow the sample interactive run of the METER-COST program (Figure 12–1). At each step in the interactive process the set of options with which the user is confronted is given along with a description of the resulting computer actions corresponding to each of the options.

After the preliminary sign on procedure to get on line to the particular computer from a terminal, the user enters a control language statement commanding the computer to begin execution of the program (this would consist of "@XQT P*S. METER-COST" for the Univac 1110 in Madison, Wisconsin). From this point forward the user will be interacting not with the computer's control system, but with the METER-COST program itself.

The program begins by describing the pieces of data that it expects the user to furnish:

"INPUT DATA:
METER LIFE, INTEREST RATE, ADDITIONAL OTHER BILLING, ANNUAL SALES SHIFTED IN KWH, NUMBER OF PEAK PERIODS, PEAK PERIOD RUNNING COSTS, PEAK PERIOD HOURS, NUMBER OF OFF-PEAK PERIODS, OFF-PEAK RUNNING COSTS, OFF-PEAK PERIOD HOURS, NEW CAPACITY AVOIDED, LRIC, NUMBER OF CUSTOMERS"

The user must then enter the desired data. Each particular piece of data is expected to be of a particular type, where there are three allowable types:

1. An alphanumeric string—e.g., "YES" or "PEAK".
2. An integer—e.g., "7200" or "− 83".
3. A real number—e.g., "25.74" or "3.48E4" [$3.48 \cdot 10^4$] or "17E5" [$17 \cdot 10^5$] or an integer.

The maximum usuable length of a line is eighty characters. Some of the pieces of data are to be expressed in free format fashion. This means two things:

1. A particular set of pieces of data can be continued from one record to another, provided each particular piece of data is contained totally on only one record.
2. On a particular record the pieces of data are separated by one or more spaces and/or commas.

The data that the program desires consists of the following nine sets of data in free format fashion in the following sequence:

1. The meter life [XL] expressed as a real number.
2. The interest rate [XI] expressed as a real number.
3. The additional other billing [OC] expressed as a real number.
4. The annual sales shifted in KWH [ASS] expressed as a real number.
5. (a) The number of peak period hours [NPPS] expressed as an integer.
   (b) For each peak period hour, $i = 1, 2, \ldots,$ NPPS, the peak period running cost [PPRC(i)] expressed as real numbers.
   (c) For each peak period hour, $i = 1, 2, \ldots,$ NPPS, the peak period hour, [PPH(i] expressed as real numbers.
6. (a) The number of off-peak periods [NOPPS] expressed as an integer.
   (b) For each off-peak period, $i = 1, 2, \ldots,$ NOPPS, the off-peak running cost [OPRC(i)] expressed as real numbers.
   (c) For each off-peak period, $i = 1, 2, \ldots,$ NOPPS, the off-peak period hour [OPPH(i)] expressed as an integer.
7. The annual KW of new capacity avoided [XNIA] expressed as a real number.
8. The long run incremental cost of a new KW [XLRIC] expressed as a real number.
9. The number of customers [XNC] expressed as a real number.

The program responds by printing out these input values along with a description of each piece of data. The program then calculates and prints out three values:

1. The breakeven meter costs;
2. The benefits;
3. The capital recovery factor.

The program then responds with "PUT IN 1. IF METER COSTS ARE KNOWN AND 2. IF NOT KNOWN SPACE AND PUT IN COST PER METER", to which the user must respond with "2." if the meter cost is not known and with "1." otherwise, followed by a space followed by the meter cost if it is known (if not known then put something in anyway; the program will then set the meter cost equal to the breakeven meter cost). The program then calculates and prints out two values:

1. The meter costs, and
2. The benefit cost ratio.

The program then responds with "TYPE IN KILOWATT HOURS SALES ON PEAK AND KILOWATTS OF PEAK CAPACITY" to which the user must respond with two real numbers in free format fashion:

1. The kilowatt hours sales on peak [SOP];
2. The kilowatts of peak capacity [XKAP].

The program then calculates and prints out five values:

1. The KWH sales on peak,
2. The KW of peak capacity,
3. The peak energy saving (and its percentage of KWH sales on peak).
4. The peak capacity avoided (and its percentage of KW of peak capacity), and
5. The percentage peak energy and power saving.

The program then signs off with "ADIOS" and control is returned to the computer's control system.

Figure 12–1. Sample Interactive Run of the METER-COST Program

```
@XQT P*S.METER-COST


 INPUT DATA:
 METER LIFE, INTEREST RATE, ADDITIONAL OTHER BILLING,
 ANNUAL SALES SHIFTED IN KWH, NUMBER OF PEAK PERIODS,
 PEAK PERIOD RUNNING COSTS, PEAK PERIOD HOURS,
 NUMBER OF OFF-PEAK PERIODS, OFF-PEAK RUNNING COSTS,
 OFF-PEAK PERIOD HOURS, NEW CAPACITY AVOIDED, LRIC,
 NUMBER OF CUSTOMERS


30.
.1
1.5
1E9
2, .02536 .01953, 1428 2086
2, .01432 .01015, 1596 3650
1E5
55.556
1E6


 METER LIFE                                                  30.00000
 INTEREST RATE                                                 .10000
 ADDITIONAL OTHER BILLING COSTS                               1.50000
 ANNUAL KWH SALES SHIFTED                            1000000000.00000
 RUNNING COST ON PEAK                                          .02190
 RUNNING COST OFF PEAK                                         .01142
  (BOTH COSTS ARE AVERAGES WEIGHTED BY HOURS, NOT BY SALES)
 ANNUAL KW OF NEW CAPACITY AVOIDED                       100000.00000
 LONG RUN INCREMENTAL COST OF A NEW KW                       55.55600
 NUMBER OF CUSTOMERS                                    1000000.00000
```

```
BREAK-EVEN METER COSTS              137.03072
BENEFITS                        16036116.37500
CAPITAL RECOVERY FACTOR                .10608


PUT IN 1. IF METER COSTS ARE KNOWN AND 2. IF NOT KNOWN
SPACE AND PUT IN COST PER METER
1. 56


METER COSTS           56.00000
BENEFIT COST RATIO     2.15527


TYPE IN KILOWATT HOURS SALES ON PEAK AND
KILOWATTS OF PEAK CAPACITY


1E10 1E6


KWH SALES ON PEAK:          10000000000.00
KW OF PEAK CAPACITY:           1000000.00
PEAK ENERGY SAVING:          708930448.00   PERCENTAGE:      7.89930
PEAK CAPACITY AVOIDED:          133926.81   PERCENTAGE:     13.39268
PERCENTAGE PEAK ENERGY & POWER SAVING:                       4.63988

ADIOS
```

Chapter 13

User's Guide to LOAD

This user's guide consists of two parts: (1) a description of how to create the input file, and (2) a description of how to run the program from an interactive terminal. While reading this guide, the reader is urged to follow the sample interactive run of the LOAD program (Figure 13–2), which follows this user's guide.

CREATING THE INPUT FILE

This part of the user's guide to the LOAD program explains how to put the input data into a data file (the storage medium may be magnetic tape, magnetic disk, punched cards, etc.) that can be readily accessed by the particular computer being used. The description in this part of the guide will be both machine-independent and medium-independent.

The data file consists of a set of sequential records, where each record contains pieces of data. Each particular piece of data is expected to be of a particular type, where there are three allowable types:

1. An alphanumeric string—e.g., "YES" or "PEAK".
2. An integer—e.g., "7200" or "– 83".
3. A real number—e.g., "25.74" or "3.48E4" [$3.48 \cdot 10^4$] or "17E5" [$17 \cdot 10^5$] or an integer.

The maximum usable length of a record is eighty characters.

Some of the pieces of data are to be expressed in free format fashion. This means two things:

1. A particular set of pieces of data can be continued from one record to another, provided each particular piece of data is contained totally on only one record.
2. On a particular record the pieces of data are separated by one or more spaces and/or commas.

The following description of the records in the data file will proceed through the records sequentially, showing where each piece of data goes in the data file.

The input data file consists of a set of records containing real numbers in free format fashion. The loads for January 1 must be first, with hours one through twenty-four, then the twenty-four loads for January 2, and so on through all 8,760 loads (or 8,784 for a leap year).

RUNNING THE PROGRAM FROM AN INTERACTIVE TERMINAL

This part of the user's guide for the LOAD program explains how to run the program from an interactive terminal. At each step in the description of the interactive process the set of options with which the user is confronted is given, along with a description of the resulting computer actions corresponding to each of the options.

After the preliminary sign on procedure to get on line to the particular computer from a terminal, there are only three fundamental control language statements that are needed:

1. The user first issues a statement to the computer to inform it that the graphics plotter is to be employed (this would consist of "@GSP, P" for the Univac 1110 in Madison, Wisconsin; the computer would then acknowledge with "GRAPHICS SYSTEM PROCESSOR V85").
2. The user then issues a statement commanding the computer to begin execution of the program (this would consist of "@XQT P*S. LOAD" for the Univac 1110 in Madison, Wisconsin). The computer then responds with "PLEASE ENTER THE YEAR THE DATA WAS TAKEN, THE NUMBER OF HOLIDAYS THAT YEAR, AND THE DATES OF THOSE HOLIDAYS (EACH ON A SEPARATE LINE)." The user then enters a record(s) consisting of two integers: the year [YEAR] and the number of holidays [NHOL]. The user then enters NHOLS records, each containing the month and day (separated by a blank space) of one of the holidays. The computer then responds with "PLEASE SUPPLY THE DATA."

3. The user then gives the program the input data to be run (e.g., this could consist of "@ADD PS*DECO." for the Univac 1110 in Madison, Wisconsin).

From this point forward the user will be interacting not with the computer's control system, but with the LOAD program itself.

The program in conjunction with the user then proceeds through a series of iterations of curve drawings. Each iteration consists of proceeding through the following steps:

1. The program will begin by asking "WHAT OUTPUT WOULD YOU LIKE? (TYPE '?' FOR A LIST OF CHOICES)". If the user chooses to respond with "?" then the program will respond with the following:

   "YOUR CHOICES ARE:
   DAILY LOAD CURVE
   PEAK DAY LOAD CURVE
   AVERAGE MONTHLY LOAD CURVE (EXCLUDING WEEKENDS AND HOLIDAYS)
   MONTHLY LOAD DURATION CURVE
   YEARLY LOAD DURATION CURVE
   (YOU NEED ONLY ENTER THE FIRST LETTER OF THE NAME)
   NOW WHAT OUTPUT WOULD YOU LIKE?"
2. If type of output desired is either a monthly load duration curve or a yearly load duration curve, then the program will respond with "DO YOU WANT A TABLE?", to which the user must respond with either "YES" or "NO". If the user responds with "YES" then the process skips to step 4. If the output desired is a daily, peak day or average monthly load curve, this step is skipped and the process moves on to step 3.
3. At this point the interactive process will follow one of the following five (a–e) procedures depending on the type of output desired:
   a. For a daily load curve the program will ask "WHICH DAY WOULD YOU LIKE?", to which the user must respond with the month and day (separated by a space).
   b. For a peak day load curve the program will compute the load curve for the day containing the hour that had the greatest load of the year. It will then respond with "THE PEAK DAY IS . . . , THE PEAK LOAD IS . . . ."
   c. For an average monthly load curve the program will ask "WHICH MONTH WOULD YOU LIKE?", to which the user must respond with the month desired.

d. For a monthly load duration curve the program will ask "WHICH MONTH WOULD YOU LIKE?", to which the user must respond with the month desired.
e. For a yearly load duration curve the program will compute the load at each of the approximately 30 · 24 = 720 hours of the month in order of decreasing load. It will then respond with "TOTAL ENERGY DEMANDED: . . . , PEAK LOAD: . . . , LOAD FACTOR: . . . ."

4. The desired graph is then drawn by the plotter, and the program responds with "GRAPH NUMBER . . . DRAWN: . . .". If the user responded in step 2 with "YES" to the question "DO YOU WANT A TABLE?", then the program will now respond with "ENTER THE % INCREMENT BETWEEN ROWS OR THE % VALUES OF THE ROWS", to which the user must respond by entering the percent by which increments are to be taken in going from 0 percent of peak load to 100 percent of peak load.
5. The program then asks "DO YOU WANT THE CURVE FLATTENED?", to which the user must respond with "YES" or "NO". If the user responds "YES" then the program proceeds to step 6; otherwise it skips to step 7.
6. The program then asks "BY WHAT PERCENTAGE DO YOU WANT THE CURVE FLATTENED? (RELATIVE TO THE ORIGINAL CURVE—PREVIOUS CHANGES ARE IGNORED)", to which the user must respond by entering the percentage by which the original curve is to be flattened. If we are dealing with either a monthly load duration curve or a yearly load duration curve then the procedure goes back to step 2; otherwise it goes back to step 4.
7. The program will now ask "DO YOU WANT TO RUN AGAIN?", to which the user must respond with "YES" or "NO". If the user responds "YES" then the procedure goes back to step 1 for another iteration of the whole procedure; otherwise the program signs off with "SO LONG" and control returns to the computer's control system.

Figure 13–1. A Sample LOAD Data File

```
EDIT,U PS*DECO.
DIT 1.39-3/8-11:11
DIT
' 1111
3250  3008  2823  2670  2632  2553  2559  2594  2703  2827  2939  3193
3383  3375  3346  3353  3486  3822  3892  3851  3868  3931  3723  3350
3233  3040  3060  3000  2988  3317  3786  4407  4627  4799  4972  5049
5083  5069  4962  4881  4931  5171  5300  5137  5188  5129  4868  4349
3970  3733  3520  3445  3426  3615  4045  4694  4837  4911  4844  4893
4919  4945  4881  4843  5095  5239  5211  5207  5259  5111  4778  4328
3869  3573  3432  3374  3351  3595  3971  4636  5025  5129  5265  5274
5238  5250  5183  5035  5207  5393  5415  5277  5226  5186  4926  4448
3985  3663  3603  3454  3442  3597  4040  4761  4957  5019  5150  5043
5039  5061  4989  4953  4986  5377  5454  5291  5274  5181  4843  4490
4003  3803  3604  3489  3480  3557  3740  4016  4187  4472  4621  4633
4633  4547  4491  4422  4522  4935  5004  4863  4806  4777  4513  4107
3687  3474  3214  3125  3103  3139  3134  3169  3233  3481  3655  3702
3810  3771  3789  3737  3783  4135  4233  4222  4163  4204  4005  3653
3445  3358  3291  3218  3253  3442  4027  4827  5011  4839  5153  5174
5141  5122  5122  5009  5205  5473  5424  5317  5289  5183  4836  4364
3785  3727  3501  3465  3479  3658  4035  4738  5053  5013  5062  5113
5111  5135  4925  4953  5109  5356  5395  5255  5283  5204  4923  4467
4054  3746  3612  3527  3523  3731  4150  4851  5115  5147  5264  5193
5205  5215  5114  5129  5290  5348  5549  5439  5430  5275  4983  4447
4033  3727  3639  3604  3588  3739  4271  4835  5114  5142  5196  5287
5225  5192  5172  5115  5220  5395  5531  5447  5490  5358  4922  4473
4040  3796  3639  3567  3630  3769  4150  4834  5123  5176  5196  5066
5113  5082  4954  4822  4944  5121  5297  5225  5238  5130  4856  4470
4013  3666  3543  3473  3440  3408  3723  4008  4208  4410  4696  4634
4612  4561  4356  4278  4429  4764  4760  4668  4663  4665  4312  3913
3556  3262  3143  3048  2995  3073  3018  3045  3126  3344  3555  3636
3722  3752  3778  3789  3867  4125  4100  4076  4129  4102  3860  3534
3202  3139  3120  3007  3060  3223  3917  4539  4941  5173  5259  5230
5195  5092  5074  4950  5287  5299  5259  5266  5214  5107  4827  4393
3766  3535  3391  3437  3402  3623  3986  4641  4906  5078  5148  5067
5024  5037  4944  4858  4915  5016  5189  5103  5083  4995  4760  4308
3894  3543  3362  3332  3347  3467  3983  4732  4940  5012  5112  4982
4894  4916  4724  4798  4913  5135  5258  5197  5043  4923  4579  4165
3753  3408  3277  3092  3209  3426  3934  4682  4966  4904  5084  4995
4986  4914  4805  4732  4888  5148  5281  5134  5148  4921  4547  4158
3686  3606  3303  3254  3238  3386  3722  4499  4770  4822  4853  4713
4922  4981  5009  4980  5082  5309  5356  5199  4853  4952  4686  4270
3866  3631  3436  3347  3333  3382  3635  3934  4255  4471  4686  4708
4696  4627  4467  4356  4393  4626  4752  4694  4633  4622  4371  3992
```

. . . and so on for the remaining

345 days (8280 hours) of the year.

Figure 13–2. A Sample Interactive Run of the LOAD Program

```
@GSP,P
GRAPHICS SYSTEM PROCESSOR V85
@XQT P*S.LOAD

 PLEASE ENTER THE YEAR THE DATA WAS TAKEN, THE NUMBER OF HOLIDAYS
 THAT YEAR, AND THE DATES OF THOSE HOLIDAYS (EACH ON A SEPARATE LINE)
1973, 3
JAN 1
JULY 4
DE 25

 PLEASE SUPPLY THE DATA
@ADD PS*DECO.

 WHAT OUTPUT WOULD YOU LIKE? (TYPE '?' FOR A LIST OF CHOICES)
?

 YOUR CHOICES ARE:
 DAILY LOAD CURVE
 PEAK DAY LOAD CURVE
 AVERAGE MONTHLY LOAD CURVE (EXCLUDING WEEKENDS AND HOLIDAYS)
 MONTHLY LOAD DURATION CURVE
 YEARLY LOAD DURATION CURVE
 (YOU NEED ONLY ENTER THE FIRST LETTER OF THE NAME)
 NOW WHAT OUTPUT WOULD YOU LIKE?
D

 WHICH DAY WOULD YOU LIKE?
JAN. 1

 GRAPH NUMBER  1 DRAWN:  LOAD  CURVE  FOR       JANUARY  1

 DO YOU WANT THE CURVE FLATTENED?
NO

 DO YOU WANT TO RUN AGAIN?
YES

 WHAT OUTPUT WOULD YOU LIKE? (TYPE '?' FOR A LIST OF CHOICES)
PEAK DAY


 THE PEAK DAY IS    DECEMBER 31; THE PEAK LOAD IS  6903.000

 GRAPH NUMBER  2 DRAWN:  LOAD  CURVE  FOR      DECEMBER 31

 DO YOU WANT THE CURVE FLATTENED?
NO
```

```
 DO YOU WANT TO RUN AGAIN?
YES

 WHAT OUTPUT WOULD YOU LIKE? (TYPE '?' FOR A LIST OF CHOICES)
AVE MON

 WHICH MONTH WOULD YOU LIKE?
JANUARY

 GRAPH NUMBER  3 DRAWN:  AVERAGE MONTHLY LOAD CURVE FOR     JANUARY

 DO YOU WANT THE CURVE FLATTENED?
NO

 DO YOU WANT TO RUN AGAIN?
YES

 WHAT OUTPUT WOULD YOU LIKE? (TYPE '?' FOR A LIST OF CHOICES)
MON. DURATION

 DO YOU WANT A TABLE?
YES

 WHICH MONTH WOULD YOU LIKE?
OCT

 GRAPH NUMBER  4 DRAWN:  MONTHLY LOAD DURATION CURVE FOR     OCTOBER

 ENTER THE % INCREMENT BETWEEN ROWS OF THE % VALUES OF THE ROWS
10


 % OF PEAK LOAD     LOAD     % OF TIME LOAD EXCEEDED
      100.        5402.00               .01
       90.        4861.80             37.50
       80.        4321.60             52.56
       70.        3721.40             67.75
       60.        3241.20             91.81
       50.        2701.00            100.00


 DO YOU WANT THE CURVE FLATTENED?
YES

 BY WHAT PERCENTAGE DO YOU WANT THE CURVE FLATTENED?
40

 DO YOU WANT A TABLE?
YES

 GRAPH NUMBER  5 DRAWN:  MONTHLY LOAD DURATION CURVE FOR     OCTOBER
```

ENTER THE % INCREMENT BETWEEN ROWS OR THE % VALUES OF THE ROWS
0,5,10,25,50,75,80,90,95,96,97,98,99,100

% OF PEAK LOAD	LOAD	% OF TIME LOAD EXCEEDED
100.	4956.43	.01
99.	4906.87	.95
98.	4857.30	2.29
97.	4807.74	7.13
96.	4758.17	12.91
95.	4708.61	22.99
90.	4460.79	47.05
80.	3965.14	68.96
75.	3717.32	86.70
50.	2478.22	100.00

DO YOU WANT THE CURVE FLATTENED?
YES

BY WHAT PERCENTAGE DO YOU WANT THE CURVE FLATTENED?
(RELATIVE TO THE ORIGINAL CURVE - PREVIOUS CHANGES ARE IGNORED)
20

DO YOU WANT A TABLE?
YES

GRAPH NUMBER 6 DRAWN: MONTHLY LOAD DURATION CURVE FOR OCTOBER

ENTER THE % INCREMENT BETWEEN ROWS OR THE % VALUES OF THE ROWS
5

% OF PEAK LOAD	LOAD	% OF TIME LOAD EXCEEDED
100.	5179.22	.01
95.	4920.25	12.50
90.	4661.29	42.21
85.	4402.33	49.47
80.	4143.37	59.28
75.	3884.41	67.75
70.	3625.45	78.37
65.	3366.49	93.96
60.	3107.53	99.87
55.	2848.57	100.00

DO YOU WANT THE CURVE FLATTENED?
NO

```
 DO YOU WANT TO RUN AGAIN?
YES

 WHAT OUTPUT WOULD YOU LIKE? (TYPE '?' FOR A LIST OF CHOICES)
YEARLY LOAD DURATION CURVE

 DO YOU WANT A TABLE?
YES


 TOTAL ENERGY DEMANDED:  3.76641+07, PEAK LOAD:  6.90300+03
  LOAD FACTOR:  6.22853-01

 GRAPH NUMBER  7 DRAWN:  LOAD DURATION CURVE FOR 1973

 ENTER THE % INCREMENT BETWEEN ROWS OR THE % VALUES OF THE ROWS
20

 % OF PEAK LOAD     LOAD     % OF TIME LOAD EXCEEDED
     100.         6903.00              .01
      80.         5522.40             4.08
      60.         4141.80            56.18
      40.         2761.20            98.81
      20.         1380.60            99.99
       0.             .00           100.00


 DO YOU WANT THE CURVE FLATTENED?
NO

 DO YOU WANT TO RUN AGAIN?
NO

 SO LONG
```

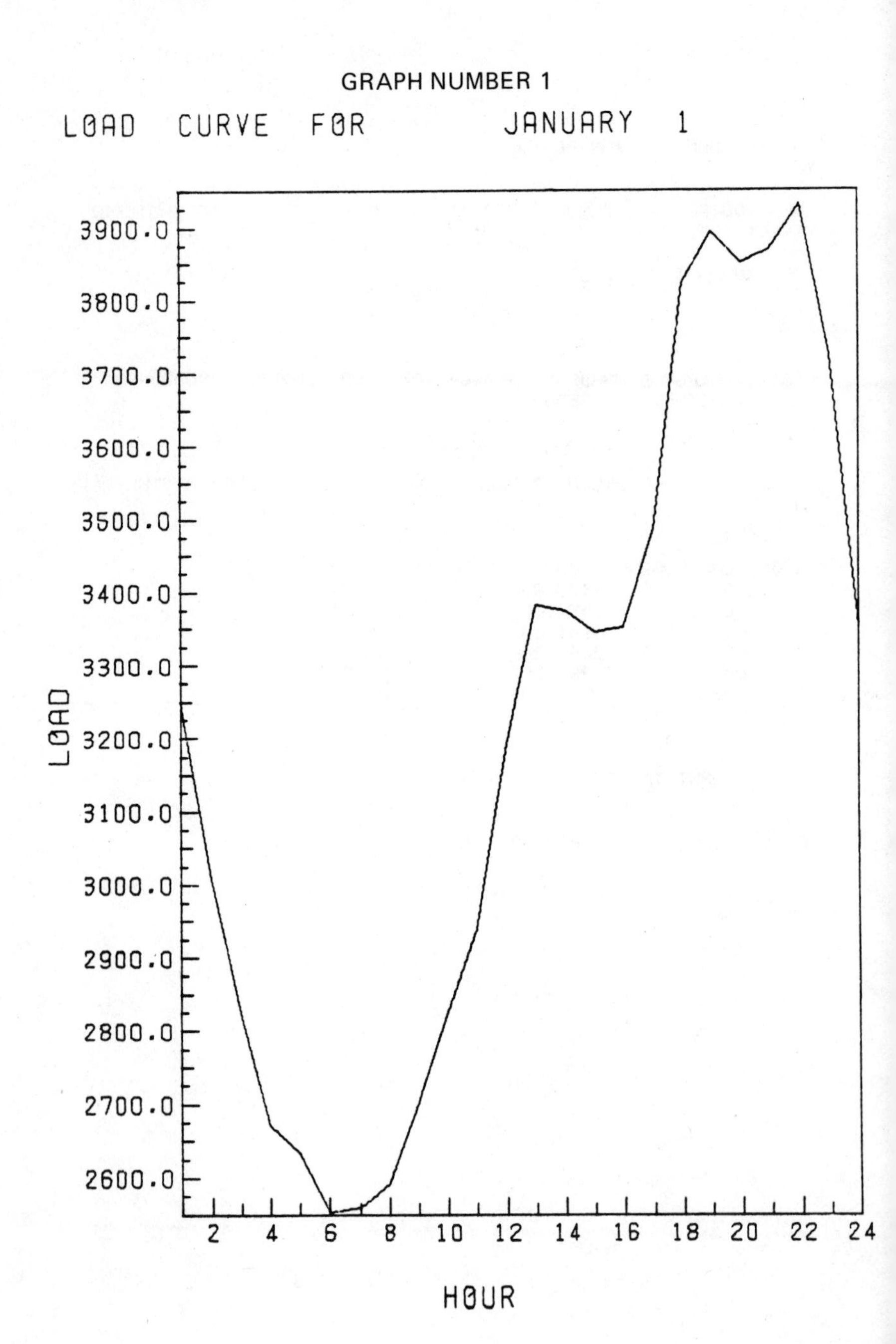
GRAPH NUMBER 1
LOAD CURVE FOR JANUARY 1
3900.0
3800.0
3700.0
3600.0
3500.0
3400.0
3300.0
3200.0
3100.0
3000.0
2900.0
2800.0
2700.0
2600.0
LOAD
2
4
6
8
10
12
14
16
18
20
22
24
HOUR

GRAPH NUMBER 2

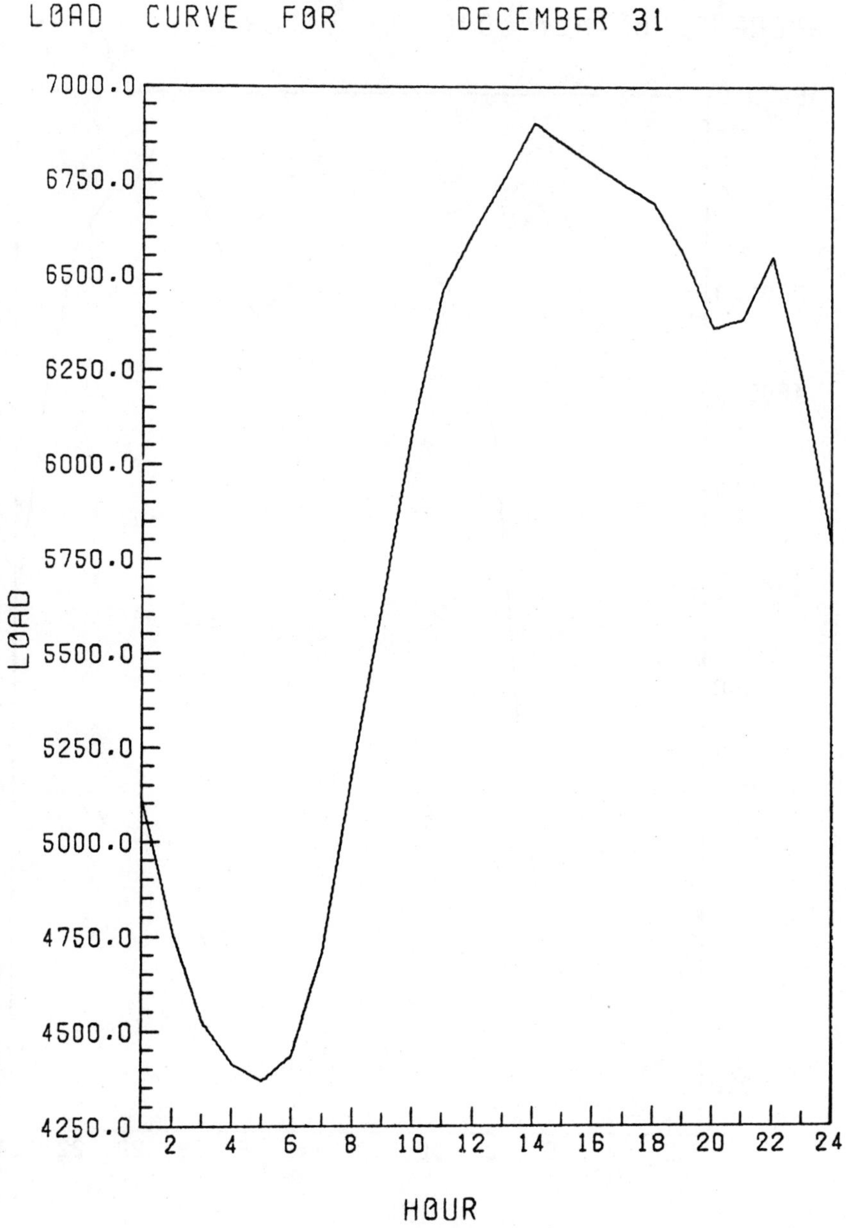

LØAD CURVE FØR DECEMBER 31

LØAD

7000.0
6750.0
6500.0
6250.0
6000.0
5750.0
5500.0
5250.0
5000.0
4750.0
4500.0
4250.0

2 4 6 8 10 12 14 16 18 20 22 24

HØUR

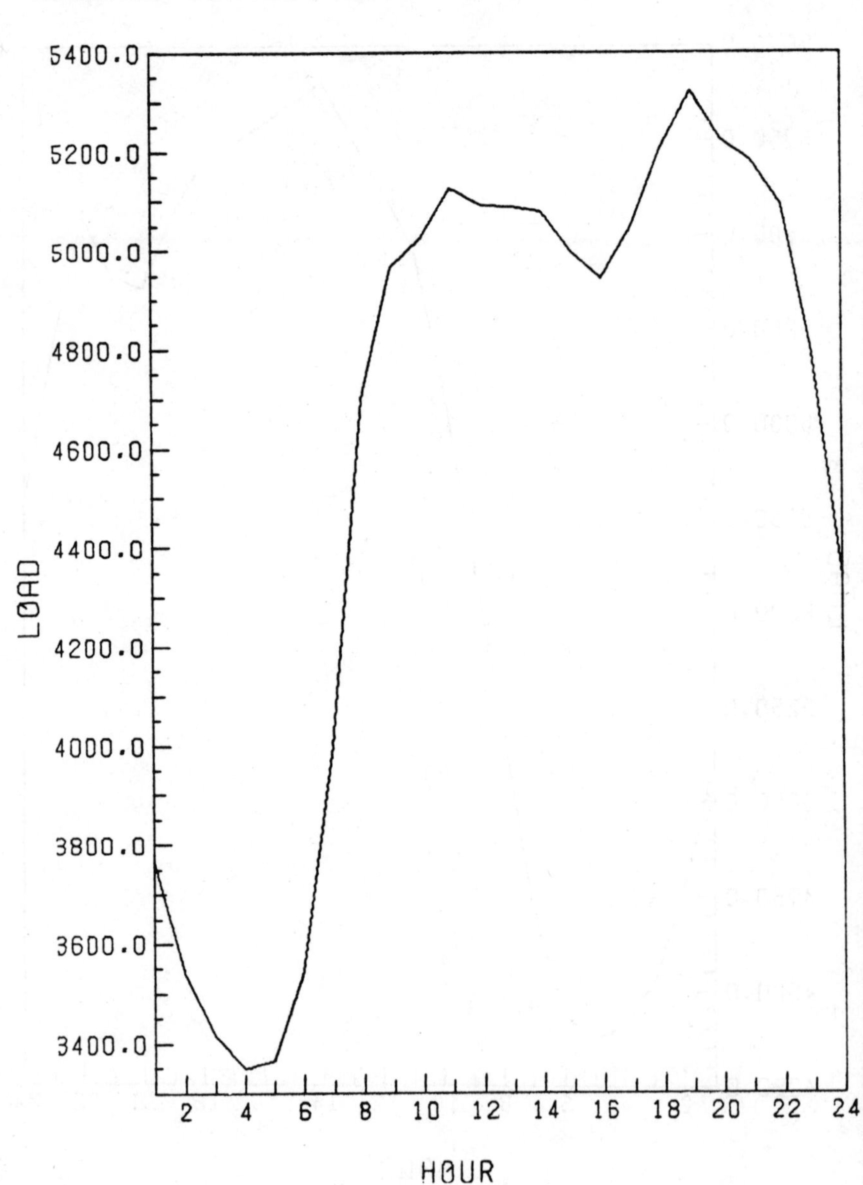
GRAPH NUMBER 3
AVERAGE MONTHLY LOAD CURVE FOR JANUARY
5400.0
5200.0
5000.0
4800.0
4600.0
4400.0
4200.0
4000.0
3800.0
3600.0
3400.0
LOAD
2
4
6
8
10
12
14
16
18
20
22
24
HOUR

GRAPH NUMBER 4

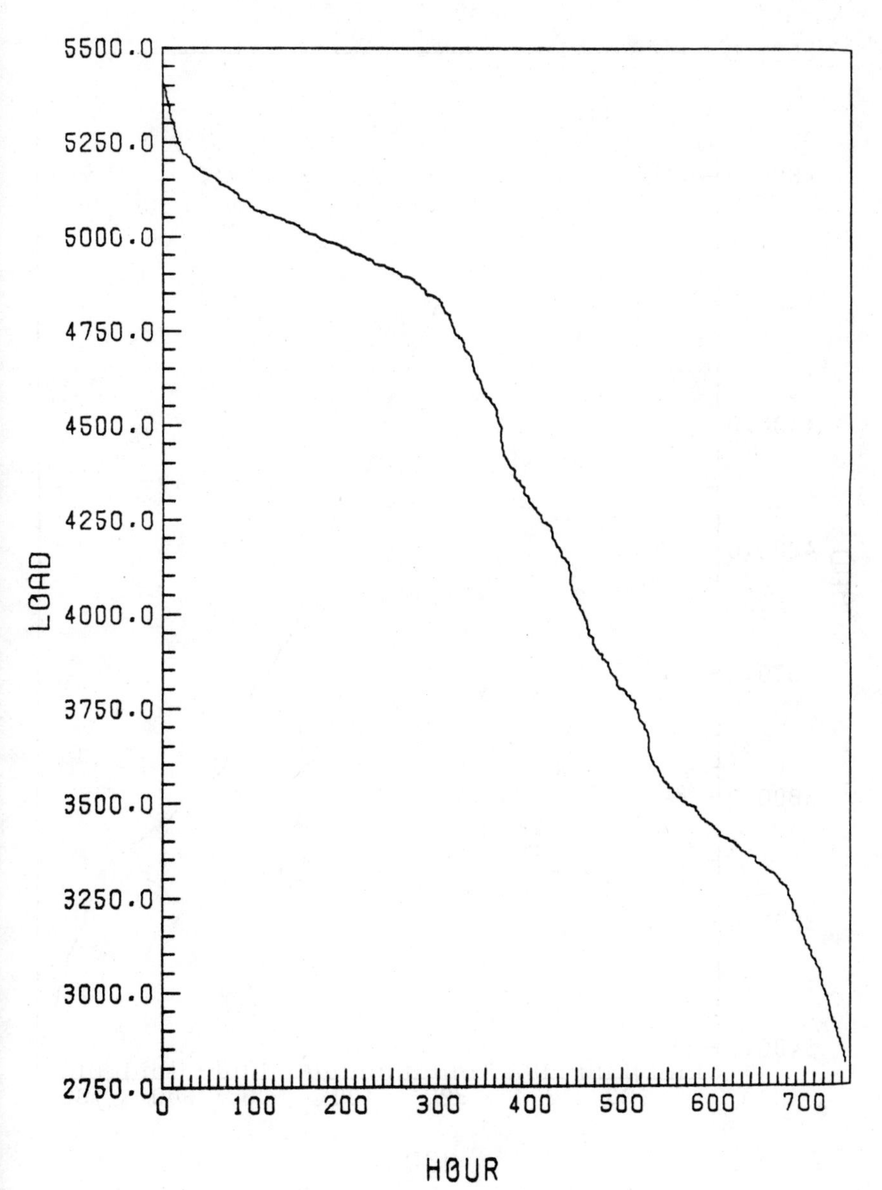

GRAPH NUMBER 5

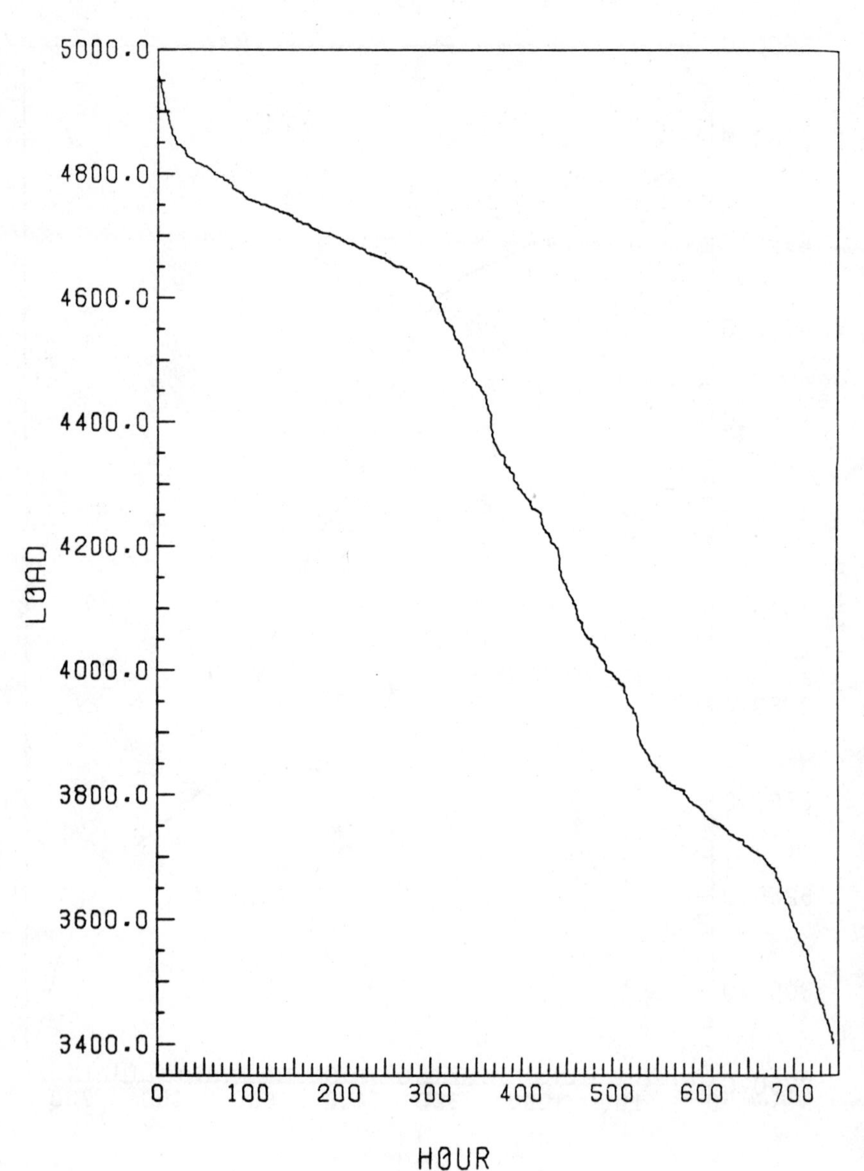

GRAPH NUMBER 6

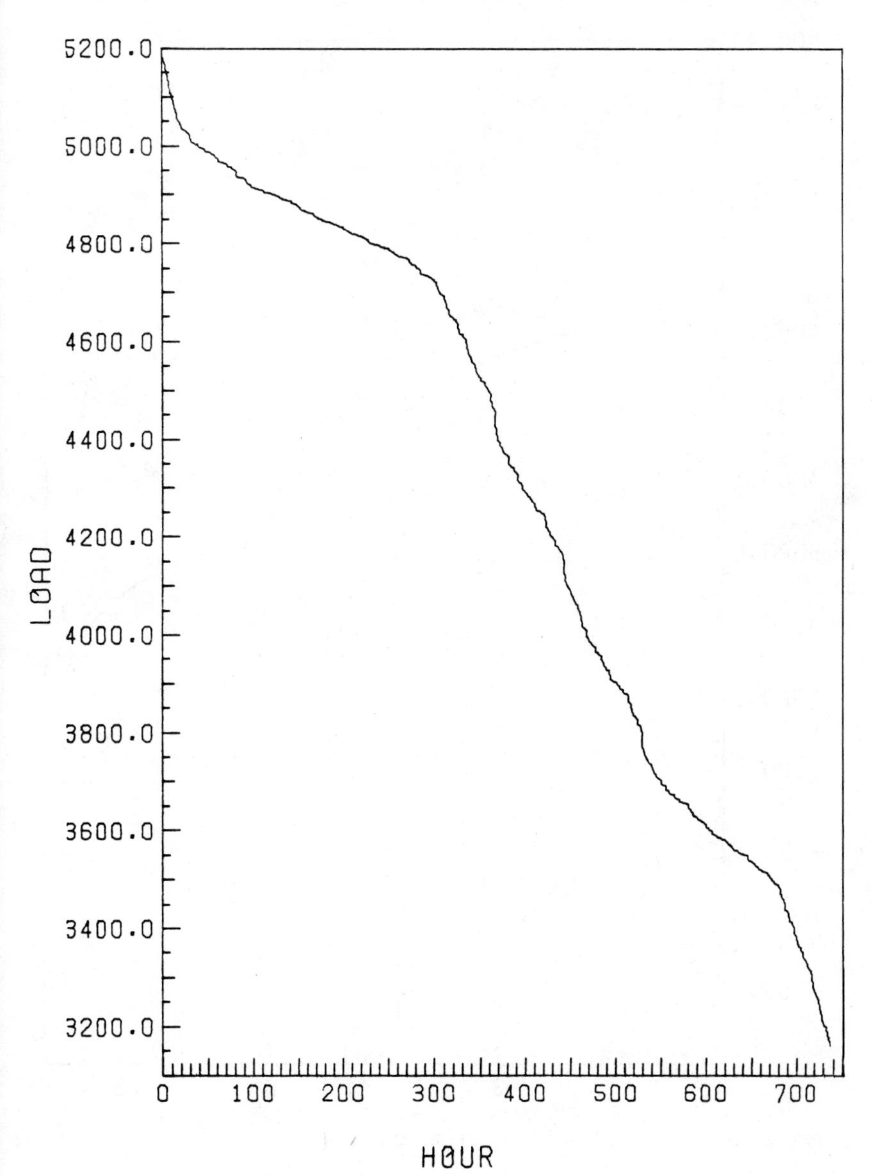

GRAPH NUMBER 7

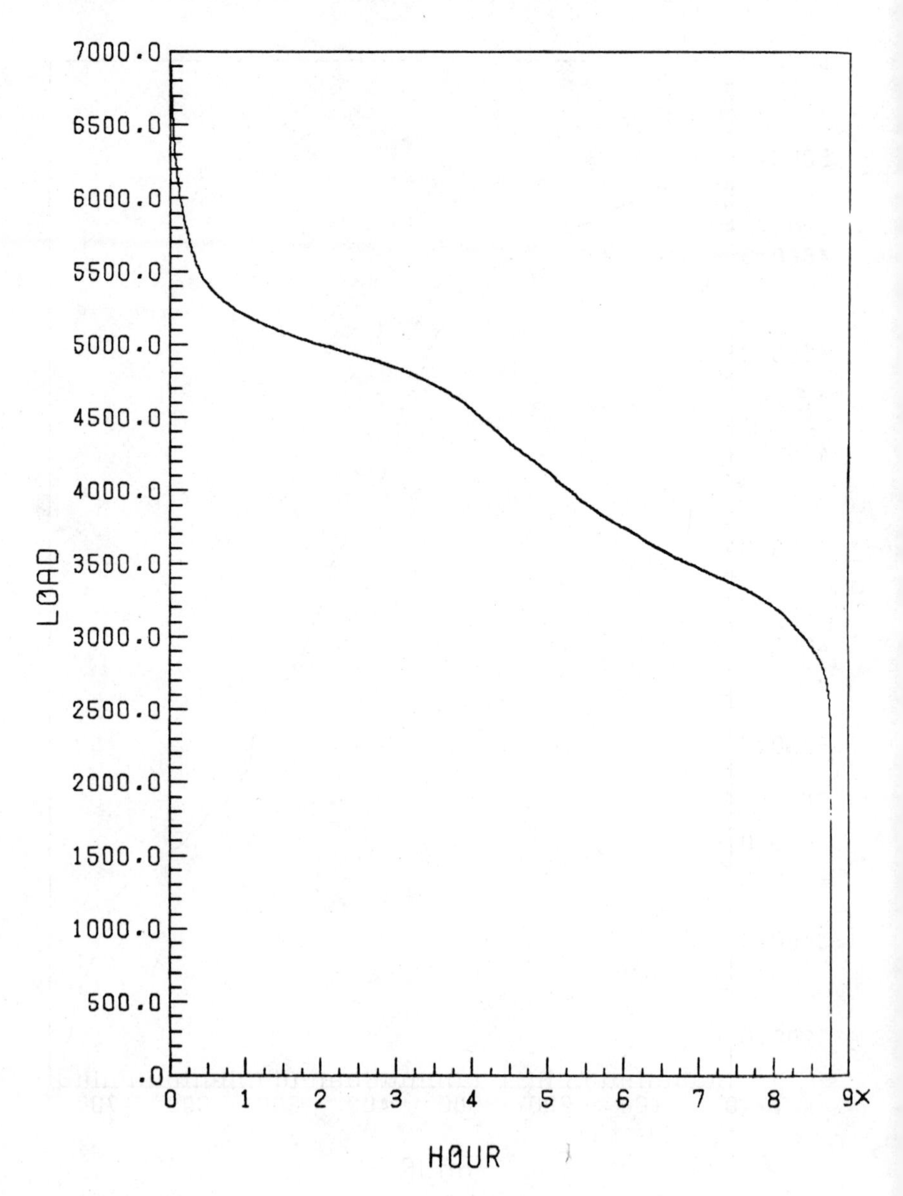

Appendixes

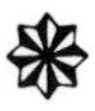

Appendix A

Metering Systems for Time of Day Pricing

This appendix presents the results of a survey* of manufacturers of electricity metering equipment that would be suitable for wide-scale implementation of time of day electricity tariffs. Continuously recording paper and magnetic tape devices, frequently used to monitor the consumption of the largest commercial and industrial consumers, are not considered because of the high cost of such devices. Where they are already in place, of course, such recording demand meters may be perfectly adequate for time of day pricing, but they would not be acquired for this purpose only.

This survey was not intended to be exhaustive, nor was any effort made to test the accuracy of the data presented. It merely presents to the reader information that was furnished us on inquiry to the manufacturers.

Among the simplest devices available are those that combine a time switch with a multiregister KWH meter. The basic problem with any of these clock-regulated meters or load management systems lies in the clock mechanism itself. The expense of checking and resetting these clocks in the case of power outages could be quite large, and therefore the systems currently used in Europe employ a spring wound carryover mechanism to operate the clock during power failures. For all these clock-activated systems, both meters and load limiters, the periods of peak are determined in advance and the clocks are set accordingly. A change in the designated peak periods requires resetting the clocks on the meters.

*Completed on December 1, 1975.

REMOTE-CONTROLLED SYSTEMS (one way communication)

A more flexible alternative to the clock mechanism uses a remote signal to communicate each day's peak period directly to the customer, either by acting directly to disconnect certain appliances for brief periods or by activating a different register on a multiregister meter and perhaps signaling the customer via a warning light that higher rates are in effect. These two operations, direct load management and time of day pricing, can of course be combined on one system, giving a utility several options.

The best known and tested of such systems are the "ripple" control systems widely used in Europe,* and radio control, which has also had limited use in the United States. The possibility of using telephone lines or cable television wires for the communication link in such a system has been explored, but these means of communication have not yet proved as convenient or reliable as power lines ("ripple" control) or radio for providing the direct link to the consumer.

The radio control system as developed by Motorola is aimed primarily at direct load management, and the manufacturer has promoted this system as offering "positive control" in contrast to a time of day metering system, which relies on customer response for its effectiveness for load management. In fact, the two systems can be combined by using the radio control system to switch the registers in a multiregister meter as well as directly controlling selected appliances. Briefly, the system operates as follows. A narrow band FM radio receiver is installed at the customer's premises. This receiver responds to a coded tone command sent to it by a radio transmitter either permanently situated in the service area or located in a land or air mobile unit. The receiver decodes the command and operates a 30 ampere relay to perform the switching function. A timing circuit within the receiver restores the switch to its original position within a five to seven minute period unless another command is sent by the transmitter. Thus if the relay were activated by a spurious tone, service on a controlled appliance would be disconnected for only a brief (five to seven minute) period of time. Precautions have also been taken to prevent controlled diversity flarebacks from appliances such as hot water heaters after an extended power outage has destroyed their natural diversity of demand. The transmitters are controlled by

*A ripple system has recently been introduced in this country in connection with electricity pricing experiments in Vermont.

a central computer maintaining two way communication with the transmitter sites. According to Motorola's most recent literature, total installed system cost for receivers and transmitters would be $8 million for 100,000 heaters, or $80 per switch (not including the cost of the central computer, which has other functions as well). If this system were to be used to implement time of day metering, the cost of the multiregister meter would be additional. Difficulties with radio control include obstruction of the signal by hills and tall buildings, and the limitation on available frequencies.

A more reliable (and somewhat more expensive) system of external switching is the "ripple" control system. A tone-coded audio frequency signal typically in the range of 150 to 350 Hz is injected into the power network at the mid or high voltage level. The signal travels through transformers and lines to the low voltage network, where individual receivers filter out the signal command and operate the switch. The major components of the system are (1) the central control console, (2) frequency generator, (3) injection or transmission stations, and (4) the individual receiver/relays. An installation for an entire city might require several transmitters at each main substation to provide adequate coverage. Also to be considered, however, is the energy cost of the signal injection equipment, which would be higher than that required for radio control. Furthermore, growth in demand must be met by an expansion of the capacity of the central injection equipment so that the signal reaches the customer at sufficient voltage.

The following summarize the features and costs of several one way (radio and ripple control) systems:

Motorola
Radio-controlled Time of Day and Load Management Metering System (one way)

Contact: James Holtzinger
Schaumburg, Illinois

			Total per point
A. Time of Day Metering			
dual register KWH meter			
control hardware	70.00		$90.00
installation	12.00		
computer, transmitter, etc.	2.00–3.00 (spread cost)		
dual register meter (subcontracted)	70.00–75.00		$160.00–165.00
B. Add Load Management*			
another radio receiver	70.00	$82.00	$242–247.00
installation	12.00		
C. Load Management Alone			
control hardware, etc. (same as A)		$90.00	
each additional appliance		$82.00	

*Space conditioning (heat and air)—off seven minutes, on thirty minutes
water heater —computer decision as to time

Brown-Boveri
Ripple System/One Way
Load Control/Time of Day

Contact: Mr. Stillhard
(201) 932–6000
North Brunswick, New Jersey

Injection: 15 KV

Points per transmitter: up to 35,000 (depending on distribution voltage and distance)

Costs: signal

transmitter	15 KVA to 2 MVA	$40,000–50,000
coupling equipment	med. distributor voltage	
control unit	memory bank	$15,000–20,000

receiver		
	1 function	$75.00
	2 function	85.00
	3 function	95.00

large quantities: 5 percent less

American made: 10–15 percent less (when in production by BBC)

total cost (receiver, transmitter, central system)		
	1 relay	$100.00
	2 relay	110.00
	3 relay	120.00

test equipment:

portable transmitter unit	$3,000–3,500
selective voltmeter-audio level	$2,400
receiver testing device	$7,000

Detail: Maximum of 15 amps/switch
higher amperage: another contact necessary

Zelweger-Ulster Ripple/One Way Load Control/Time of Day	Contact: Peter Schnieper (704) 392–7421 Charlotte, North Carolina

Injection: uses any KV

Costs: signal at substation	$1200–1500/MVA system capacity
transmitter hardware	or ≈ $15.00/receiver
control network	
coupling	
receiver (1 function)	$65.00
add functions (up to 4)	15.00
installation:	variable
Total costs: 1 function	$80.00
2 function	95.00
3 function	110.00
4 function	125.00
Testing equipment:	
portable transmitter	$2,000.00
voltmeter-audio level	100.00
transmission testing equipment	included in central control

Plessey
Ripple/One Way
Load Control/Time of Day

Contact: Al Neumann
(213) 341–7770
Los Angeles, California

Injection: 7 or 35 KV
Points per transmitter: 10,000 to 20,000
Signaling volts: 1 to 1½ V

must subcontract:
meters
switches

Costs: signal

transmission hardware (at 35 KV)	$40,000
auto load control	4,800
auto program control	4,300
central control (automatic)	19,000 (manual at less cost)
up to 3 parallels (sets of information)	
up to 10 parallels	+6,000
control relays (2 amps) 1 function	38.00/relay
(20 amps) 1 function	40.00/relay
(20 amps) 2 function	64.00/relay
Total cost:	$70.00/point

Detail: Load shed above certain KV consumption
time of day: await development of inexpensive adapter

Weston-Schlumberger
Ripple System/One Way
Load Control/Time of Day

Contact: Bob Fuller
Don Terrell
(213) 821–8084
Los Angeles, California

Receivers/MVA transformer capacity			10,000/12KV
Cost: signal, injection, shunt			$75,000/12KV
circuit, generator			$300,000/69KV
receivers:	1 function		$50.00
	3 function		$75.00
		installation	$40.00
signal injection:	210 HZ audio signal—1 percent of distribution voltage		
installation:	69KV $40,000 injection station		
	$14,000 distribution injection station		

Landis and Gyr
Ripple System/One Way
Load Control/Time of Day

Contact: John Stalder
(914) 592–4400
Elmsford, New York

Load management (shedding)

Time of day metering

Cost:

signal		$1,000/1 MVA transformer capacity
receivers:	1 function	$50.00
	2 function	65.00
	3 function	75.00
signal injection		10.00
installation		25.00
		$85.00 → 135.00/point
meter		cost variable

Number of receivers/MVA transformer capacity: 150

AUTOMATIC METER READING (AMR) SYSTEMS

In recent years, several companies have developed systems that are designed to read customer meters remotely. Usually, this capability is coupled with load-shedding functions for one or more circuits at the point of consumption. The following information was furnished by manufacturers.

Datrix LMS
Load Management System

Contact: Brian Travis
(813) 961–8000
Tampa, Florida

Services: AMR
load shedding
load shifting
load research
demand metering
system and line control
service disconnect/connect

System: remote unit: transponder/encoder
intermediate collector: 1 million/minute
central control: computer

Transmission: remote → intermediate → central: radio frequency
powerline
Rf/powerline
communication
system

Installation: on existing or new meter

Maintenance: none expected; designed for modular repair

Additional components: none

Test history: 500 LME packages installed, orders for six more.

Availability: 120 days

Cost: A. load management evaluation package (LME package)
400 meters, minicomputer, relay hardware,
$250,000.00 switches (on-off by command),
150 heaters, 250 hot water heaters

B. load management system + AMR + $150.00/point
demand metering + time of day metering,
16 appliance control, rate analysis,
installation included

DARCO Telemetering Systems
Automatic Meter Reading
and Usage Control

Contact: Floyd English
(402) 333–9858
Omaha, Nebraska

Services: auto meter reading

load shedding
load shifting
demand metering
visual display at point of consumption

can add gas and water battery backup for AMR (15–18 hours during outage)
4 part time of day metering

System: remote unit encoder (magnetic annular ring) and need switch

intermediate console—10,000 units/console → 130,000

central control—computer or use existing utility billing computer

Transmission: remote → console via telephone lines

console → central via telephone lines

Installation: on existing KWH meter, water and gas

Maintenance: solid state

Add components: time of day, timed load shed, demand load shed, biofeedback

Test history: Iowa Light and Power, with United Telephone System 1973

Availability: now

Cost: basic AMR, includes battery backup and alert; large-scale integrated circuit; electric, gas and water hookup.

basic AMR	remote unit:	49.95 (1)
basic AMR + time of day (4 part)	add:	39.95 (2)
basic AMR + timed* load shed—add to (1) per load:		15.00 (3)
basic AMR + timed and demand* load shed, add to (1):		59.95 (4)
basic AMR + time of day metering + timed and demand load shed add to (1) & (2) & (3) or (1) & (2) & (4):		

Total = 104.90 → 149.85 (5)

*Timed load control: switching device preset to time of day and day of week. Times off and timed on.

Timed and demand load control: switching device turns off at a preset KW maximum consumption, stays off seven minutes, monitors itself again for KW max over fifteen minute period.

General Electric
AMRAC: Automatic Meter Reading and Control

Contact: Paul B. Robinson
(603) 692–2100
Somersworth, New Hampshire

Services: automatic meter reading
—time of day for main meter in up to four pricing periods
—alternatively, demand for main meter
—periodic read for up to three auxiliary meters (2nd electric, water, gas) (all meter data represent absolute readings of meter dials)
load shedding and customer altering
—up to five external devices
communication for dispatch of distribution feeder
additional services: survey metering, initial and final reads, monitoring suspicious meters, demand from 5 percent of time of day meter terminal units

System: remote equipment: meter encoder, meter terminal unit (electronics)
intermediate collector
central computer
operation: computer causes simultaneous reading and storing of all time of day meters in designated register of meter terminal units; computer causes transmission of stored data at minimum rate of 3,333 meters per hour on each telephone trunk.

Transmission: power line between meter terminal units and intermediate
telephone or equivalent between central and multiple party-lined intermediates
error detection codes used in both directions.

Installation:

Maintenance:

Additional components: no transformer bypass, but repeaters may be needed in some circumstances.

Test history:

Availability: "when utilities support these new tariffs"

Cost:

encoder	20.00
time of day meter terminal unit including capability for five external loads and alerts	110.00
all other, including computer	20.00
	$150.00
contractor for each load controlled	$20–25.00

American Science and Engineering
Load Management and Automatic
Metering System

Contact: R.E. Abbott
(617) 868–1600
Cambridge, Massachusetts

Services:	automatic meter reading	service disconnect/connect
	load shed	detects errors/failures
	load shift	records continuous KWH
	load research	4 part daily rate
	demand metering	distribution system control
	time of day metering	

System: remote unit—encoder/transponder
intermediate collector—command sequencer
meters/30–40 minutes (substation control unit)
central control—computer

Transmission: remote to intermediate—powerline 506 KHZ optimal
intermediate to central—telephone or microwave

Installation: new meter or retrofit encoder to existing meter

Maintenance: replacement

Additional components: no transformer bypasses repeaters; traps recommended for power factor correcting capacitors

Test history: three years in Jersey Central Power and Light

Current programs: New Jersey experiment; Wisconsin Electric Power Company

Availability: order now (all capabilities); preproduction units deliver March 1976; production LSI units deliver September 1976

Cost: production hardware (all elements of system) including computer, SCUs, encoders, transponders at approximately $150 per point to $175 per point including water heat control relay

Typical cost detail: data dispatch computer (for 120,000)

2½ sets and accessories	$ 0.4M
substation control units (319) 4.2K@	1.34M
transponders (120,000) 98.00@	12.00M
auxiliary switching devices (120,000) $40.00 @	4.8M
	$18.54M

+10 to 15 percent documentation, field support, spares, application engineering, custom software, training

Automated Technology Corporation
RAMRAC Remote Automatic Meter
Reading & Control

Contact: S.R. Calabro
(201) 489–7250
Hackensack, New Jersey

Services:	automatic meter reading load shed load shift load research demand metering	records continuous KWH reads and stores indefinitely can be read every fifteen to thirty minutes add gas, water metering
System:	remote unit: optical encoder (light-sensitive diodes) intermediate collector: 500 units a piece/ 125 seconds central control: computer	
Transmission:	remote to intermediate—powerline intermediate to central powerline	2–350 KHZ range
Installation:	on existing meter or new meter	
Maintenance:	replacement	
Additional components:	no transformer bypass no distribution carrier traps	
Testing history:	Consolidated Edison Company of New York; Ohio Power Co.	
Availability:	now	

Cost:

(1) one way meter reading (cost at 100,000 units) encoder, transmitter meter, satellite w/tape storage $60,00

(2) two way interrogation and load management

optical encoder	20.00 @	100.00 @
meter, electronics	60.00 @	
satellite	20.00 @	
computer	1.00*	

hardware, overhead, line testing
observeillance
(people) + $25.00
extras: switching device (signal provided)
$3.00 to $5.00
alert light (3 minute warning)
$3.00

*Cost divided over large order.

Westinghouse
Automated Load Management
and Meter Reading

Contact: John Goodman
Sam Jordan
(919)834–5271
Raleigh, North Carolina

Services: automatic meter reading; service disconnect/connect

load shedding:
1. close-open/command
2. close-command open-timed

shifting (time of day); status monitoring and block

demand metering; uniquely addressing

System: remote unit—encoder/meter

coupling points; AMR read 100,000 meter/3 hours; 4 peak hour readings/day

central control: mini computer

Transmission: remote → intermediate—powerline
intermediate → central—telephone

Installation: added on to existing meter

Maintenance: replacement

Additional components: no transformer bypasses; may need line repeaters and carrier traps

Test history: Carolina Power Light—AMR; (333) meters/3KW demand reads

Ohio Edison, West Penn Power, Consumers Power, Florida Power and Light

Availability: 1980—Low cost systems given below

Now—prices three to five times those given below

Cost:

	1980–LSIC Total	Now Total
load management	$100.00	$500.00
load management + AMR + demand metering	150.00	700.00
AMR + 4 period time of day metering + load management (for 1,000 or more)	145.00	700.00

Readex Electronics, Inc.
AMR Automatic Meter Reading

Contact: Donald W. Rouse
(716) 624–2150
Haneoye Falls, New York

Services:
- automatic meter reading
- load shed (three loads)
- load shift (two meters, three rates each)
- load research (every fifteen minutes)
- gas, water metering
- detects errors
- backup battery during outage

System: remote unit: adapter and switch, electronic counter
intermediate collector
central control: computer

Transmission: remote → intermediate—radio and powerline
intermediate → central—radio

Installation: variable

Maintenance: large-scale integrated circuitry

Additional components: transmission costs and adaptations negligible

Test history: automatic meter reading—eight utilities in New York State

Availability: (three to six months) early 1976 for 1,000; nine months to one year for 100,000

Cost:

Item	Quantity	Cost
AMR	(100,000)	$103.45 @
AMR & load shedding	(100,000)	143.34 @
AMR & time of day metering	(100,000)	143.45 @
AMR & load shedding and time of day metering	(100,000)	163.45 @
additional meters read (water, gas, etc.) add	(100,000)	47.00 @
AMR and other systems cost/1,000		600 → 900.00 @
command unit, computer and software		85,000.00

Co Axial Scientific Corporation
Cable Transmission AMR System

Contact: Steve McVoy
(813) 349–2770
Sarasota, Florida

Services: AMR
time of day metering
load research

(since this system is primarily a reporting system, load management for switching on/off appliances would require much more expensive hardware than that offered below)

Room on wide band for many other services: TV
burglar alarm
two way educational programming
data retrieval

System: remote unit—simple transducer
central unit—computer

Transmission: cable

Testing history: pay TV in Columbus, Ohio

Available: when transducer for utility meter retrofit is available

Cost: customer without cable:

	Components	Total
transmission lines	$25.00	
data circuitry	25.00	
installation	10.00	$60.00

customer with cable:

data circuitry	$25.00	
installation	10.00	$35.00

computer cost: $15,000 for service to 15,000 customers $1.00/pt.

SUMMARY

AMR, Load Management, Time of Day, Demand Metering
Approximate Cost/Remote Unit 100,000 Units or More
(for detail see preceding pages pertaining to each system)

Availability			
now	ATC:	automatic metering and load management	$100–125.00
now	DATRIX:	AMR + load management + time of day metering + demand metering	150.00
	AS&E:	AMR + load management + time of day metering + demand metering	
March 1976		prototype/preproduction hardware	
		remote meter	650.00
		add per controlled appliance	40.00
September 1976		production hardware—LSI	
		remote meter	125.00
		add per controlled appliance	40.00
"When utility conviction makes large investment advisable"	GE:	automatic time of day metering, capability for three other meters, control of five loads or alerts	150.00
		above including contractor for one load	175.00
	WESTINGHOUSE:		
now		load management (three appliances)	500.00
		AMR, 4 period time of day metering	700.00
1980		load management (three appliances)	100.00
		AMR, 4 period time of day metering	145.00
Availability			
	READEX:		
9 months to 1 year		AMR	130.00
		AMR + load shed *or* AMR + time of day metering	143.45
		AMR + load shed + time of day metering	163.45

now	DARCO:	
	AMR system	49.95
	AMR and load management	64.95–109.90
	AMR and time of day (4 part)	89.90
	AMR and time of day and load management	104.90–149.85

CONTACTS FOR METER COST INFORMATION

I. Manufacturers

Darco Telemetering Systems
Floyd English, president
268 N. 115th Street
Omaha, Nebraska
(402) 333–9858

Readex Electronics, Inc.
Donald W. Rouse, vice president
68 East Street
Honeoye Falls,
New York 14427
(716) 624–2150

American Science
and Engineering, Inc.
Ralph Abbott
955 Massachusetts Avenue
Cambridge, Massachusetts 02139
(617) 868–1600

General Electric Company
Paul Robinson
Main Street
Somersworth,
New Hampshire 03878
(603) 692–2100

Westinghouse Electric Corporation
John R. Goodman
Automatic Metering Division
Raleigh, North Carolina 27603
(919) 834–5271

Automated Technology Corporation
S.R. Calabro, president
300 Hudson Street
Hackensack, New Jersey 07601
(201) 489–7250

Datrix Corporation
Brian Travis
13902 N. Dale Mabry
Tampa, Florida 33624
(813) 961–8000

Motorola Communications and
Electronics, Incorporated
James S. Holtzinger
Schaumburg, Illinois 60172

Landis and Gyr
John Stalder
4 Westchester Plaza
Elmsford, New York 10523
(914) 592–4400

Zelweger Uster Corporation
Peter Schnieper, manager
Ripple Control Division
4404 Chesapeake Drive
Charlotte, North Carolina 28216
(704) 392–7421

Weston-Schlumberger
Bob Fuller
Los Angeles, California
(213) 821–8084

Plessey
Al Neumann
Los Angeles, California
(213) 341–7770

Brown-Boveri
Mr. Stillhard
North Brunswick, New Jersey
(201) 932–6000

II. Buyers: Federally Funded Projects

Connecticut
Jacqueline Smith (203) 566–3696

Arizona
Ed Hyland
Arizona Public Service Corporation
Phoenix (602) 271–7408

New Jersey
Charles Richman
New Jersey State Energy Commission

Arkansas
Beth King, George Brazil
Arkansas Power and Light
Justice Building
Little Rock 72201

Vermont
C.A. Whitehair
Vermont Public Service Board
7 School Street
Montpelier 05602

III. Buyers: Utility-Funded Projects

Arkansas
Arkansas Power and Light
(see federally funded)

Wisconsin
Gary Lokken
Wisconsin Electric Power Company
Milwaukee

 *Appendix B*

Experimentation to Measure the Effects of Time of Day or Peak Load Pricing in the Sale of Residential Electricity: A Survey of Issues and Answers*

INTRODUCTION

The intent of this appendix is to provide a synopsis of the main methodological and practical issues surrounding the measurement of residential customer responsiveness to alternative electric rate structures. Our focus is justifiably placed owing to the fact that there now are several ongoing, federally funded projects aimed at discovering whether or not time of day or peak load rates for the residential sector will result in sufficient customer response to warrant the increased metering costs associated with them. Additional projects may soon be funded, making it even more important that firm guidelines be established on matters of statistical design, compensation of subjects, etc., so that the results of the various experiments will be of equal validity.

At the heart of the matter of sample design is the question of reliance on an economic model of customer behavior on which to base an optimal allocation of observations among cells. It is apparent that significant efficiencies of design can be achieved if the model intended for ultimate use in analyzing the data to be obtained from a pricing experiment is used at this early stage. But there are a variety of plausible demand models to choose from, each implying a different set of maintained hypotheses and, perhaps, widely disparate "optimal" allocations. So, which should be used? In the face of a lack of consensus as to the appropriate model, perhaps a very non-

*Prepared by Dennis Aigner, Professor of Economics, University of Wisconsin, Madison.

informative design structure ought to be used, namely ANOVA (analysis of variance). Then, once a design is decided upon, what of the practical matters of implementation?

These are the questions to be explored below. We begin the discussion with a detailed exposition of the process by which an optimal allocation of observations among cells is calculated, based on one of the plausible demand models that could be used to analyze pricing data (Aigner, 1975). An alternative model is then considered (Wenders and Taylor, 1975). Finally, some of the more practical considerations involved in implementing an experiment are discussed, in particular the matter of compensation of selected households, which draws heavily on the paper of Wenders and Taylor (1975) and a Rand project proposal (1973).

SPECIFICATION OF A MODEL FOR ANALYSIS—THEORETICAL CONSIDERATIONS

The microeconomic theory of consumer's behavior is undoubtedly among the most fully developed and widely understood parts of the science of economics. Most graduate students and an increasing number of undergraduates are exposed to it on a formal level through such books as Henderson and Quandt's *Microeconomic Theory* (1971).

Given a utility function for the individual consumer written in terms of, say, m commodities and a budget constraint on total expenditure, it is a fairly simple exercise, assuming exogenous prices for the commodities in question, to develop implicit "demand" functions. These functions relate the optimum level of consumption for each good to all their prices and the consumer's total expenditure (or, "income"). A large amount of information about these functions is obtained with quite weak assumptions about the shape and nature of the utility function. Any operational system of demand equations, the specification of which is the goal of this section, should either conform to the general restrictions that emerge from the theory or, at least, should allow those restrictions to be tested.*

To review briefly, let $x_l, \ldots, x_m$ be the optimal consumption levels of the m commodities, with $p_l, \ldots, p_m$ their respective prices and z the consumer's total expenditure, to be allocated among purchases of the goods. Then, in the system of demand functions that

*For present purposes, as will become clear, we are more interested in developing an operational model for a specific purpose than one to "test" the theory.

relate the x_js to the p_js and z, the following general restrictions must hold:

Homogeneity

If all prices and z are increased by the same factor of proportionality, then the optimum quantities demanded remain the same. Technically, the form of each demand function must be homogeneous of degree zero in prices and money income. A convenient form of this restriction is

$$\Sigma_{j=1}^{m} \frac{p_j}{x_i} \cdot \frac{\partial x_i}{\partial p_j} = - \frac{z}{x_i} \cdot \frac{\partial x_i}{\partial z}, \qquad i = 1, \ldots, m \tag{B.1}$$

which says that for any one of the commodities, say the ith, the sum of all direct and cross-price elasticities must equal the negative of the income elasticity of demand for that good.

Adding Up

The demand equations must be such that the sum of expenditures on the various commodities equals total expenditure, i.e., money income. This implies

$$\Sigma_{i=1}^{m} \frac{\partial (p_i x_i)}{\partial z} = 1, \tag{B.2}$$

which, in words, says that the marginal propensities to consume must add to one over the m commodities, so that a dollar increase in z is completely used up through marginal adjustments in the *expenditure* levels of the goods.

Symmetry

A change in any one of the exogenous prices works itself out through two simultaneous but decomposable effects, the so-called *income* and *substitution* effects. Formally,

$$\frac{\partial x_i}{\partial p_j} = k_{ij} - x_j \frac{\partial x_i}{\partial z} \qquad i, j = 1, \ldots, m \tag{B.3}$$

where k_{ij} is interpreted to be the response in x_i to the change in p_j (other things held constant) such that the consumer is no better or worse off (in utility) than he was before the price changed: the *substitution effect.* If $i = j$, so that we are concerned with the direct price effect on x_i of a change in p_i, equation (B.3) shows it being expressed as the sum of two things, a movement along the indifference curve, k_{ii} (which can be shown always to be negative in sign), and a movement to a new indifference curve, indicated by the term $-x_i \partial x_i / \partial z$, the *income effect.* For this same case, if $\partial x_i / \partial z > 0$, then clearly $\partial x_i / \partial p_i < 0$, which says an increase in the price of a commodity always reduces *its* consumption if it is a "normal" good, i.e., if $\partial x_i / \partial z > 0$, *ceteris paribus.*

When $i \neq j$, the sign of k_{ij} is ambiguous, so no such straightforward statement can be made. However, it must be the case that $k_{ij} = k_{ji}$, the symmetry of cross-price "pure" substitution effects. If the sign of (B.3) is positive, commodities i and j are termed "gross substitutes" for one another ("gross complements" if (B.3) is negative).

Homogeneity Again

Given (B.1), (B.2), and (B.3) it also must be true that*

$$\Sigma_{i=1}^{m} \; p_i k_{ij} = 0. \tag{B.4}$$

Equation (B.4) is *implied* by the other three sets of restrictions.

Moving from the esoteric to the practical matter of specifying the *form* of demand functions requires a big leap. For, functional forms that lend themselves to statistical estimation often are theoretically consistent only with very specific and not too interesting utility functions. There is a rather large literature on the subject that we will not detail here.** Instead, we present two potentially useful specifications, one which is already well known in applications and one which has been implemented only recently.

The first and by far most well-known specification is the *linear expenditure system.* Writing $y_i = x_i p_i$, each equation has the form

$$y_i = p_i \gamma_i + \beta_i (z - \Sigma_{j=1}^{m} p_j \gamma_j) \qquad i = 1, \ldots, m \tag{B.5}$$

with interpretations and restrictions as follows: y_i is (obviously) expenditure on the ith good. The γ_js are interpreted as the minimum required quantities," with $x_j > \gamma_j$; thus, $p_i \gamma_i$ is the "minimum" expenditure to obtain a subsistence level quantity of good i. Following this interpretation, $\Sigma_{j=1}^{m} p_j \gamma_j$ measures "subsistence income," whereas $z - \Sigma_{j=1}^{m} p_j \gamma_j$ is "supernumerary income," to be allocated in the

*Another way of writing (B.4) is, in these terms, $\Sigma_{j=1}^{m} p_j k_{ij} = 0$.

**For a good source book, the reader is referred to Phlips (1974).

proportions $\beta_l, \ldots, \beta_m$. The β_is are the *marginal* budget shares, with $0 < \beta_i < 1$ and $\Sigma_{i=1}^m \beta_i = 1$.

Some manipulation demonstrates that the corresponding direct and cross-price *elasticities* for (B.5) are given by:

$$\eta_{ii} = -1 + \frac{\gamma_i (1 - \beta_i)}{x_i}, \qquad i = 1, \ldots, m \tag{B.6}$$

$$\eta_{ij} = -\gamma_j \frac{p_j \beta_i}{y_i}, \qquad i,j = 1, \ldots, m$$

Thus, if $\gamma_i > 0$ it is seen that $-\eta_{ii} < 1$, so that the direct price effect is *inelastic*. The sign of η_{ij} likewise depends on the sign of γ_j. If $\gamma_j < 0$, meaning the jth good is price elastic, then $\eta_{ij} > 0$, and the goods i and j are gross substitutes. However, k_{ij} is *always* positive, which says that in terms of the pure cross-substitution effect, goods i and j *must* be substitutes.

More importantly, it can be shown that this system of expenditure equations is consistent with a utility function of the form

$$U(x_l, \ldots, x_m) = \Sigma_{i=1}^m \beta_i \log(x_i - \gamma_i), \tag{B.7}$$

with $0 < \beta_i < 1$, $\Sigma_{i=1}^m \beta_i = 1$, and $x_i > \gamma_i$ for all i. In (B.7) it is seen that the utility accruing to the individual from holding any of the goods is *additive* in the sense that $U(x_l, \ldots, x_m) = \Sigma_{i=1}^m U_i(x_i)$. This is indeed a strong assumption on the form of consumer preferences. However, for present purposes its implications may not be so unattractive, especially if we look upon (B.5) as a description of demand relationships for electricity use during different periods of the day rather than for electricity consumption as one "good" among the totality of commodities (energy-related and otherwise) purchased and consumed. In the former application, the fact that electricity at different times of the day, as different "goods," is restricted to be pure substitutes is not counterintuitive.

One practical drawback of the linear expenditure system (B.5) is that while it is linear in z and the p_js, it is nonlinear in parameters. This attribute does not cause any great difficulties from an analysis or estimation point of view, although something other than a "linear" least squares method is required. As a model on which to build a sampling design, however, the nonlinearity does cause concern. For, the usual approach to a nonlinear model would have us "linearize" it and base the design on the linear approximation. While for some situations this may appear to be an innocuous enough simplification, in the present case the linearized model will not meet the conditions and general restrictions of demand theory as does (B.5).

An attractive alternative economic model with likewise quite specific implications for the form of the demand (or expenditure) equations of interest has recently been proposed by Christensen et al (1975). The basic theoretical construct is the *transcendental logarithmic* utility function (the *translog*, for short).

The version of the translog we adopt for use here relates the utility obtained when optimizing levels of consumption are inserted to prices and money income. Specifically, we take as the form of the *indirect utility function* the translog function

$$-\ln V = \alpha_o + \Sigma_{i=1}^{m} \alpha_i \ln p_i^* + \frac{1}{2} \Sigma_{i=1}^{m} \Sigma_{j=1}^{m} \beta_{ij} \ln p_i^* \ln p_j^* , \tag{B.8}$$

where $p_i^* = p_i/z$, and the parameters satisfy the normalization $\Sigma_{i=1}^{m} \alpha_i = 1$. The utility function that corresponds to (B.8) is not additive; neither is (B.8) itself. Thus, in contrast to the previous model, the nature of consumer preferences entertained by the specification is less restrictive. If, however, (B.8) is made homothetic ($\Sigma_{i=1}^{m} \beta_{ij} = 0$) and additive ($\beta_{ij} = 0$ for $i,j = 1, \ldots, m$ but $i \neq j$), it can be shown that the corresponding utility function is itself additive.

The set of equations that is derived from (B.8), analogous to the expenditure system (B.5), is

$$w_i = \frac{\alpha_i + \Sigma_{j=1}^{m} \beta_{ij} \ln p_j^*}{\Sigma_{j=1}^{m} \alpha_j + \Sigma_{i=1}^{m} \Sigma_{j=1}^{m} \beta_{ij} \ln p_j^*}, \quad i = 1, \ldots, m \tag{B.9}$$

where $w_i = y_i/z$, the share of the budget devoted to commodity i. The corresponding expressions for the elasticities of interest are:

$$\eta_{ii} = -1 + \frac{\beta_{ii}/w_i - \Sigma_{j=1}^{m} \beta_{ji}}{1 + \Sigma_{l=1}^{m} \Sigma_{j=1}^{m} \beta_{lj} \ln p_j^*}, \tag{B.10}$$

the direct price elasticity, and the cross-price elasticity,

$$\eta_{ij} = \frac{\beta_{ij}/w_i - \Sigma_{l=1}^{m} \beta_{lj}}{1 + \Sigma_{l=1}^{m} \Sigma_{k=1}^{m} \beta_{lk} \ln p_k^*}. \tag{B.11}$$

The expenditure elasticity for any of the goods, as in the linear expenditure system, is not restricted to be of a particular (constant) magnitude.

As written, (B.9) is also nonlinear in parameters, and therefore presents no apparent advantages in that respect. However, if it is further assumed that the translog indirect utility function is explicitly *homothetic*, that is, all expenditure elasticities equal unity, then the equations (B.9) simplify greatly. Homotheticity is implied by $\Sigma_{i=1}^{m} \beta_{ij} = 0$ for all j, which results in

$$w_i = \alpha_i + \Sigma_{j=1}^{m} \beta_{ij} \ ln \ p_j^* \qquad i = 1, \ldots, m \qquad \text{(B.12)}$$

with

$$\eta_{ii} = -1 + \frac{\beta_{ii}}{w_i} \qquad \text{(B.13)}$$

and

$$\eta_{ij} = \frac{\beta_{ij}}{w_i} . \qquad \text{(B.14)}$$

Under the homotheticity assumption, the translog model is very attractive. The budget share equations are linear in parameters, which allows a straightforward use of (B.12) as the basis for a sampling design. Symmetry of pure cross-substitution effects can easily be imposed via the restrictions $\beta_{ij} = \beta_{ji}$, $i \neq j$, $i,j = 1, \ldots, m$. The question is, of course, at what cost do we get the simplified system (B.12)? Homotheticity means that a proportional increase in z will result in a *like* proportional increase in the consumption of each good. While that assumption appears dubious in a general expenditure study where z is total expenditure on *all* goods, for the more limited uses we have in mind—where z is taken to be expenditure on electricity only, to be allocated according to consumption during different periods of the day or season of the year—it may be more tenable.* At least homotheticity is less stringent an assumption than additivity, in the sense that it puts fewer parameter restrictions on the utility function.

*It should be mentioned, however, that in a recent empirical study by Christensen and Manser (1974) where homotheticity was *tested* as a restriction in a translog model of meat consumption, it was decisively rejected. I can't help but think that different kinds of meat hold more promise of nonhomothetic behavior that the same product, electricity, at different times of the day. But, that remains to be seen.

In any event, for the obvious virtues of the assumption, it may well make sense to impose it at the point of experimental design but to test it in the context of a more general model for analysis.* In what follows we accept this view and use the translog model given by (B.12) as our maintained hypothesis.

SPECIFICATION AND ESTIMATION OF A MODEL FOR ANALYSIS–ECONOMETRIC CONSIDERATIONS

Implementation of (B.12) requires the specification of stochastic terms representing either inherent randomness in the underlying behavior being modeled or sampling assumptions (or both). Following common usage, we append additive disturbances to (B.12) and write

$$w_i = \alpha_i + \Sigma_{j=1}^{m} \beta_{ij} \; ln \; p_j^* + \underline{X}_i' \underline{\gamma} + u_i \qquad i = 1, \ldots, m \qquad \text{(B.15)}$$

for a typical observation (a household), where $\underline{X}_i'$ is a $[1 \times (K-m)]$ row vector of values taken on by relevant socioeconomic variables (e.g., household income, family size, geographic locale, etc.), $\underline{\gamma}$ is a corresponding $[(K-m) \times 1]$ vector of unknown coefficients, and u_i is a random variable with zero mean and constant (over observations) variance σ_{ii}. Further, while independence in sampling is assumed, we allow disturbances for the same observation but different equations to be correlated. Specifically, for the "typical" observation represented in (B.15), we allow a nonzero covariance between u_i and u_l, σ_{il}, for $i, l = 1, \ldots, m$ and $i \neq l$. This assumption is consistent with the idea that while observed budget shares for each household are presumed to have been generated by maximizing the same utility function conditional on values taken on by the various variables in $\underline{X}_i$, they are the result of a joint optimizing process such that the error in setting an optimum level of the ith good is related to a similar error in the observed level of the lth good.

Now, assuming we have available observations on n households gathered according to the foregoing specifications, we define the following vectors and matrices:

$$\underset{(n \times 1)}{\underline{w}_i} = \begin{pmatrix} w_{1i} \\ \vdots \\ w_{ni} \end{pmatrix}, \qquad i = 1, \ldots, m$$

*The same can be said for the symmetry restrictions.

a vector of observations on the ith budget share;

$$\underset{\sim}{\underline{p}}_j^* = \begin{pmatrix} ln\ p_{ij}^* \\ \vdots \\ ln\ p_{nj}^* \end{pmatrix}, \qquad j = 1, \ldots, m$$

a vector of observations on the jth (normalized) price;

$$\underset{[n \times (K-m)]}{X} = \begin{pmatrix} \underline{X}_l' \\ \hdashline \vdots \\ \hdashline \underline{X}_n' \end{pmatrix},$$

the matrix of observations on relevant socioeconomic variables;

$$\underset{[n \times (K+1)]}{Z} = \left(\imath \;\vdots\; \underset{\sim}{\underline{p}}_l^* \;\vdots\; \cdots \;\vdots\; \underset{\sim}{\underline{p}}_m^* \;\vdots\; X \right),$$

where $\imath$ is an $(n \times 1)$ column of ones:

$$\underset{(n \times 1)}{\underline{u}_i} = \begin{pmatrix} u_{li} \\ \vdots \\ u_{ni} \end{pmatrix}, \qquad i = 1, \ldots, m$$

the vector of disturbances for the ith equation; and

$$\underset{[(K+1) \times 1]}{\underline{\beta}_i} = \begin{pmatrix} \alpha_i \\ \beta_{il} \\ \vdots \\ \beta_{im} \\ \gamma_{il} \\ \vdots \\ \gamma_{i,K-m} \end{pmatrix}, \qquad i = 1, \ldots, m$$

the vector of unknown parameters in the ith equation.

Combining the above definitions into a cohesive statement of the working model, we have

$$\begin{pmatrix} \underline{w}_l \\ \vdots \\ \underline{w}_m \end{pmatrix} = \begin{pmatrix} Z & & 0 \\ & \ddots & \\ 0 & & Z \end{pmatrix} \begin{pmatrix} \underline{\beta}_l \\ \vdots \\ \underline{\beta}_m \end{pmatrix} + \begin{pmatrix} \underline{u}_l \\ \vdots \\ \underline{u}_m \end{pmatrix} \tag{B.16}$$

or,

$$\underset{(mn \times 1)}{\underline{w}} = \underset{[mn \times m(K+1)]}{\underline{\Xi}} \quad \underset{[m(K+1) \times 1]}{\underline{\beta}} + \underset{(mn \times 1)}{\underline{u}}$$

where $E(\underline{u}) = 0$ and

$$\underset{(mn \times mn)}{\Sigma} = E(\underline{uu'}) = \Omega \otimes I_n\,, \tag{B.17}$$

with

$$\underset{(m \times m)}{\Omega} = \begin{pmatrix} \sigma_{ll} & \cdots & \sigma_{lm} \\ \vdots & \ddots & \vdots \\ \sigma_{ml} & & \sigma_{mm} \end{pmatrix} \tag{B.18}$$

and I_n is an $(n \times n)$ identity matrix.

The equations in (B.16) are in the form of Zellner's "seemingly unrelated" regressions but with the same matrix of observations on independent variables appearing in each equation. Alternatively, (B.16) is *multivariate regression.*

Whether Ω is known or not, as long as there are no parameter constraints across equations, ordinary least squares (OLS) are generalized least squares (GLS) yield the *same* parameter estimates,* $\hat{\underline{\beta}}$, with variance-covariance matrix (assuming Ω is known)

$$E(\hat{\underline{\beta}} - \underline{\beta})\,(\hat{\underline{\beta}} - \underline{\beta})' = \Omega \otimes (Z'Z)^{-1}\,. \tag{B.19}$$

*Cf., Goldberger (1970).

In the usual situation, of course, Ω is unknown. Writing $\hat{\underline{u}}_i$ as the vector of calculated residuals corresponding to the LS estimate $\hat{\underline{\beta}}_i$, the elements of Ω can be unbiasedly estimated by

$$\hat{\sigma}_{il} = \frac{1}{n-(K+1)} \hat{\underline{u}}_i' \hat{\underline{u}}_l ,$$

thereby yielding an operational version of (B.19).

An interesting feature of the model from an econometric point of view that has some design ramifications is the fact that since for every observation $\Sigma_{i=1}^{m} w_i = 1$ and a column of ones appear in Z, it must be true that $\Sigma_{i=1}^{m} u_i = 0$. That is, there is a constraint on the disturbances across equations for each observation that implies that Ω is singular. As mentioned previously, since OLS equation by equation provides the best linear unbiased estimator for $\underline{\beta}$, the singularity of Ω is of no immediate consequence. However, because of it the following restrictions will hold among *estimated* coefficients:

$$\Sigma_{i=1}^{m} \hat{\alpha}_i = 1, \tag{B.20}$$

$$\Sigma_{i=1}^{m} \hat{\beta}_{ij} = 0, \qquad j = 1, \ldots, m$$

$$\Sigma_{i=1}^{m} \hat{\gamma}_{ik} = 0, \qquad k = 1, \ldots, K-m$$

which implies that any one equation can be discarded at the outset for purposes of estimation, its coefficients being calculated by coefficient estimates for the remaining $(m-1)$ equations in conjunction with (B.20). Thus, for example, were but two periods of the day considered for the pricing experiment, with "peak" and "off-peak" prices, a one equation design model would suffice even if the one cross-equation symmetry constraint were to be imposed at the outset.

For the case $m > 2$, for purposes of estimation and as a basis for sampling design, one equation can likewise be ignored. If symmetry is to be imposed in the estimation, then is it no longer true that OLS and GLS constrained estimators coincide. The appropriate estimator (GLS) is given by:*

$$\hat{\hat{\underline{\beta}}} = \hat{\underline{\beta}} - CR'(RC \qquad {}^{1} R\hat{\underline{\beta}} , \tag{B.21}$$

*See Theil (1971), pp. 338–45, for a more detailed exposition of the restricted estimator in an expenditure system.

where $\underline{\hat{\beta}}$ is the unconstrained OLS estimator defined by

$$\underset{[(m-1)(K+1)\times 1]}{\underline{\hat{\beta}}} = \begin{pmatrix} (Z'Z)^{-1} Z' \underline{w}_l \\ \hdashline \vdots \\ \hdashline (Z'Z)^{-1} Z' \underline{w}_{m-1} \end{pmatrix},$$

$$\underset{[(m-1)(K+1)\times(m-1)(K+1)]}{C} = \underset{[(m-1)\times(m-1)]}{\hat{\Omega}} \otimes \underset{[(K+1)\times(K+1)]}{(Z'Z)^{-1}}$$

and

$$R\underline{\beta} = 0,$$

which reflects the linear constraints to be imposed. In the above, note that the dimensionality of all relevant vectors and matrixes defined over the number of equations (m) has been reduced because of the discarded equation. R is of dimension $[q \times (m-1)(K+1)]$, where q is the number of linear constraints imposed. Alternatively, the symmetry hypothesis can be tested via the statistic

$$F = \frac{(m-1)n - (m-1)(K+1)}{q} \cdot \tag{B.22}$$

$$\frac{\underline{\hat{\beta}}' R' \left\{ R \left[\hat{\Omega} \otimes (Z'Z)^{-1} \right] R' \right\}^{-1} R \underline{\hat{\beta}}}{(\underline{w} - \Xi \underline{\hat{\beta}})' (\hat{\Omega}^{-1} \otimes I_n \check{\hat{}} \, \underline{w}) - \Xi \underline{\hat{\beta}})},$$

where, again, the dimensionality of w and Ξ has been correspondingly reduced to reflect discarding of the mth equation. In (B.21) and (B.22), $\hat{\Omega}$ is a consistent estimate of Ω obtained either through the use of OLS residuals or via the observed budget shares, as suggested by Theil (1971).* (B.22) is approximately an F-statistic with q and $m[n-(K+1)]$ degrees of freedom if the u_is in (B.15) are assumed to be distributed normally.

Without imposition of the symmetry constraint, the numerical results are invariant to which equation is discarded. With symmetry imposed, this is not the case. However, it is known that an iterative procedure, whereby $\hat{\Omega}$ is updated at each step by using the most

*p. 341.

recent parameter estimates to reestimate its elements, converges to "stable" values that do not depend on the equation discarded at the outset.* In any event, stopping at a single iteration provides consistent parameter estimates and a well-defined (though asymptotic) test theory.

Without imposition of the homotheticity constraint, the correct budget share equations are not (B.15) but, rather, have the form of (B.9) with suitable modifications to include relevant socioeconomic variables and an additive disturbance. While we do not detail methods for estimation in that case here, they are available as straightforward extensions of methods for single equation nonlinear regression to the multiequation model.**

SAMPLING DESIGN—GENERAL CONSIDERATIONS†

In this section we present a general framework for designing a sample in an optimal fashion, among the objectives being precision of estimation of direct and cross-price effects of time of day electricity pricing subject to a budget and/or other relevant constraints. Allowance is made also for policymakers' specific interest in alternative tariff structures to be felt in the final design. We begin the exposition assuming that a single equation regression model is the framework for ultimate analysis and extend the design model thus developed to the multivariate regression case.

In the notation of the previous section, let the regression model of interest be

$$\underset{(n \times 1)}{\underline{w}} = \underset{[n \times (K+1)]}{Z} \; \underset{[(K+1) \times 1]}{\underline{\beta}} + \underset{(n \times 1)}{\underline{n}}, \qquad \text{(B.23)}$$

with $E(\underline{u}) = 0$ and $E(\underline{uu}') = \sigma^2 I_n$, as it would be if there were but one commodity represented in (B.16). The regressor matrix, Z, depends, row for row, on a matrix of *design variables* of dimension $(n \times G)$, where $G \leq K$.†† This specification appropriately focuses

*These fully iterated estimates are the maximum likelihood estimates under a normality assumption for the u_is of (B.15). Cf., Goldberger (1970).

**Cf., Gallant (1975). The translog model without homotheticity imposed has been implemented in Christensen and Manser (1974).

†This section draws heavily on the work of Conlisk and Watts (1969). For a general recerence on experimental design, see Cochran and Cox (1957), especially Chapter 8.

††So, for example, the design variables may include $p_l, \ldots p_m$ and z whereas a row of z involves, correspondingly, $ln\ p_l^*, \ldots, ln\ p_m^*$.

attention on the design variables at the stage of sampling design and the regressor variables at the analysis stage.

The *design problem* is to choose the rows of the design matrix, hence the rows of Z, in an optimal way. To simplify matters, it is assumed that at least over the relevant column partition of Z (the partition of variables subject to experimental control) row selection is limited to a set of r *admissible* rows ($r < n$). In the row space of the design matrix these admissible rows of Z correspond to *design points*, selected in advance so as to give adequate coverage to the *design space.* Actual determination of these points (how many of them and their exact specification) is an artful matter that depends on a variety of things, among them *a priori* knowledge of the relevant range of variation for policy purposes of each design variable, interest in particular combinations of values to be taken on by design variables, etc. In any event, the design problem is thus reduced to the problem of selecting r nonnegative integers, $n_l, \ldots, n_r$, where $\Sigma_{h=1}^{r} n_h = n$, corresponding to the selection of admissible row #1 of Z (denoted $\underline{Z}_l'$) n_1 times, row #2 n_2 times, etc., so that $Z'Z = \Sigma_{h=1}^{m} n_h \underline{Z}_h' \underline{Z}_h$.*

Next, an objective function must be formulated that adequately reflects the goals of analysis as functions of $n_l, \ldots, n_r$. We take the primary goal of analysis to be precise estimation of the direct and cross-price elasticities given by equations (B.13) and (B.14) for the homothetic translog budget share equations (B.12). In addition, we may be interested in precise estimation of the ith budget share for given values of the p_j^*s and other, socioeconomic variables.† In either case, we are interested in linear functions of basic model parameters, the elements of $\underline{\beta}$. Let the set of such linear functions of interest be denoted by $P\underline{\beta}$, where P is a $[H \times (K+1)]$ matrix whose rows reflect particular linear functions of $\underline{\beta}$. For example, in order to represent (B.13), the relevant row of P would look like $(-1, 0, \ldots, 0, 1/w_i, 0, \ldots 0)$, with the term $1/w_i$ placed in the position corresponding to β_{ii}. To represent interest in all individual coefficients, P would be specified as a $[(K+1) \times (K+1)]$ identity matrix, and so on.

Because (B.23) is written as a classical linear regression model, OLS will yield best linear unbiased estimates of the elements of $\underline{\beta}$. Their variance-covariance matrix is given by the familiar expression $\sigma^2 (Z'Z)^{-1}$. Likewise, the best linear unbiased estimator for $P\underline{\beta}$ is $P\hat{\underline{\beta}}$,

*In what follows, we are assuming for exposition convenience that all the variables in Z are controlled. This will not be the normal case in practice, in which case the "optimality" of sample design applies only to that subset of variables under experimental control.

†That is, the "height" of the response surface at a particular point.

with $(H \times H)$ variance-covariance matrix $V(P\hat{\underline{\beta}}) = \sigma^2 P(Z'Z)^{-1}P'$.

Finally, suppose W is given as a diagonal matrix (of dimension $(H \times H)$) of "weights" to be applied to the functions of $P\hat{\underline{\beta}}$, reflecting their "policy importance," and that we adopt as our objective function the weighted trace of $V(P\hat{\underline{\beta}})$; that is,

$$\begin{aligned} \phi(n_1, \ldots, n_r) &= \sigma^{-2} \; tr\, WV(P\hat{\underline{\beta}}) \\ &= \sigma^{-2} \; tr\, P'WPV(\hat{\underline{\beta}}) \\ &= tr\left[D(\Sigma_{h=1}^{r} \; n_h \; \underline{Z}_h' \; \underline{Z}_h)^{-1} \right], \end{aligned} \tag{B.24}$$

where $D = P'WP$.*

$\phi(n_1, \ldots, n_r)$ is now to be *minimized* subject to a cost constraint. (The model (B.23) is already an *implicit* constraint on ϕ.) Letting C_h be the unit cost of an observation at the hth design point, and denoting by C the total budget, we have $\Sigma_{h=1}^{r} C_n n_h \leq C$. As may be the case in the present application, the C_h s can themselves depend on values taken on by variables at each design point.

Given (B.24) and the cost constraint, our problem is as follows,

$$\underset{n_h}{\text{minimize}} \; \phi(n_1, \ldots, n_r) = tr\left[D(\Sigma_{h=1}^{r} \; n_h \; \underline{Z}_h' \; \underline{Z}_h)^{-1} \right] \tag{B.25}$$

subject to:

$$\Sigma_{h=1}^{r} \; C_h \, n_h \leq C$$

$$n_h \geq 0, \qquad h = 1, \ldots, r$$

which, strictly speaking, is an integer programming problem. Little is lost, undoubtedly, by treating the n_h s as continuous variables in any actual computation and rounding.

The nature of a solution to (B.25) will be such that the budget constraint holds at equality. Thus, in solution all design points included must have the same marginal effectiveness (per dollar of cost) in reducing the criterion function. Moreover, since ϕ is homogeneous of degree minus one in the n_h s, the optimal *proportional* sample allo-

*The weighted trace function is not the only available metric for summarizing multiple objectives, but it is quite convenient. For a discussion of alternatives, see Conlisk and Watts (1969), p. 154.

cations, $f_h^* = n_h^* / n^*$, are independent of C (although a larger value of C implies a larger total sample size).

Extension of the design problem (B.25) to the multivariate regression case is not difficult conceptually, but it does put on additional demands at the point of implementation. The matrix formulation (B.16) is already in the form of (B.23) except for the fact that the variance-covariance of disturbances is not of the form $\sigma^2 I$ but instead is (B.17). Hence, the correct expression for $V(P\hat{\underline{\beta}})$ is, using (B.19),

$$V(P\hat{\underline{\beta}}) = P[\Omega \times (Z'Z)^{-1}]P' \qquad \text{(B.26)}$$

and for the criterion function,

$$\phi(n_1, \ldots, n_r) = tr\left\{D[\Omega \otimes (\Sigma_{h=1}^{r} n_h \underline{Z}_h' \underline{Z}_h)^{-1}]\right\} \qquad \text{(B.27)}$$

where $D = P'WP$, as before. Besides requiring in advance of computation elements of the weighting matrix, W, we now need Ω in order to proceed. Extension to this more general case also encompasses a single equation model with nonspherical disturbances, a case of some interest if, for example, the investigator wishes to weight each row of Z to reflect anticipated heteroskedasticity or to correct for attrition of observations over the life of the experiment in particular cells.

SAMPLING DESIGN—A SPECIFIC ILLUSTRATION

In order to illustrate the material of the previous section, we have undertaken to solve a specific design problem, using (B.15) as the underlying econometric model with $m = 2$. That is, we assume that only two prices are to be offered: for "peak" and "off-peak" electricity. No seasonal shift in the rate structure is allowed for in this example. With $m = 2$, as was pointed out above, the design problem can be based on a single equation model.

The independent variables we consider are (1) an intercept constant, (2) "peak" price per KWH deflated by average monthly bill (expressed as a logarithm), (3) "off-peak" price per KWH deflated by average monthly bill (expressed as a logarithm), (4) household income, and (5) an urban-rural dummy. Thus, the basic accounting period is one month over observation units, which are households. No doubt there are other relevant independent variables to consider, such as the geographic area in which the household is located (corresponding to service by different utility companies), family size, etc. As will become apparent shortly, even with the limited set of independent variables chosen, the size of the design problem becomes large very quickly.

Table B–1 shows the set of values assigned to design variables used in the illustrative problem. The eight pairs of prices cover a wide range of rate differentials, from 1:1 ("control") to 13:1. It was felt that this range should cover most, if not all, realistic pricing structures. It is to be noted that the "realism" of these differentials depends also on the number of hours per day designed "peak." We have implicitly assumed that consumption during the day is equally divided between peak and off-peak hours, which gives an average price of 3.5 cents per KWH over all pairs. A particular differential may be consistent with numerous actual utility cost structures in conjunction with their respective definitions of the "peak" period. So, while only eight pairs of prices are used, they really apply to many more than eight alternative pricing structures, where by "pricing structure" we now mean a pair of KWH rates combined with a designation of the number of peak hours per day.

The three values for "average monthly bill" derive from evaluating the midpoint monthly use for three quantity classes—0–600 KWH per month, 600–1,500 KWH per month, and over 1,500 KWH per month—at 3.5 cents per KWH. In the open class we use 2,000 KWH as the class mean. Likewise, based on income classes of $0–10,000, $10,000–20,000, and over $20,000, we have constructed the household income variable from interval midpoints, with $25,000 being used as the mean income for the open interval.

Finally, a (0,1) dummy variable is included to capture (control

Table B–1. Values of Design Variables

Intercept Constant	*"Peak" Price (cents per KWH)*	*"Off-peak" Price (cents per KWH)*	*Average Monthly bill (dollars)*	*Household Income (1,000 dollars)*	*Urban-rural Dummy*
1.0	6.5	0.5	10.50	5.0	0.0
	6.25	0.75	15.75	15.0	1.0
	6.0	1.0	70.00	25.0	
	5.5	1.5			
	5.0	2.0			
	4.5	2.5			
	4.0	2.0			
	3.5	3.5			

for) any behavioral differences in response by persons in rural as opposed to urban environments.* Each row of the *design matrix* therefore consists of six variables and there is a total of 144 design points to consider (1 × 8 × 3 × 3 × 2), whereas the regressor matrix has a total of 144 admissible rows with values of five independent variables as elements in each row. While $Z'Z$ is only a (5 × 5) matrix and hence easily invertible, the nonlinear programming problem to be solved for an optimal allocation of observations, (B.25), involves 144 unknowns.

Other things that need to be specified in setting up the design problem are the D-matrix and the budget constraint. For this example we assume $P = I$ and $W = I$, which says we are interested in the regression coefficients themselves rather than the height of the response surface at any particular point. Moreover, each coefficient is "equally interesting." This probably does not correspond to most people's ranking, in terms of policy importance, of the estimable parameters and functions of parameters that appear explicitly in or can be derived from (B.15). For, from the point of view of a cost-benefit analysis of pricing for residential customers, the cross-price elasticity is probably the single most important parameter, followed by the own price elasticities. Therefore, the results we present should be viewed as more suggestive than definitive, as they apply to a "neutral" view of the policy importance of estimated regression coefficients and no importance is attached to estimation of the height of the response surface at any particular point, which would be of interest if we wanted to predict the share of peak use in the monthly bill of a particular class of customer faced with a particular pair of rates.

Various suggestions have been made regarding the compensation scheme to be used in the experiment, which bears on the calculation of a cost per observation to be incorporated into the design problem. However, questions of the duration of the experiment and the compensation scheme to be used have more important implications for the interpretation of results than for cost calculations, so we have not attempted to use a complicated scheme at this point. It is assumed that the total budget (for the life of the experiment) is $250, 000, with a fixed cost per observation of $250 to cover costs of metering and any compensation. This yields a target sample size of $n = 1000$.

The optimal sample allocation to design points for our illustrative

*In the design problem, nothing further need be specified about this dummy variable. In the analysis stage, of course, we must *define* "urban" and "rural." For example, in the 1970 census, 66 percent of the population of Wisconsin lived in "urban" areas, defined to be areas with populations of 2,500 or more.

problem is presented in Table B−2. Perhaps surprisingly, of 144 admissible points, *only fourteen appear with nonzero numbers of observations allocated to them.* As is expected in such designs, the tendency is to allocate observations to extreme values in the range of each design variable. So, we see no intermediate values of prices, average monthly bill and household income represented. The reason for this result is simply that, *ceteris paribus*, precision of estimation of regression coefficients is inversely related to variation in the independent variables. And variation is maximized when observations are placed at the extremes in the ranges of independent variables. To the extent that nonlinearities and/or correlations between independent variables are present, there may be exceptions to this general principle and deviation from an otherwise "balanced" design, where equal numbers of observations are allocated to every design point.

As was mentioned in the previous section, since the n_h s are treated as continuous variables in the solution algorithm and then rounded to integer values, there will be some discrepancy between the total of nonzero n_h s and the n implied by the budget constraint. For the case in point, this amounts to sixteen observations. A way to force the final solution to come closer to $n = 1000$ is to adjust the budget constraint upward slightly. In terms of the pricing structure pairs, "controls" represent 62 percent (608/984) of the final optimal allocation.

Another important facet of the results in Table B−2 is that some of the chosen design points correspond to combinations of values of design variables that seem unlikely to occur. For instance, the combinations of a low average monthly bill with a high income or a high monthly bill with a low income probably should not be admissible. Or, if such combinations are to be admitted, some sort of nonlinear (interaction) relationship should be specified that at least makes such occurrences "rare."

Table B−3 presents the optimal allocation of observations to design points, assuming a perfect positive correlation between average monthly bill and income. This reduces the number of admissible rows in the design matrix to forty-eight, of which twelve are included in the optimal design. As anticipated, intermediate price pairs are now drawn into the picture, as is the intermediate level of average monthly bill (income). The proportion of "controls" is drastically reduced from the previous case, to thirty-seven percent of the total sample size.

Comparison of the function value under an optimal allocation of observations for this latter example with that obtained from a "balanced" design (equal numbers of observations per cell) shows that the present scheme is more than twice as efficient. Even so, further

Table B–2. Optimal Allocation of Observations to Design Points

Values of Design Variables						
Intercept Constant	*"Peak" Price (¢/KWH)*	*"Off-peak" Price (¢/KWH)*	*Average Monthly Bill (dollars)*	*Household Income (dollars)*	*Urban-rural Dummy (0 = urban), 1 = rural)*	n_h
1.0	6.5	0.5	10.50	5,000.	0.0	112
1.0	6.5	0.5	10.50	5,000.	1.0	67
1.0	6.5	0.5	10.50	25,000.	0.0	6
1.0	6.5	0.5	10.50	25,000.	1.0	36
1.0	6.5	0.5	70.00	5,000.	0.0	54
1.0	6.5	0.5	70.00	5,000.	1.0	25
1.0	6.5	0.5	70.00	25,000.	0.0	15
1.0	6.5	0.5	70.00	25,000.	1.0	61
1.0	3.5	3.5	10.50	5,000.	0.0	298
1.0	3.5	3.5	10.50	5,000.	1.0	152
1.0	3.5	3.5	70.00	5,000.	0.0	7
1.0	3.5	3.5	70.00	5,000.	1.0	91
1.0	3.5	3.5	70.00	25,000.	0.0	54
1.0	3.5	3.5	70.00	25,000.	1.0	6
						$n = 984$

Table B–3. Optimal Allocation of Observations to Design Points, Assuming a Perfect Positive Correlation Between Income and Average Monthly Bill

	Values of Design Variables				
Intercept Constant	*"Peak" Price (¢/KWH)*	*"Off-peak" Price (¢KWH)*	*Average Monthly Bill (dollars)*	*Urban-rural Dummy (0 = urban; 1 = rural)*	n_h
1.0	6.5	0.5	10.50	0.0	40
1.0	6.5	0.5	10.50	1.0	16
1.0	6.5	0.5	70.00	0.0	59
1.0	6.5	0.5	70.00	1.0	110
1.0	5.5	1.5	15.75	0.0	156
1.0	5.5	1.5	15.75	1.0	127
1.0	5.0	2.0	15.75	0.0	76
1.0	5.0	2.0	15.75	1.0	40
1.0	3.5	3.5	10.50	0.0	154
1.0	3.5	3.5	10.50	1.0	85
1.0	3.5	3.5	70.00	0.0	64
1.0	3.5	3.5	70.00	1.0	71
					n = 998

efficiency gains can be achieved through use of the so-called "finite selection model" developed in conjunction with the national health insurance experiment conducted by Rand under the auspices of The Office of Economic Opportunity, as described by Morris (1973), to which the reader is referred for details.

AN ALTERNATIVE MODEL

The illustrative problem just considered is included primarily to give the reader a feeling for how the rather abstract material of preceding sections is made operational. As we have already mentioned, there are numerous refinements to be made to the specification of the design model before we can be fully satisfied that the "optimal" allocation produced is really satisfactory. Most of these points have been touched on in the previous section. We return here to what appear to be the most difficult of them.

The use of the familiar static theory of consumer behavior as a basis for our econometric specification no doubt leaves much to be desired. In particular, a household's ability to respond to alternative pricing schemes is a function of the stock and vintage of its electrical applicances, which suggests a dynamic investment model as the appropriate starting place for improving the theoretical basis of our model. (Even with the present econometric specification, we should probably introduce appliance stock and vintage variables into the design problem in anticipation of their potential usefulness, and at least guard against other important but unforeseen variables through careful randomization among subsets of the population defined by admissible design points.)

A model that explicitly recognizes the short-run dependency of electricity consumption on the household's stock of appliances is the "utilization" model first used by Fisher and Kaysen in their 1962 book and further developed for the present application by Wenders and Taylor (1975).

The suggested form for the system of demand equations in the short run is

$$q_{ij} = (\alpha_{ij} + \beta_{ij}\mu + \gamma_{ij}\Pi_1 + K_{ij}\Pi_2 + \xi_{ij}p)s_i \quad \text{(B.28)}$$

for $i = 1, \ldots, I$ and $j = 1,2,$

where:

q_{ij} = KWH consumed in "end use" category i during period j ($j = 1,2$ corresponds to, e.g., peak/off peak),

s_i = stock of appliances devoted to the ith "end use," assumed given in the short run and measured in watts (maximum rating),

μ = household income,

p = "price" of all other goods,

Π_1 = "peak" price per KWH,

Π_2 = "off-peak" price per KWH.

Wenders and Taylor consider this framework with more elaborate pricing structures incorporated (two and three part tariffs), but we have limited attention to the scheme considered in the previous section for obvious reasons.*

Other than the direct orientation toward the stock of appliances in this model, the only substantive difference between it and (B.25) is the inclusion of the "price" of all other goods, p, in each demand function, which we suppressed from consideration in the translog model as if cross-price effects between electricity and the consumption of other commodities in the short-run were negligible.

What sets the Wenders and Taylor model apart as a basis for sample design is that, depending on the definitions of appliance "end use" categories used, the set of equations needed to characterize each household's behavior *will differ over households.* This presents some difficulty in implementing the design methodology previously developed, as we will now show.

For example, consider the following stylized problem. There are two end use categories; say A and B, corresponding to home heating and water heating. Households may possess either electric space heating, electric water heating, or both. Abstracting for ease of presentation from the treatment of time of day rates, assume that within either single end use category a linear regression equation is the appropriate underlying model.**

Then we have:

Category A

$$\underline{y}_A = X\underline{\beta}_B + \underline{u}_A$$

*It should be noted that these other tariffs can likewise be incorporated into the previous model.

**As if we rewrote (B.28) as q_{ij}/s_i and added an error term. This we can do without altering the substance of the econometric specification because s_i doesn't vary over households.

with sample size n_A, $E(\underline{u}_A) = 0$, $E(\underline{u}_A \underline{u}'_A) = \sigma_A^2 I$,

Category B

$$\underline{y}_B = X\underline{\beta}_B + \underline{u}_B$$

with sample size n_B, $E(\underline{u}_B) = 0$, $E(\underline{u}_B \underline{u}'_B) = \sigma_B^2 I$,

Category AB

$$\underline{y}_A = X\underline{\beta}_A + \underline{u}_A \qquad \text{or} \qquad \begin{pmatrix} \underline{y}_A \\ \underline{y}_B \end{pmatrix} = \begin{pmatrix} X & 0 \\ 0 & X \end{pmatrix} \begin{pmatrix} \underline{\beta}_A \\ \underline{\beta}_B \end{pmatrix} \begin{pmatrix} \underline{u}_A \\ \underline{u}_B \end{pmatrix}$$

$$\underline{y}_B = X\underline{\beta}_B + \underline{u}_B \qquad\qquad y = \underline{\overline{X}}\,\underline{\beta} + \underline{u}$$

with sample size n_{AB}, $E(\underline{u}) = 0$, and

$$E(\underline{uu}') = \begin{pmatrix} \sigma_A^2 I & \sigma_{AB} I \\ \sigma_{AB} I & \sigma_B^2 I \end{pmatrix} = \Omega \otimes I .$$

Each category uses a common regressor (design) matrix, X, but with differing row dimension. From what we know about the design problems *within* each category, were we to limit attention to either A or B or AB, the methodology already given would suffice to find an optimal allocation of observations among the admissible rows of X. But, of course, since the best values for n_A, n_B and n_{AB} are unknown, we must consider their determination in concert with the allocation of observations among rows of X for each subproblem.

Adopting the criterion function

$$\phi = \phi_A + \phi_B + \phi_{AB} \tag{B.29}$$

for illustrative purposes, with ϕ_A being the weighted trace function for category A, and like definitions for categories B and AB, the grand problem is to solve for the values $n_{A1}, \ldots, n_{Ar}, n_{B1}, \ldots, n_{Br}, n_{AB1}, \ldots, n_{ABr}$ by minimizing (B.29) subject to an appropriate budget constraint. Then $n_A = \Sigma_{h=1}^{r} n_{Ah}, n_B = \Sigma_{h=1}^{r} n_{Bh}$ and $n_{AB} = \Sigma_{h=1}^{r} n_{ABh}$ come by definition.

Interestingly, it can be shown that the problem just described is separable: that is, its solution is equivalent to solving first for n_A, n_B and n_{AB}, and then performing an internal allocation of observations among admissible rows of X in each category.

It is beyond the scope of this survey to report on the details of proof of the needed separability theorem or to develop fully the ideas leading up to it. The main result is that *given* optimal allocations within each group the problem is one of solving for n_A, n_B and n_{AB} in:

$$\min_{n_A, n_B, n_{AB}} = \left[\frac{\sigma_A^2}{n_A} + \frac{\sigma_B^2}{n_B} + \frac{\sigma_A^2 + \sigma_B^2}{n_{AB}}\right] \tag{B.30}$$

subject to:

$$n_A + k_1 n_B + k_2 n_{AB} \leq \frac{C}{\theta}$$

$$n_A, n_B, n_{AB} \leq 0$$

where k_1 and k_2 are known factors that reflect the notion that Bs and ABs may have different observation costs attached to them as compared to As (or each other), and θ is the average cost per observation for As. Conversely, once optimal values for n_A, n_B, and n_{AB} are determined, the internal allocation among the admissible rows of X is straightforward. In fact, since each subproblem is based on the same design matrix, and since we know from previous results that the *proportional* allocation will not vary over sample size, the internal allocation problem need only be solved once.

The stylized example just presented captures the essential features of the design problem based on the Wenders and Taylor framework, although a realistic and literal application would be more complicated computationally. An interesting question that has not yet been answered concerns how an optimal design based on this model compares to the one previously computed, since both rely on the same design matrix.

Unfortunately, robustness of the optimal design over different model specifications that use the same set of design variables is apparently not a feature of the methodology just presented, based on the limited sensitivity analysis we have so far attempted. Therefore, model selection is a critical step in the process. Not that a different model cannot be used to analyze the data than the one on which the sample design is based. But design points that contain useful information (as judged by their inclusion in the optimal design) for one model may not for another; therefore, we face the problem of inefficiency of design whenever there is some doubt about the model used.

Given that everyone who considers the problem we have addressed here accepts the notion that nonlinearities in (perhaps) all variables should be allowed for, one approach is to use a quadratic function (with product terms) as an approximation to any specific (nonlinear) model. The virtues of this suggestion are obvious. Its drawback is primarily that many more parameters are needed to specify the approximator function than are required to determine (B.25), for instance. Thus, a given number of observations will be spread over more design points, reducing the anticipated precision of estimation for any one of the parameters and resulting in a larger value for any general criterion function (like (B.24)).

PRACTICAL MATTERS OF DESIGN IMPLEMENTATION

After such an extended treatment of methodological issues, we should no doubt reserve at least equal space for the practical matters of design implementation. With an optimal design in hand, how is the necessary random sample to be selected? How are households with the required characteristics to be found to fill the cells? Indeed, how *should* the cells themselves be defined? What of the policy-related questions that must be answered? There are a myriad other questions to be posed at the practical level. But unfortunately, many of them are specific to any particular application and hence are difficult to treat in a comprehensive way. Therefore, we shall concentrate on the two most important issues that seem amenable to general treatment, and comment only briefly on several others.

First, on the matter of an "appropriate" compensation scheme (given that compensation must be offered), there seem to be two main alternatives that have been proposed, a lump sum or other payment scheme that is unaffected by the customer's response to experimental rates, and some method of reimbursement whenever the monthly bill based on experimental rates exceeds the customer's otherwise "normal" bill for that month. We should also distinguish immediately two possible motives for any such compensation scheme: in the first, payment is purely a participation incentive, whereas in the second, payment is directed at further control of the experimental situation.

The lump sum idea is more or less consistent with the first of these motives and is endorsed both by Wenders and Taylor and by the Rand group. The customer will experience both income and substitution effects from time of day rates being offered, and these effects will be measured via various parameters and functions of parameters in the adopted econometric model. Without some care in setting up the experimental rates, of course, it is possible that a particular customer would be faced with large relative increases from his normal monthly bill unless he drastically changes his use pattern, which is a desirable situation from the point of view of the experiment but possibly undesirable from a customer relations and/or legal viewpoint. This is the reason we forced all the pairs of rates in our illustration to *average* 3.5 cents per KWH, the "control" rate. Nevertheless, if the results are to be of much use in the future, the entire response surface must be considered, and that requires the offering of a variety of experimental rates—some presently cost-justified, some perhaps not—which apparently poses some nontrivial legal complications.

Under the alternative compensation scheme, the potential income effect is being partially controlled by "guaranteeing" that the customer will pay no more than his normal monthly bill under the experimental pricing structure. If the goal is to isolate the substitution effect experimentally, this idea is in the right direction. However, it does have the deleterious feature of being one-sided: The customer is not forced to repay any gains he may make in reducing his monthly bill through an effective modification of his use pattern. Moreover, there would be no need to try to isolate the substitution effect experimentally if the econometric model were an approximately correct expression of customer behavior and/or isolation of the substitution effect is *not* of interest.

For these reasons, any compensation scheme that is related to actual response to time of day pricing is to be avoided. Schemes that maintain a maximum degree of detachment of the payment from actual behavior, like the lump sum idea, are preferable, and at worst can be regarded as effecting the income component of response in a neutral way. From an experimentalist viewpoint, the best compensation scheme is to have no compensation at all.

Next, there is the matter of the duration of the experiment. The question is, What can we infer about "permanent" response from a limited duration experiment? There are several things to be said. First, no matter how carefully we may be able to mask the fact that it is an experiment by guaranteeing a particular rate structure for, say, three years with the option (on the customer's part) of renewal, the customer must be made aware of the possibilities for changed use patterns through purchase of appliances or special devices.* Then, previous experience with similar large-scale social experiments** has indicated that short-run substitution effects will tend to be magnified in the limited duration experiment to the extent that there is bias being introduced into customer response because they know it is not a "permanent" program. This result comes primarily from the fact that, in these other experiments, the income effect is biased toward zero. There are ways to control for such biases, at least in part, at the analysis stage. But, more importantly, since in the present context we are concerned only with a small part of the customer's total income and expenditure (and not his total income, per se, as in these comparable experiments), the income effect is probably negligible already, and so, therefore, is the bias.

This all suggests that the results may be insensitive to the kind of compensation scheme used but says nothing about how long a period of time is "long enough" for the experiment to run. Since in recent times the price of electricity has changed several times and no doubt will change soon again, any guarantee of rate stability beyond twelve months is probably a bonus as far as customer expectations are concerned. A longer period is required, however, to make possible the kinds of investment decisions needed to take advantage of time of day rates.†

Finally, our orientation in this essay has been from a purely cross-section viewpoint, which begs the question of seasonal differentials, which may be the most important differential to consider for some utilities. In time series analysis, it is a simple matter to incorporate a shift in the rate structure into the model and to test its significance through the specification of a seasonal dummy variable. The rate schedule would then exhibit a "kink" (actually, it would be a step function) over the summer-winter seasons. In a purely cross-section setting, of course, there is no way to represent this more complex pricing structure. The econometric model given in (B.16) and (B.17) can easily be expanded to characterize a *pooling* of cross-section and time series observations, as if we considered each household to be observed monthly over a twelve month period. In that setting we can explicitly treat a seasonally shifting rate structure from the points of view of sampling design and of analysis of the effect of seasonality

*If such devices are not readily available commercially, although technically, feasible, the utilities may want to embark on some development and limited production themselves.

**See, e.g., Metcalf (1974).

†Wenders and Taylor suggest a time horizon of seven years. The Rand group proposes a horizon of at least thirty months.

in the peak versus off-peak pricing structure. But this suggestion presupposes that the behavioral response to time of day pricing is the same except for a shift in level over seasons, quite a stringent assumption. Because of the complexities involved in realistically modeling the complete seasonal/time of day response, it may be that the best alternative at this point is to treat the seasonal and time of day problems as separate experiments.

REFERENCES

Aigner, Dennis J. 1975. "Sample Design for an Electricity Pricing Experiment. University of Wisconsin. Mimeo.

Christensen, L.R.; Dale W. Jorgenson; and Lawrence J. Lau. 1975. "Transcendental Logarithmic Utility Functions." *American Economic Review* LXV (3): 367–83.

Christensen, Laurits R., and Marilyn E. Manser. 1974. "Estimating U.S. Consumer Preferences for Meat, 1947–1971." Workshop Paper No. 7403, Social Systems Research Institute, University of Wisconsin-Madison. Forthcoming in *Journal of Econometrics.*

Cochran, William G., and Gertrude M. Cox. 1957. *Experimental Designs.* 2nd. ed John Wiley and Sons.

Conlisk, John, and Harold Watts. 1969. "A Model for Optimizing Experimental Designs for Estimating Response Surfaces." *Proceedings of the Social Statistics Section—American Statistical Association.* pp. 150–56.

Gallant, A.R. 1975. "Seemingly Unrelated Nonlinear Regressions." *Journal of Econometrics* 3(1): 35–50.

Goldberger, Arthur S. 1970. "Criteria and Constraints in Multivariate Regression." Workshop Paper No. 7026, Social Systems Research Institute, University of Wisconsin-Madison.

Henderson, James M., and Richard Quandt. 1971. *Microeconomic Theory.* 2nd. ed. McGraw-Hill Book Company.

Metcalf, Charles E. 1973. "Making Inferences from Controlled Income Maintenance Experiments." *American Economic Review* 58 (June): 478–83.

———. 1974. "Predicting the Effects of Permanent Programs from a Limited Duration Experiment." *J. Human Resources* 9(4): 530–55.

Morris, Carl. 1973. "Statistical Design Aspects for the Health Insurance Study." WN–8383/1–OEO, The Rand Corporation.

Phlips, Louis. 1974. *Applied Consumption Analysis.* North-Holland Publishing Co.

The Rand Corporation. 1973. "Analysis of the Desirability and Effects of Alternative Electric Rate Structures." Project Proposal to the Federal Energy Administration.

Theil, Henri. 1971. *Introduction to Econometrics.* John Wiley and Sons.

Wenders, John T., and Lester D. Taylor. 1975. "Time-of-Day and Seasonal Pricing Experiments in the Sale of Electric Power." University of Arizona. Mimeo.

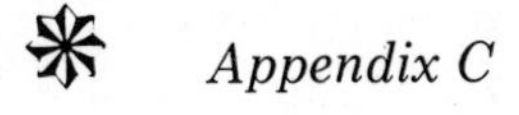

FORTRAN Program Listings

Author's Note: Regretfully, the following pages are the best we could reproduce from the computer read-outs. Any reader needing further clarification may write to:

Professor Charles Cicchetti
Department of Economics
The University of Wisconsin
at Madison.

MARGINALCOST
(and associated subprograms)

```
@PRT,S P*S.MARGINALCOST
FURPUR-MACC  2.04-01/06-13:58

P*S.MARGINALCOST
 1  C THIS PROGRAM ("MARGINALCOST") COMPUTES THE COST TO AN ELECTRICAL UTILITY
 2  C PROVIDING AN EXTRA KWH AT VARIOUS TIMES OF THE YEAR
 3  C The MAP statements in P*S.MCMAP indicate the subroutines used
 4  C The statements in P*S.MCCOMPILE compile those routines
 5  C Variable and Subroutine Names:
 6  C  VARS     PROC in P*S.VARSPROC
 7  C  NVLP     maximum allowed number of Voltage Levels (a PARAMETER variable)
 8  C  NYP      maximum allowed number of Years of fuel savings (PARAMETER)
 9  C  NFP      maximum Number of Facility types for a voltage stage (PAR.)
10  C  NOBSP    maximum Number of OBServations of historical t&d data (PAR.)
11  C  NPERP    maximum Number of PERiods (PAR.)
12  C  NPLNTP   maximum Number of PLaNTs moving forward or back (PAR.)
13  C  NVL      Number of Voltage Levels
14  C  KALL     = 'YES' iff user Knows ALL the loss over loads
15  C  -- see input worksheet "inputs for MARGINALCOST" for the rest of
16  C     the input variables --
17  C  CRF      Capital Recovery Factor
18  C  MCKWGC   Marginal Cost per Kw of Generating Capacity ($/kw - all costs
19  C             are in $ unless stated otherwise)
20  C  MCKWTD   Marginal Cost per K  of Transmission and Distribution capacity
21  C  MCEKWH   Marginal Cost (in cents) of Energy per KWH
22  C  CALMDP   Cumulative Average Loss Multipliers for Demand at Peak at the
23  C             various voltage levels
24  C  CMLMEP   Cumulative Marginal Loss Multipliers for Energy at Peak
25  C  CMLMEO   Cumulative Marginal Loss Multipliers for Energy Off Peak
26  C  PRPEAK(I) = 'PEAK' iff the Ith period is a peak period, otherwise
27  C             it = 'OFF PK'
28  C  ALMDP    Average Loss Multipliers for Demand at Peak (simple)
29  C  HRSPER   number of HouRS in the PERiods
30  C  MCKWHG   Marginal Cost (in cents) per KWH of Generating capacity
31  C  MCKWHT   Marginal Cost per KWH of T&d (Transmission and Distribution)
32  C             (in cents/kwh)
33  C  FLAG     = 'STOP' - a FLAG to indicate the end of the variables in VARSB
34  C  VARSB    COMMON Block containing these VARiableS
35  C  NCHVRP   maximum Number of Changing VaRiables (PARAMETER)
36  C  NVLCVP   maximum Number of VaLues of a Changing Variable (PAR.)
37  C  FIRCHG   = 'YES' iff any changes would be the FIRst CHanGes
38  C  NFI      unsubsripted temporary holding place for an NF(I)
39  C  NCHVAR   Number of Changing VARiables
40  C  CHVARN(I) = n means that CHanging VARiable number I is V(n) (see
41  C             note 3 of the documentation)
42  C  NVLCHV(I) = Number of VaLues taken on by the Ith CHanging Variable
43  C  RUNNO    RUN NO.
44  C  NORUNS   NO. of RUNS to be made (using different values for the
45  C             changing variables)
46  C  NVAL(I) = Number of the current VALue of the Ith changing variable
47  C  NVAR     unsubscripted temporary holding place for CHVARN(N)
48  C  NHOLS    Number of HOLidays
49  C  IMAGE    array containing the IMAGE of the date of a holiday
50  C  MONTH    the number of the MONTH of a holiday
```

```
51   C   DAYMO    the number of the DAY of the MOnth of a holiday
52   C   DYSPST(I) = the number of DaYS PaST in the year by the first day
53   C               of the Ith month
54   C   HOLDYR   the Days of the YeaR that are HOLidays
55   C   PRDSCR   array with the PeRIod DeSCRIPtions
56   C   YEAR     the YEAR during which the holidays fell on the given dates
57   C   V        an array EQUIVALENCEd to the variables in VARSB
58   C   VALCHV(I,J) = the Jth VALue of the Ith CHanging Variable
59   C   NEW      the NAMELIST name used for reading the NEW values of the changed
60   C               (not "changing") variables
61   C   DAYYR    DEFINE function that finds the number of the DAY of the YeaR
62   C               of a given date
63   C   DATE     subroutine that reads the image of a DATE in arg 1 and returns
64   C               the number of the month and day in args 2 and 3
65   C   INPTPR   subroutine that PRints the INPuTs
66   C   UPLIM    the UPper LIMit of a range of values for a changing variable
67   C   INCR     the INCRement used in stepping through the range
68   C   LOSSM    subroutine that computes the LOSS Multipliers
69   C   GENCAP   subroutine that computes MCKWGC
70   C   TRANDS   subroutine that computes MCKWTD
71   C   PERHRS   subroutine that computes HRSPER
72   C   MCKWH    subroutine that computes MCKWHG, MCKWHT, fills PRPEAK
73   C               and prints HRSPER
74   C   ENERGY   subroutine that computes MCEKWH
75   C   SUMARY   subroutine that prints the SUMMARY table of total marginal cost
76           INCLUDE VARS,LIST
77           PARAMETER MCHVRP=10, NVLCVP=100
78           INTEGER FIRCHG,NFI,NCHVAR,CHVARN(NCHVRP),NVLCHV(NCHVRP),RUNNO,
79        1          NORUNS,N,NM1,NVAL,NVAR,REPLY,I,J,K,NI,DONE,NHOLS
80        2          ,IMAGE(12),MONTH,DAYMO,DYSPST(12)/0,31,59,90,120,
81        3          151,181,212,243,273,304,334/HOLDYR,PRDSCR,YEAR
82           DIMENSION V(1),VALCHV(NCHVRP,NVLCVP)
83           EQUIVALENCE (V(1),NVL)
84           NAMELIST /NEW/NVL,KALL,LOLP,DLDLP,DLDLO,
85        1                   KPEAK,LP,LO,KLOL,NPLNTS,
86        1                   NEKWGC,CGP,AFOM,FY,NY,FS,IR,NYA,RM,
87        1                   NOBS,NF,F,
88        1                   CCUF,AOMCF,FUTDAT,
89        1                   CL,ACL,INUF,
90        1                   NPER,PERNAM,NPPS,NPP,PRDSCR,NHOLS,YEAR,HOLDYR,
91        1                   IFCKWH,V
92           COMMON /HOURBL/HOLDYR(15),PRDSCR(NPERP,12)
93           DEFINE DAYYR(MONTH,DAYMO) = DYSPST(MONTH) + DAYMO
94
95           FIRCHG = 'YES'
96           PRINT 10
97   10      FORMAT (//' HELLO.  PLEASE FURNISH INITIAL DATA')
98
99   C read initial data:
100          READ, NVL
101          READ 20, KALL
102  20      FORMAT (12a6)
103          IF (KALL .EQ. 'YES') READ, (LOLP(J),DLDLP(J),DLDLO(J),J=1,NVL)
104          IF (KALL .NE. 'YES') READ 20, KPEAK
105          IF (KALL .NE. 'YES') READ, LP,LO,(KLOL(J),J=1,NVL)
106          READ, IR,RM,NPLNTS
107          DO 25 J = 1,NPLNTS
```

```
108            READ, NEKWGC(J),CGP(J),AFOM(J),NYA(J),NI,(FS(J,I),I=1,NI)
109     25     NY(J) = NI
110           DO 30 I = 1,NVL
111            READ, NFI,(CCUF(I,J),AOMCF(I,J),J=1,NFI)
112     30     NF(I) = NFI
113           READ 20, FUTDAT
114           IF (FUTDAT .EQ. 'YES') GO TO 45
115           RFAD, NOBS
116           DO 40 I = 1,NVL
117            NFI = NF(I)
118     40     READ, ((F(I,J,K),K=1,NOBS),J=1,NFI)
119           READ, ((CL(I,K),K=1,NOBS),I=1,NVL)
120           GO TO 60
121     45    READ, (ACL(I),I=1,NVL)
122           DO 50 I = 1,NVL
123            NFI = NF(I)
124     50     READ, (INUF(I,J), J=1,NFI)
125     60    READ, NPER
126           DO 70 K = 0,2,2
127     70     READ 20, ((PERNAM(I,J+K),J=1,2),I=1,NPER)
128           READ 20, ((PRDSCR(I,J),J=1,12),I=1,NPER)
129           READ, NPPS,(NPP(I),I=1,NPPS)
130           READ, NHOLS,YEAR
131           DO 72 I = 1,NHOLS
132            READ 20, IMAGE
133            CALL DATE(IMAGE,MONTH,DAYMO)
134            HOLDYR(I) = DAYYR(MONTH,DAYMO)
135     72    CONTINUE
136           READ, (IFC[illegible]H(J),J=1,NPFR)
137
138     C print inputs:
139     74    PRINT 75
140     75    FORMAT (/' DO YOU WANT THE INPUTS PRINTED? (THEY''RE LONG)')
141           READ 20, REPLY
142           IF (REPLY .EQ. 'YES') CALL INPTPR(YEAR,NHOLS)
143     C get values of changing variables:
144     80    NCHVAR = 0
145           DO 130 I = 1,10000
146            IF (V(I) .EQ. 'STOP') GO TO 135
147            IF (V(I) .NE. -1) GO TO 130
148            IF (NCHVAR .EQ. 0) PRINT 85
149     85     FORMAT (/' PLEASE SUPPLY THE VALUES OF THE CHANGING VARIABLES')
150            PRINT 87, I
151     87     FORMAT ('     (VARIABLE NUMBER',I5,':)')
152            NCHVAR = NCHVAR + 1
153            CHVARN(NCHVAR) = I
154            READ, VALCHV(NCHVAR,1)
155            DO 90 J = 2,100
156     90      READ (0,-,ERR=100) (VALCHV(NCHVAR,K),K=1,J)
157     100    NVLCHV(NCHVAR) = J - 1
158            NI = NVLCHV(NCHVAR)
159            READ (0,-) (VALCHV(NCHVAR,J),J=1,NI)
160            IF (NVLCHV(NCHVAR).NE.3 .OR. VALCHV(NCHVAR,2).GE.0) GO TO 130
161     C (compute values within the range:)
162            UPLIM = -VALCHV(NCHVAR,2)
163            INCR  =  VALCHV(NCHVAR,3)
164            IF (INCR .LE. 0) INCR = (UPLIM - VALCHV(NCHVAR,1))/2
```

```
165          DO 110 J = 2,100
166           VALCHV(NCHVAR,J) = VALCHV(NCHVAR,J-1) + INCR
167           DONE = 100*(UPLIM-VALCHV(NCHVAR,J))/(UPLIM-VALCHV(NCHVAR,1))
168    110     IF (DONE .LE. 0) GO TO 120
169    120    NVLCHV(NCHVAR) = J
170    130   CONTINUE
171
172    135   RUNNO = 1
173    C compute NORUNS - if large, ask if user is serious:
174          NORUNS = 1
175          IF (NCHVAR .EQ. 0) GO TO 240
176    C if there are no changing variables, jump to 240
177          DO 140 N = 1,NCHVAR
178    140    NORUNS = NORUNS*NVLCHV(N)
179          IF (NORUNS .LE. 10) GO TO 180
180          PRINT 150, NORUNS
181    150   FORMAT (/' YOU HAVE ASKED FOR ',I8,' RUNS;'/
182         1 ' DO YOU WISH TO RESUPPLY THE VALUES OF THE CHANGING VARIABLES?')
183          READ 20, REPLY
184          IF (REPLY .NE. 'YES') GO TO 180
185          PRINT 170
186    170   FORMAT (' THEN PLEASE DO SO, EXACTLY AS BEFORE')
187          GO TO 80
188    C if there are changing variables, choose values for them and print them:
189    180   PRINT 190, RUNNO
190    190   FORMAT (/////' *** RUN NUMBER ',I3,' - VALUES OF CHANGING VARIABLE
191         1'        ,'S:'//' CHANGING VARIABLE NO.    VARIABLE NO.',7X,'VALUE')
192          DO 220 N = 1,NCHVAR
193           PROD = 1
194           IF (N .EQ. 1) GO TO 205
195           NM1 = N - 1
196           DO 200 J = 1,NM1
197    200     PROD = PROD*NVLCHV(J)
198    205    NVAL = 1 + MOD((RUNNO-1)/PROD,NVLCHV(N))
199           NVAR = CHVARN(N)
200           V(NVAR) = VALCHV(N,NVAL)
201           PRINT 210, N,NVAR,V(NVAR)
202    210    FORMAT (I11,I18,F22.4)
203    220   CONTINUE
204          PRINT 230
205    230   FORMAT (//)
206    C if there are no changing variables we've jumped to here:
207    C compute the marginal costs:
208    240   CALL LOSSM
209          IF (KGNCAP .NE. 'YES') CALL GENCAP
210          IF (KTDCAP .NE. 'YES') CALL TRANDS
211          CALL PERHRS(HRSPER,NPER,NHOLS,YEAR)
212          CALL MCKWH
213          IF (KENCST .NE. 'YES') CALL ENERGY
214          CALL SUMARY
215          IF (RUNNO .GE. NORUNS) GO TO 250
216          RUNNO = RUNNO + 1
217          GO TO 180
218    C take care of changes:
219    250   PRINT 260
220    260   FORMAT (///' ARE THERE ANY CHANGES YOU WISH TO MAKE IN THE DATA?')
221          READ 20, REPLY
```

```
222           IF (REPLY .EQ. 'YES') GO TO 280
223           PRINT 270
224   270     FORMAT (//' AU REVOIR'///)
225           STOP
226   280     IF (FIRCHG .EQ. 'YES') PRINT 290
227   290     FORMAT (/' ENTER THE NEW VALUE(S) AS IN THIS EXAMPLE:'/
228          1 ' (NEVER TYPE IN COLUMN ONE - IT IS IGNORED - AND END LINES',
229          2 ' AT COMMAS)'/
230          3 ' $NEW NEKWGC = 5E5,  AFOM = 75E6,'/
231          4 ' CGP = 200E6, V(33) = 2 * .05'/
232          5 ' $END'//)
233           IF (FIRCHG .NE. 'YES') PRINT 300
234   300     FORMAT (/' ENTER THE NEW VALUE(S) AS BEFORE (PRECEDING CHANGES',
235          1 ' REMAIN IN EFFECT)'//)
236   310     READ (5,NEW,ERR=320)
237           FIRCHG = 'NO'
238           RUNNO = 1
239           GO TO 74
240   320     PRINT 330
241   330     FORMAT (//' THERE WAS AN ERROR IN THOSE CHANGES:  PLEASE TRY',
242          1 ' AGAIN' //)
243           GO TO 310
244           END
PRT     COMPLETED..
@PRT,S P•S.INPTPR

P•S.INPTPR
  1   C THIS SUBROUTINE IS REFERENCED BY MARGINALCOST (see P•S.MARGINALCOST)
  2           SUBROUTINE INPTPR(YEAR,NHOLS)
  3           INCLUDE VARS
  4           COMMON /HOURBL/HOLDYR(15),PRDSCR(NPERP,12)
  5           INTEGER I,J,K,NI,NFI,YEAR,NHOLS,HOLDYR,PRDSCR
  6           PRINT 15
  7   15      FORMAT (/' DATA FOR LOSS MULTIPLIERS:')
  8           PRINT, NVL
  9           PRINT 20, KALL
 10   20      FORMAT (12X,A6)
 11           IF (KALL .EQ. 'YES') PRINT, (LOLP(J),DLDLP(J),DLLLO(J),J=1,NVL)
 12           IF (KALL .NE. 'YES') PRINT 20, KPEAK
 13           IF (KALL .NE. 'YES') PRINT, LP,LQ,(KLOL(J),J=1,NVL)
 14           PRINT 22
 15   22      FORMAT (/' DATA FOR GENERATION COST:')
 16           PRINT, IR,RH,NPLNTS
 17           DO 25 J = 1,NPLNTS
 18            NI = NY(J)
 19   25       PRINT, NEKWGC(J),CGP(J),AFOM(J),NYA(J),NI,(FS(J,I),I=1,NI)
 20           PRINT 27
 21   27      FORMAT(/' DATA FOR TRANSM. & DISTR. COST:')
 22           DO 30 I = 1,NVL
 23            NFI = NF(I)
 24   30       PRINT, NFI,(CCOF(I,J),AOMCF(I,J),J=1,NFI)
 25           PRINT 20, FUTDAT
 26           IF (FUTDAT .EQ. 'YES') GO TO 45
 27           PRINT, NOBS
 28           DO 40 I = 1,NVL
 29            NFI = NF(I)
 30   40       PRINT, ((F(I,J,K),K=1,NOBS),J=1,NFI)
```

```
31          PRINT, ((CL(I,K),K=1,NOBS),I=1,NVL)
32          GO TO 60
33    45    PRINT, (ACL(I),I=1,NVL)
34          DO 50 I = 1,NVL
35           NFI = NF(I)
36    50     PRINT, (INUF(I,J), J=1,NFI)
37    60    PRINT 65
38    65    FORMAT (/' DATA FOR KWH CHARGES:')
39          PRINT, NPER
40          DO 70 K = 0,2,2
41    70     PRINT 75, ((PERNAM(I,J+K),J=1,2),I=1,NPER)
42    75    FORMAT (3X,12A6)
43          PRINT 75, ((PRDSCR(I,J),J=1,12),I=1,NPER)
44          PRINT, NPPS,(NPP(I),I=1,NPPS)
45          PRINT, NHOLS,YEAR
46          PRINT 80, (HOLDYR(I), I=1,NHOLS)
47    80    FORMAT (' NUMBERS OF THE DAYS OF THE YEAR WHICH ARE HOLIDAYS:',
48         1        5I4/(18I4))
49          PRINT 90
50    90    FORMAT (' INCREMENTAL FUEL COSTS:')
51          PRINT, (IFCKWH(J),J=1,NPER)
52          END
PRT    COMPLETED..
@PRT,S P*S*GENCAP

P*S*GENCAP
 1   C THIS SUBROUTINE IS REFERENCED BY MARGINALCOST (see P*S*MARGINALCOST)
 2   C Variables particular to this routine:
 3   C  PVFS     Present Value (in the first year of fuel savings of the current
 4   C              plant) of the Fuel Savings from that Plant
 5   C  ACC      Annuitized Capital Cost of the current plant
 6   C  CIGC     Cost (moved to the first year of the fuel savings of the first pla
 7   C              of Increasing Generating Capacity (from the current plant)
 8   C  ACGCKW   Annual Cost of increasing Generating Capacity per Kw (including th
 9   C              reserve margin)
10   C  MCKWGC   takes losses into account and adds up contributions from all plant
11   C  NUNITS   Number of UNITS, ie sets of plants coming on line together
12   C  NEKWGT   Number of Extra KW of Generating capacity, Total, provided
13   C              by a unit
14   C  RERUN    = .TRUE. iff have asked about NSTD already
15          SUBROUTINE GENCAP
16          INCLUDE VARS
17          INTEGER J,NOPLNT,I,NYNPL,NUNITS,NPLNTI
18          LOGICAL RERUN
19          DIMENSION MCKWG(NPLNTP,NVLP)
20          DATA RERUN/.FALSE./FY/NPLNTP*0/
21          IF (IR .GT. 1) IR = IR/100
22          IF (RM .GT. 1) RM = RM/100
23          NUNITS = 0
24          CIGC = 0
25          NEKWGT = 0
26          IF (NPLNTS .LE. 1 .OR. RERUN) GO TO 5040
27          RERUN = .TRUE.
28          PRINT 5010
29  5010    FORMAT (/' DO YOU WANT THE NONSTANDARD CASE, WHEREBY FUTURE',
30         1      ' PLANTS ARE TREATED AS'/' DISTINCT UNITS AND DISCOUNTED?')
31          READ 5020, NSTD
```

```
32  5020  FORMAT (A6)
33         IF (NSTD .NE. 'YES') GO TO 5040
34         PRINT 5030, NPLNTS
35  5030  FORMAT (' PLEASE SUPPLY CHRONOLOGICALLY THE',I2,' YEARS WHEN',
36       1        ' THE PLANTS COME ON LINE')
37         READ, (FY(I), I=1,NPLNTS)
38  5040  DO 6090 J = 1,NVL
39  6090   MCKWGC(J) = 0
40         NPLNT1 = NPLNTS + 1
41         DO 6115 NOPLNT = 1,NPLNT1
42          IF (NOPLNT .GT. NPLNTS) GO TO 6102
43          CRF = IR/(1 - (1+IR)**-NYA(NOPLNT))
44          PVFS = 0
45          NYNPL = NY(NOPLNT)
46          DO 6100 J = 1,NYNPL
47  6100     PVFS = PVFS + (1+IR)**-(J-1)*FS(NOPLNT,J)
48          ACC = CRF*CGP(NOPLNT)
49          IF (NOPLNT .EQ. 1) GO TO 6106
50          IF (FY(NOPLNT) .EQ. FY(NOPLNT-1)) GO TO 6108
51  C    after the last plant of a unit, compute cost per kw for that unit
52  6102     ACGCKW = (CIGC/NEKWGT)*(1+RM)
53          DO 6104 J = 1,NVL
54           MCKWG(NUNITS,J) = CALMOP(J)*ACGCKW
55  6104     MCKWGC(J) = MCKWGC(J) + MCKWG(NUNITS,J)
56          IF (NOPLNT .GT. NPLNTS) GO TO 6115
57  C    within a unit, add up costs & capacities of plants
58  6106    NUNITS = NUNITS + 1
59          CIGC = 0
60          NEKWGT = 0
61  6108    CIGC = CIGC+((ACC+AFOM(NOPLNT))-PVFS)/(1+IR)**(FY(NOPLNT)-FY(1))
62          NEKWGT = NEKWGT + NEKWGC(NOPLNT)
63  6115  CONTINUE
64         PRINT 6120
65  6120  FORMAT (//T10,'MARGINAL ANNUAL COST OF GENERATING CAPACITY',
66       1        ' ($/KW)'/T10,50('-')//
67       1        ' VOLTAGE LEVEL (1=HI VOLTAGE)      MARGINAL COST')
68         IF (NUNITS .EQ. 1) GO TO 6150
69         PRINT 6130, (J, J=1,NUNITS)
70  6130  FORMAT (38X,'TOTAL   UNIT:',I2,2(I5,3X)/
71       1        (44X,3(I5,3X)))
72         DO 6135 J = 1,NVL
73  6135    PRINT 6140, J,MCKWGC(J),(MCKWG(I,J),I=1,NUNITS)
74  6140  FORMAT (I15,F29.3,3F8.3/(44X,3F8.3))
75         RETURN
76  6150  PRINT 6160, (J,MCKWGC(J), J=1,NVL)
77  6160  FORMAT (I15,F29.3)
78         RETURN
79         END
PRT     COMPLETED..
@PRT,S P*S.MCMAP

P*S.MCMAP
  1       LIB IRP-DC*LIB
  2       IN P*S.MARGINALCOST,.DATE,.INPTPR,.LOSSM,.GENCAP,.TRANDS
  3       IN P*S.PERHRS,.PERIN,.DAYWK
  4       IN P*S.MCKWH,.ENERGY,.SUMARY
PRT     COMPLETED..
```

```
@PRT,S P•S.MCCOMPILE

P•S.MCCOMPILE
 1       @PDP,SF P•S.VARSPROC,P•S.VARSPROC
 2       @FOR,SZC P•S.MARGINALCOST
 3       @FOR,SZC P•S.INPTPR
 4       @FOR,SZC P•S.LOSSM
 5       @FOR,SZC P•S.GENCAP
 6       @FOR,SZC P•S.TRANDS
 7       @FOR,SZC P•S.PERHRS
 8       @FOR,SZC P•S.MCKWH
 9       @FOR,SZC P•S.ENERGY
10       @FOR,SZC P•S.SUMARY
PRT     COMPLETED..
@PRT,S P•S.VARSPROC

P•S.VARSPROC
 1       VARS  PROC
 2       C THIS PROC IS INCLUDED IN THE ROUTINES OF MARGINALCOST (SEE P•S.MARGINAL(
 3             PARAMETER NVLP=5, NYP=25, NFP=5, NOBSP=20, NPERP=6, NPLNTP = 5
 4             IMPLICIT REAL (A-Z)
 5             INTEGER NVL,KALL,KPEAK,IY,NY,
 6            1        NOBS,NF,FUTDAT,NPER,PERNAM,NPPS,NPP,
 7            1        PRPEAK,HRSPER,NPLNTS
 8             COMMON /VARSB/NVL,KALL,LOLP(NVLP),DLDLP(NVLP),DLDLO(NVLP),
 9            1              KPEAK,LP,LO,KLOL(NVLP),CRF,MCKWGC(NVLP),
10            1              NPLNTS,IR,RM,NEKWGC(NPLNTP),CGP(NPLNTP),AFOM(NPLNTP)
11            1              ,FY(NPLNTP),NY(NPLNTP),FS(NPLNTP,NYP),NYA(NPLNTP),
12            1              MCKWTD(NVLP),NOBS,NF(NVLP),F(NVLP,NFP,NOBSP),
13            1              CCUF(NVLP,NFP),AOMCF(NVLP,NFP),FUTDAT,
14            1              CL(NVLP,NOBSP),ACL(NVLP),INUF(NVLP,NFP),
15            1              NPER,PERNAM(NPERP,4),NPPS,NPP(NPERP),
16            1              MCEKWH(NVLP,NPERP),IFCKWH(NPERP),
17            1              CALMDP(NVLP),CMLMEP(NVLP),CMLMEO(NVLP),PRPEAK(NPERP)
18            1              ,ALMDP(NVLP),HRSPER(NPERP),MCKWHG(NVLP),MCKWHT(NVLP)
19            1              ,FLAG
20             DATA FLAG/'STOP'/
21         END
PRT     COMPLETED..
@PRT,S P•S.DATE

P•S.DATE
 1   C THIS SUBROUTINE IS REFERENCED BY MARGINALCOST AND LOAD (see
 2   C P•S.MARGINALCOST and P•S.LOAD)
 3   C   DATEIM(I) = Ith character in the DATE Image stored in IMAGE
 4   C   MONNM(I) = first I characters in the MONth NaMe
 5          SUBROUTINE DATE(IMAGE,MONNO,DAY)
 6          IMPLICIT INTEGER (A-Z)
 7          DIMENSION IMAGE(12),DATEIM(72),FORMT(3)/'(',' ','X,I2)'/
 8         1           MO(12)/'JA','F','MAR','AP','MAY','JUN','JUL',
 9         2                  'AU','S','O','N','D'/
10         3            ,MONNM(3)
11          MONNO = 0
12          DAY = 0
13          DECODE (IMAGE,10) DATEIM
14   10     FORMAT (72A1)
15          DO 20 I = 72,1,-1
16   20      IF (DATEIM(I) .NE. ' ') GO TO 30
```

```
17  30      IM2 = I - 2
18          ENCODE (COLUMN,40) IM2
19  40      FORMAT (I6)
20          FORMT(2) = COLUMN
21          READ (0,FORMT,ERR=80) DAY
22          DO 50 J = 1,3
23           MONNM(J) = 6H
24  50       FLD(0,6*J,MONNM(J)) = FLD( ,6*J,IMAGE(I))
25          DO 60 I = 1,12
26           DO 60 J = 1,3
27  60        IF (MONNM(J) .EQ. MO(I)) GO TO 70
28          RETURN
29  70      MONNO = I
30  80      RETURN
31          END
PRT     COMPLETED..
@PRT,S P*S.LOSSM

P*S.LOSSM
 1  C THIS SUBROUTINE IS REFFRENCED BY MARGINALCOST (see P*S.MARGINALCOST)
 2  C Variables particular to this routine:
 3  C   PEAKK    = '*' iff PEAK loss-over-loads are Known but not off-Peaks
 4  C   OFFK     = '*' iff OFF peak loss-over-loads are Known but not Peaks
 5  C   NUMBER   array with the names of the first ten NUMBERs
 6  C   ULOL     Unknown Loss-Over-Loads
 7  C   MLMEP    simple Marginal Loss Multipliers for Energy on Peak
 8  C   MLMEO    Marginal Loss Multipliers for Energy Off peak
 9  C   LK       the Load during the time (peak or off-peak) when the LOLs are Known
10  C   LU       the Load when the LOLs are Unknown
11  C When KALL is not 'YES' the formula energy lost = const*(input energy)**2
12  C  is used - DLDLs are just twice the LOLs, and the LK and LPs are
13  C  used to eliminate the unknown "const"
14          SUBROUTINE LOSSM
15          INCLUDE VARS
16          INTEGER J,PEAKK,OFFK,NUMBER(10)
17          DIMENSION ULOL(NVLP),MLMEP(NVLP),MLMEO(NVLP)
18          DATA NUMBER/'ONE','TWO','THREE','FOUR','FIVE','SIX','SEVEN',
19         1            'EIGHT','NINE','TEN'/
20          PEAKK = '     '
21          OFFK =  '     '
22          IF (KALL .EQ. 'YES') GO TO 5150
23          IF (KPEAK .NE. 'PEAK') GO TO 5110
24          LK = LP
25          LU = LO
26          GO TO 5120
27  5110    LK = LO
28          LU = LP
29  5120    DO 5140 J = 1,NVL
30           ULOL(J) = (KLOL(J)/LK)*LU
31           IF (KPEAK .NE. 'PEAK') GO TO 5130
32           LOLP(J) = KLOL(J)
33           DLDLP(J) = KLOL(J)*2
34           DLDLO(J) = ULOL(J)*2
35           GO TO 5140
36  5130     LOLP(J) = ULOL(J)
37           DLDLP(J) = ULOL(J)*2
38           DLDLO(J) = KLOL(J)*2
```

```
39   5140  CONTINUE
40         IF (KPEAK .EQ. 'PEAK') PEAKW = '*'
41         IF (KPEAK .NE. 'PEAK') OFFY  = '*'
42   5150  DO 5160 J = 1,MVL
43          ALMDP(J) = 1/(1-LOLP(J))
44          MLMEP(J) = 1/(1-DLDLP(J))
45          MLMEO(J) = 1/(1-DLDLO(J))
46   5160  CONTINUE
47         CALMDP(1) = ALMDP(1)
48         CMLMEP(1) = MLMEP(1)
49         CMLMEO(1) = MLMEO(1)
50         DO 5170 J = 2,NVL
51          CALMDP(J) = ALMDP(J)*CALMDP(J-1)
52          CMLMEP(J) = MLMEP(J)*CMLMEP(J-1)
53          CMLMEO(J) = MLMEO(J)*CMLMEO(J-1)
54   5170  CONTINUE
55         PRINT 5180, PEAKK,PEAKK,OFFK,ALMDP(1),CALMDP(1),MLMEP(1),
56        1             CMLMEP(1),MLMEO(1),CMLMEO(1),(ALMDP(J),CALMDP(J),
57        2             MLMEP(J),CMLMEP(J),MLMEO(J),CMLMEO(J),NUMBER(J-1),
58        3             NUMBER(J),NUMBER(J),J=2,NVL)
59   5180  FORMAT (//T25,'LOSS MULTIPLIERS'/T25,16('-')//' VOLTAGE',T29,
60        1        'FOR DEMAND',T54,'FOR ENERGY'/'  STAGE',T30,
61        2        'ON PEAK',A1,T48,'ON PEAK',A1,T62,'OFF PEAK',A1/
62        3        23X,'  SIMPLE CUMULATIVE',' SIMPLE CUMUL.  SIMPLE CUMUL.'/
63        4        ' FROM GENERATION TO HIGH',F7.4,F8.4,3X,2F7.4,F8.4,F7.4/
64        5        ' VOLTAGE CUSTOMERS AND'/' HIGH SIDE OF STAGE ONE'/
65        6        ' TRANSFORMERS'//
66        7       (' FROM HIGH SIDE OF STAGE',F7.4,F8.4,3X,2F7.4,F8.4,F7.4/
67        8        1X,A5,' TRANSFORMERS TO'/' STAGE ',A5,' CUSTOMERS'/
68        9        ' AND HIGH SIDE OF STAGE'/1X,A5,' TRANSFORMERS'//))
69          IF (KALL .NE. 'YES') PRINT 5190
70   5190  FORMAT (' * THESE MULTIPLIERS ARE CALCULATED DIRECTLY FROM'/
71        1        '   INPUT LOSS FIGURES;  THE OTHERS ARE ESTIMATED')
72          RETURN
73          END
ET    COMPLETED..
PR1,S P.S.TRANDS

P.S.TRANDS
 1  C THIS SUBROUTINE IS REFERENCED BY MARGINALCOST (see P.S.MARGINALCOST)
 2  C Variables particular to this routine:
 3  C  ACUF(i,j) = Annual Cost per Unit of the jth Facility at the ith voltage stage
 4  C  L(i,j) = Load at the ith voltage level (including loads "downstream",
 5  C            at lower voltage levels) for the jth observation of historical data
 6  C  FNUFKW(i,j) = Estimated (from regression) Number of Units of Facility
 7  C            J at the ith voltage level needed per KW of total load (L) there
 8  C  CKWTDL  annual Cost per kW of T&D without Losses
 9  C  EF1(i,j) = anticipated Expenditure on the jth Facility at v. l. i
10  C  E(i) = Planned Expenditure at voltage level i
11  C  AL      Additional Loads that are anticipated
12     CAPCST  total CAPacity CoSTs - gen. + trans. & distr.
13        SUBROUTINE TRANDS
14        INCLUDE VARS
15        INTEGER I,J,K,NFI,NVLM1,I2,I3,IM1,I2P1
16        DIMENSION ACUF(NVLP,NFP),L(NVLP,NOBSP),ENUFKW(NVLP,NFP),
17       1          CKWTDL(NVLP),EF(NVLP,NFP),E(NVLP),AL(NVLP)
18       2          ,CAPCST(NVLP)
19        DO 7120 I = 1,NVL
20         NFI = NF(I)
```

```
21              DO 7120 J = 1,NFI
22    7120        ACUF(I,J) = CCUF(I,J)*CRF + AOMCF(I,J)
23              IF (FUTDAT .EQ. 'YES') GO TO 7190
24    C historical data/regression method --
25              DO 7140 K = 1,NOBS
26    7140        L(NVL,K) = CL(NVL,K)
27              NVLM1 = NVL - 1
28              DO 7150 I = NVLM1,1,-1
29                DO 7150 K = 1,NOBS
30    7150        L(I,K) = CL(I,K) + ALMDP(I+1)*L(I+1,K)
31              DO 7160 I = 1,NVL
32    7160        CKWTDL(I) = 0
33              DO 7180 I = 1,NVL
34                NFI = NF(I)
35                DO 7170 J = 1,NFI
36                  SUMLF = 0
37                  SUML  = 0
38                  SUMF  = 0
39                  SUML2 = 0
40                  DO 7165 K = 1,NOBS
41                    SUMLF = SUMLF + L(I,K)*F(I,J,K)
42                    SUML  = SUML  + L(I,K)
43                    SUMF  = SUMF  + F(I,J,K)
44                    SUML2 = SUML2 + L(I,K)*L(I,K)
45    7165          CONTINUE
46                  ENUFKW(I,J) = (NOBS*SUMLF-SUML*SUMF)/(NOBS*SUML2-SUML*SUML)
47                  CKWTDL(I) = CKWTDL(I) + ACUF(I,J)*ENUFKW(I,J)
48    7170        CONTINUE
49    7180      CONTINUE
50              GO TO 7230
51    C when future data is available --
52    7190      CONTINUE
53              DO 7210 I = 1,NVL
54                E(I) = 0
55                NFI = NF(I)
56                DO 7210 J = 1,NFI
57                EF(I,J) = ACUF(I,J)*INUF(I,J)
58    7210        E(I) = E(I) + EF(I,J)
59              AL(NVL) = ACL(NVL)
60              NVLM1 = NVL - 1
61              DO 7220 I = NVLM1,1,-1
62    7220        AL(I) = ACL(I) + ALMDP(I+1)*AL(I+1)
63              DO 7225 I = 1,NVL
64    7225        CKWTDL(I) = E(I)/AL(I)
65    C both methods rejoin --
66    7230      CONTINUE
67              MCKWTD(1) = CKWTDL(1)
68              CAPCST(1) = MCKWGC(1) + MCKWTD(1)
69              DO 7260 I = 2,NVL
70                MCKWTD(I) = 0
71                IM1 = I - 1
72                DO 7250 I2 = 1,IM1
73                  I2P1 = I2 + 1
74                  PROD = 1
75                  DO 7240 I3 = I2P1,I
76    7240          PROD = PROD * ALMDP(I3)
77                  MCKWTD(I) = MCKWTD(I) + CKWTDL(I2)*PROD
78    7250        CONTINUE
```

```
79            MCKWTD(I) = MCKWTD(I) + CKWTDL(I)
80            CAPCST(I) = NCKWGC(I) + MCKWTD(I)
81   7260   CONTINUE
82   C Print results:
83          PRINT 7270, (I,MCKWTD(I),CAPCST(I),I=1,NVL)
84   7270   FORMAT (//'  MARGINAL ANNUAL COST OF TRANSMISSION AND '
85        1         ,'DISTRIBUTION CAPACITY ($/KW)'/2X,69('-')//' VOLTAGE ',
86        1         'LEVEL ',
87        2         '(1=HI VOLTAGE)    MARGINAL COST    GEN. + TRANSM. '
88        3         ,'& DISTR.'/(I15,F28.3,F20.3))
89          RETURN
90          END
PRT    COMPLETED.
@PRT,S P.S.PERHRS

P.S.PERHRS
 1   C THIS SUBROUTINE IS REFERENCED BY MARGINALCOST (see P.S.MARGINALCOST)
 2   C Variable and Subroutine Names particular to this routine:
 3   C  INPUTS   this array is the same as PRDSCR
 4   C  DAYYRP   array with the numbers of the DAYs of the YeaR that sPecify
 5   C             the Periods
 6   C  NDATES   Number of DATES used to specify the Periods
 7   C  DAYS     numbers of the DAYS of the week that are included in the Periods
 8   C  NODAYS   NO. of DAYS of the week that are included in the periods
 9   C  EIHOL(I) = 'INCL' iff HOLidays are Included in the ith Period,
10   C            = 'EXCL' iff they are Excluded and = 'IGNORE' if they are ignored
11   C  HOUR     the HOURS that specify the Periods
12   C  PERIN    subroutine that for all PERiods fills IN the above 6 arrays
13   C  WKDAY    internal FUNCTION that gives the number of the DAY of the Week
14   C             (Mon = 1) that the arg.th day of the year falls on
15   C  DYWKFD   the number of the DaY of the WeeK that the First Day of
16   C             the year falls on (this is cyclic with Period 7x4=28 years)
17   C  INOUTF   = 'IN' iff the arg 1st day of the week is IN the arg 2nd Period,
18   C            = 'OUT' otherwise (an internal FUNCTION)
19   C  NDAYS    Number of DAYS in a stretch of period (between two specified
20   C             dates)
21          SUBROUTINE PERHRS(HRSPER,NPER,NHOLS,YEAR)
22          PARAMETER NPERP = 6
23          IMPLICIT INTEGER (A-Z)
24          DIMENSION HRSPER(NPERP)
25          COMMON /HOURBL/HOLDYR(15),INPUTS(NPERP,12)
26        1        /PERBLK/DAYYRP(NPERP,10),NDATES(NPERP),DAYS(NPERP,8)
27        2                ,NODAYS(NPERP),EIHOL(NPERP),HOUR(NPERP,2)
28
29          DO 10 I = 1,NPER
30   10       HRSPER(I) = 0
31          CALL PERIN(NPER)
32   C first calculate the number of days in each Period & store in HRSPER:
33   C  take care of holidays:
34          DO 50 HOL = 1,NHOLS
35           DAY = WKDAY(HOLDYR(HOL))
36           DO 40 PER = 1,NPER
37            NDATE = NDATES(PER) - 1
38            DO 20 I = 1,NDATE,2
39   20        IF (HOLDYR(HOL).GE.DAYYRP(PER,I) .AND. HOLDYR(HOL).LE.
40        1         DAYYRP(PER,I+1)) GO TO 30
41   C  (if this holiday does not fall within the stretch between any pair of
42   C   dates for this Period, GO TO 40:)
```

```
43             GO TO 40
44   30        IF (EIHOL(PER) .EQ. 'IGNORE') GO TO 40
45             INOUT = INOUTF(DAY,PER)
46             IF (EIHOL(PER).EQ.'INCL' .AND. INOUT.EQ.'OUT')
47            1      HRSPER(PER) = HRSPER(PER) + 1
48   C   (If holidays are included in this period but this holiday [# HOL]
49   C    does not fall on a day of the week already included add a day -
50   C    eg if the period is Dec. 1 - Dec. 31, sat, sun, incl and Cristmas
51   C    falls on a Tues we need to add a day, but if it falls on Sun
52   C    it will be counted later because all Suns are included)
53             IF (EIHOL(PER).EQ.'EXCL' .AND. INOUT.EQ.'IN')
54            1      HRSPER(PER) = HRSPER(PER) - 1
55   C   (If holidays are excluded in this period but this holiday falls
56   C    on a day of the week included in the period, deduct a day from the
57   C    count. Then later the day of this holiday will get counted
58   C    in because of its day of the week but the -1 we just added in
59   C    will cancel it out as desired.)
60   40        CONTINUE    QNEXT PER(IOD)
61   50      CONTINUE     QNEXT HOL(IDAY)
62   C now count the number of days in the periods' dates that are the
63   C    right days of the week:
64           DO 80 PER = 1,NPER
65             NDATE = NDATES(PER) - 1
66             DO 70 I = 1,NDATE,2
67              NDAYS = DAYYRP(PER,I+1) - DAYYRP(PER,I) + 1
68              HRSPER(PER) = HRSPER(PER) + (NDAYS/7)*NODAYS(PER)
69   C   (for each of the NDAYS/7 [an integer] complete weeks in this
70   C    stretch of dates, there are NoDAYS(PER) days included)
71   C   (now starting after those NDAYS/7 complete weeks, go day by day
72   C    through the end of the stretch counting the number of 'IN' days:)
73              START = DAYYRP(PER,I) + (NDAYS/7)*7
74              FINISH = DAYYRP(PER,I+1)
75              IF (FINISH .LT. START) GO TO 70
76              DO 60 J = START,FINISH
77   60           IF (INOUTF(WKDAY(J),PER) .EQ. 'IN') HRSPER(PER) = HRSPER(PER)+1
78   70        CONTINUE
79   C finally, multiply the number of days in the period by the number
80   C   of hours per day included (worrying about whether or not the
81   C   hours span midnight) to get the real HRSPER:
82             FACTOR = 0
83             IF (HOUR(PER,2) .LT. HOUR(PER,1)) FACTOR = 1
84             HRSPER(PER) = HRSPER(PER)*(HOUR(PER,2) - HOUR(PER,1) + 1
85          1                 + 24*FACTOR)
86   C Phew!!
87   80      CONTINUE
88           RETURN
89
90           FUNCTION INOUTF(DAY,PER)
91           IMPLICIT INTEGER (A-Z)
92           NDAY = NODAYS(PER)
93           IF (NDAY .EQ. 0) GO TO 105
94           DO 100 I = 1,NDAY
95   100      IF (DAY .EQ. DAYS(PER,I)) GO TO 110
96   105     INOUTF = 'OUT'
97           RETURN
98   110     INOUTF = 'IN'
99           RETURN
100
101          FUNCTION WKDAY(I)
```

```
02          IMPLICIT INTEGER (A-Z)
03          DIMENSION DYWKFD(28)/3,5,6,0,1,3,4,5,6,1,2,3,4,6,0,1,2,4,5,6,
04         1                     0,2,3,4,5,0,1,2/
05          SUB = MOD(YEAR,28) + 1
06          WKDAY = MOD(I + DYWKFD(SUB),7) + 1
07          RETURN
08          END
RT     COMPLETED..
PRT,S P*S.PERIN
P*S.PERIN
  1   C THIS SUBROUTINE IS REFERENCED BY PERHRS (see P.S.PERHRS)
  2   C Variables and Subroutine names particular to this routine:
  3   C  BCORD    DEFINE function = .TRUE. iff CHAR(arg) is a Blank, Comma OR Dash
  4   C  BEGFLD   DEFINE function = .TRUE. iff a FieLD BEGins in column arg ("fields"
  5   C               are separated by blanks, commas or dashes )
  6   C  ENDFLD   DEFINE function = .TRUE. iff a FieLD ENDs in column arg
  7   C  IMAGE    array with the IMAGE of a date
  8   C  INPUT    array with the current period's description, the INPUT to the routine
  9   C  DAY      array with the current period's specifying DAY numbers
 10   C  DASHQ    [for "DASH?"] DASHQ(I) = '-' iff DAY(I) was specified with
 11   C               a DASH following it.  It = ' ' otherwise
 12   C  CHAR(I) = the Ith CHARacter of the current INPUT [= ' ' if I = 73]
 13   C  NDATE    Number of the current DATE
 14   C  COL      temporary holding area for a COLumn number
 15   C  START    like COL
 16   C  MVCFST   a routine from the library IRP-DC.LIB that MoVes Characters
 17   C  MONNO    NO. of the MONth found in IMAGE
 18   C  DAYNO    number of the DAY of the MOnth found in IMAGE
 19   C  NDAY     Number of the current DAY specification
 20   C  NHOUR    Number of the current HOUR specification
 21   C  CHARNO   Fieldata NO. for a CHARacter
 22   C  DAYWK    subroutine that gives the number of the DAY of the Week
 23   C               (arg 2) of the day with name arg 1
 24          SUBROUTINE PERIN(NPER)
 25          PARAMETER NPERP=6
 26          IMPLICIT INTEGER (A-Z)
 27          LOGICAL BCORD,BEGFLD,ENDFLD
 28          DIMENSION IMAGE(12),INPUT(12),DAY(8),DASHQ(8),CHAR(73)
 29         1          ,DYSPST(12)/0,31,59,90,120,151,181,212,243,273,304,334/
 30          COMMON /PERBLK/DAYYRP(NPERP,10),NDATES(NPERP),
 31         1          DAYS(NPERP,3),NODAYS(NPERP),EIHOL(NPERP),HOUR(NPERP,2)
 32         2      /HOURBL/HOLDYR(15),INPUTS(NPERP,12)
 33          BCORD(I) = CHAR(I).EQ.' '.OR.CHAR(I).EQ.','.OR.CHAR(I).EQ.'-'
 34          BEGFLD(I) = BCORD(I-1).AND..NOT.BCORD(I)
 35          ENDFLD(I) = .NOT.BCORD(I).AND.BCORD(I+1)
 36          DAYYR(MONTH,DAYNO) = DYSPST(MONTH) + DAYNO
 37
 38          DO 320 PER = 1,NPER
 39
 40           DO 10 I = 1,8
 41   10        DASHQ(I) = 6H
 42           DO 20 J = 1,12
 43   20        INPUT(J) = INPUTS(PER,J)
 44           DECODE (INPUT,25) CHAR
 45   25      FORMAT (72A1)
 46           CHAR(73) = 6H
 47   C determine the date specifications (DAYYRP,NDATES):
```

```
 48              COL = 2
 49              NDATE = 0
 50              IF (BCORD(I)) GO TO 30
 51              START = 1
 52              GO TO 60
 53   30         DO 40 I = COL,72
 54   40          IF (BEGFLD(I)) GO TO 50
 55   50         START = I
 56   60         FLDS = 0
 57              DO 70 I = START,72
 58               IF (.NOT.ENDFLD(I)) GO TO 70
 59               FLDS = FLDS + 1
 60               IF (FLDS .GE. 2) GO TO 80
 61   70         CONTINUE
 62   80         NCHAR = I + 1 - START
 63              DO 85 J = 1,12
 64   85          IMAGE(J) = 6H
 65              CALL MVCEST(INPUT,START,IMAGE,1,NCHAR)
 66   C    (this moves NCHAR characters from INPUT, starting at char. no. START,
 67   C    to IMAGE [starting at char. no. 1])
 68              CALL DATE(IMAGE,MONNO,DAYMO)
 69              IF (DAYMO .EQ. 0 .OR. MONNO .EQ. 0) GO TO 90
 70   C     (if we have run out of dates DATE will not find either a
 71   C      month or a day in IMAGE, and this statement will send us to 90)
 72              NDATE = NDATE + 1
 73              DAYYRP(PER,NDATE) = DAYYR(MONNO,DAYMO)
 74              COL = I + 1
 75              GO TO 30
 76   90         IF (NDATE .NE. 0) GO TO 93
 77   C   (if no dates are specified, set default dates!)
 78              COL = 1
 79              DAYYRP(PER,1) = 1
 80              DAYYRP(PER,2) = 365
 81              NDATE = 2
 82              GO TO 105
 83   C   (if any of the date pairs span Jan 1, eg dec 1 - mar 1, insert
 84   C    two more dates, make it eg dec 1 - dec 31, jan 1 - mar 1 which
 85   C    is equivalent but doesn't louse up PERHRS)
 86   93         NDATE1 = NDATE - 1
 87              DO 100 J = 1,NDATE1,2
 88               IF (DAYYRP(PER,J) .LE. DAYYRP(PER,J+1)) GO TO 100
 89               JP1 = J + 1
 90               DO 96 K = NDATE,JP1,-1
 91   96           DAYYRP(PER,K+2) = DAYYRP(PER,K)
 92               DAYYRP(PER,J+1) = 365
 93               DAYYRP(PER,J+2) = 1
 94               NDATE = NDATE + 2
 95   100        CONTINUE
 96   105        NDATES(PER) = NDATE
 97
 98   C determine the day specifications (DAYS,NODAYS):
 99              NDAY = 1
100              GO TO 140
101   110        DO 120 I = COL,72
102               IF (NDAY.NE.1.AND.CHAR(I).EQ.'-') DASHC(NDAY-1) = '-'
103   120         IF (BEGFLD(I)) GO TO 130
104   130        START = I
```

```
105  140      DAYNAM = 6H
106           CALL MVCFST(INPUT,START,DAYNAM,1,2)
107  C   (this moves the first two characters [all that are needed] of the
108  C    current day name from INPUT, starting at char. no. START, into
109  C   DAYNAM which is sent off to DAYWK to be converted to a number
110  C   [DAY(NDAY)].  'WE' for "weekend" is assigned number 8)
111           CALL DAYWK(DAYNAM,DAY(NDAY))
112           IF (DAY(NDAY) .EQ. 0) GO TO 150
113  C   (again, if we have run out of days this sends us to 150)
114           COL = START + 1
115           NDAY = NDAY + 1
116           GO TO 110
117  150      NDAY = NDAY - 1
118           IF (DAY(1) .NE. 0) GO TO 160
119  C  if no days are specified set the default days "1-7":
120           DAY(1) = 1
121           DAY(2) = 7
122           DASHQ(1) = '-'
123           NDAY = 2
124  160      NDAYS = 0
125           DO 190 I = 1,NDAY
126            IF (DASHQ(I) .NE. '-') GO TO 180
127            START = DAY(I)
128            STOP = DAY(I+1) - 1
129            DO 170 J = START,STOP
130             NDAYS = NDAYS + 1
131             DAYS(PER,NDAYS) = J
132  170       CONTINUE
133            GO TO 190
134  180       NDAYS = NDAYS + 1
135            DAYS(PER,NDAYS) = DAY(I)
136  190      CONTINUE
137           DO 200 I = 1,NDAYS
138  200      IF (DAYS(PER,I) .EQ. 8) GO TO 210
139           GO TO 220
140  C  if 'WE' was entered, register Sat and Sun:
141  210      DAYS(PER,I) = 6
142           NDAYS = NDAYS + 1
143           DAYS(PER,NDAYS) = 7
144  220      NODAYS(PER) = NDAYS
145
146  C determine the holiday specifications (EIHOL):
147           EIHOL(PER) = 'IGNORE'
148           DO 230 I = COL,72
149  230       IF (BEGFLD(I)) GO TO 240
150  240      IF (CHAR(I) .EQ. 'E') EIHOL(PER) = 'EXCL'
151           IF (CHAR(I).EQ.'I' .OR. CHAR(I).EQ.'H') EIHOL(PER) = 'INCL'
152           IF (CHAR(I) .NE. 'O') GO TO 245
153           EIHOL(PER) = 'INCL'
154           NODAYS(PER) = 0
155
156  C determine the hour specifications (HOUR):
157  C (start at the right end of the IMAGE and work left until both
158  C hours are found)
159  245      COL = 72
160           NHOUR = 2
161  250      DO 260 I = COL,1,-1
```

```
162  260       IF (ENDFLD(I)) GO TO 270
163  270      START = I
164           CHARNO = FLD(0,6,CHAR(START))
165           IF (CHARNO.GT.57 .OR. CHARNO.LT.48) GO TO 310
166  C   (this statement sends us to 310 if there are no hours specified
167  C    and hence the first char. encountered in the scan is not a number)
168           DO 280 I = START,1,-1
169  280       IF (BEGFLD(I)) GO TO 290
170  290      COL = I - 1
171           NCHAR = START - COL
172           HOURIN = 6H
173           CALL MVCFST(INPUT,I,HOURIN,1,NCHAR)
174  C   (this extracts the hour number from INPUT and puts it into HOURIN)
175           DECODE (HOURIN,300) HOUR(PER,NHOUR)
176  C   (and this converts it from Hollerith format to integer)
177  300      FORMAT (I)
178           IF (NHOUR .EQ. 1) GO TO 315
179           NHOUR = 1
180           GO TO 250
181  310      HOUR(PER,1) = 1
182           HOUR(PER,2) = 24
183
184  315      CONTINUE
185  320    CONTINUE        DNEXT PER(100)
186         RETURN
187         END
PRT    COMPLETED..
@PRT,S P.S.DAYWK

P.S.DAYWK
  1  C THIS SUBROUTINE IS REFERENCED BY PERIN (see P.S.PERIN)
  2  C  NAME(I) = the first I characters of the NAME of the day
  3         SUBROUTINE DAYWK(DAYNAM,DAYNO)
  4         IMPLICIT INTEGER (A-Z)
  5         DIMENSION NAME(2),DY(7)/'M','T','W','TH','F','SA','SU'/
  6
  7         DAYNO = 0
  8         DO 10 J = 1,2
  9          NAME(J) = 6H
 10  10      FLD(0,6*J,NAME(J)) = FLD(0,6*J,DAYNAM)
 11         DO 20 I = 1,7
 12          DO 20 J = 1,2
 13  20       IF (NAME(J) .EQ. DY(I)) GO TO 30
 14         GO TO 40
 15  30     DAYNO = I
 16  40     IF (NAME(2).EQ.'TH' .OR. NAME(1).EQ.'R') DAYNO = 4
 17         IF (NAME(2) .EQ. 'WE') DAYNO = 8
 18         RETURN
 19         END
PRT    COMPLETED..
@PRT,S P.S.MCKWH

P.S.MCKWH
  1  C THIS SUBROUTINE IS REFERENCED BY MARGINALCOST (see P.S.MARGINALCOST)
  2        SUBROUTINE MCKWH
  3        INCLUDE VARS
```

```
 4          INTEGER I,J,PKPER
 5
 6   C Print HRSPER:
 7          PRINT 8100, ((PERNAM(I,J), J=1,2), I=1,NPER)
 8   8100   FORMAT (//T25,'LENGTH OF PERIODS (HOURS)'/
 9         1        T25,25('-')//1X,10A6)
10          PRINT 8110, ((PERNAM(I,J), J=3,4), I=1,NPER)
11   8110   FORMAT (1X,10A6)
12          PRINT 8120, (HRSPER(I), I=1,NPER)
13   8120   FORMAT (I9,4I12)
14
15   C fill PRPEAK:
16          HRSPK = 0
17          DO 8200 I = 1,NPERP
18   8200    PRPEAK(I) = 'OFF PK'
19          DO 8300 I = 1,NPPS
20           PKPER = NPP(I)
21           HRSPK = HRSPK + HRSPER(PKPER)
22   8300    PRPEAK(PKPER) = 'PEAK'
23
24   C compute marginal cost per kwhs:
25          DO 8400 I = 1,NVL
26           MCKWHG(I) = 100*MCKWGC(I)/HRSPK
27   8400    MCKWHT(I) = 100*MCKWTD(I)/HRSPK
28          RETURN
29          END
PRT    COMPLETED..
@PRT,S P*S.ENERGY

P*S.ENERGY
 1               SUBROUTINE ENERGY
 2               INCLUDE VARS
 3               INTEGER I,J
 4               DO 9100 I = 1,NVL
 5                DO 9100 J = 1,NPER
 6                 IF (PRPEAK(J) .EQ. 'PEAK') MCEKWH(I,J) = IFCKWH(J)*CMLMEP(I)
 7                 IF (PRPEAK(J) .NE. 'PEAK') MCEKWH(I,J) = IFCKWH(J)*CMLMEO(I)
 8        9100   CONTINUE
 9               PRINT 9110, ((PERNAM(I,J),J=1,2),I=1,NPER)
10        9110   FORMAT (//T20,'MARGINAL COST OF ENERGY (CENTS/KWH)'
11              1           /T20,35('-')
12              1           //' VOLTAGE',T30,'PERIOD'/'  STAGE ',10A6)
13               PRINT 9120, ((PERNAM(I,J),J=3,4),I=1,NPER)
14        9120   FORMAT (' (1= HI)',10A6)
15               DO 9130 I = 1,NVL
16        9130    PRINT 9140, I,(MCEKWH(I,J),J=1,NPER)
17        9140   FORMAT (I5,6F12.3)
18               RETURN
19               END
PRT    COMPLETED..
@PRT,S P*S.SUMARY

P*S.SUMARY
 1  C THIS SUBROUTINE IS REFERENCED BY MARGINALCOST (see P*S*MARGINALCOST)
 2  C Variables particular to this routine:
 3  C   PERNMP(I,J) = NaMe of the Ith peak PERiod (as j = 1,4)
 4  C   PERNMO(I,J) = NaMe of the Ithe Off Peak PERiod (as j = 1,4)
```

```
 5      NOFFPP   Number of OFF Peak Periods
 6   C  OFFPP    number of the current OFF Peak Period
 7   C  MEKWHP   MCEKWH for just the Peak periods
 8   C  MEKWHO   MCKWH for just the Off Peak Periods
 9   C  TOTMC    TOTal Marginal Costs
10          SUBROUTINE SUMARY
11          INCLUDE VARS
12          INTEGER I,PERIOD,J,PERNMP(NPERP,4),VL,NOFFPP,PERNMO(NPERP,4)
13         1        ,OFFPP
14          DIMENSION MEKWHP(NPERP),TOTMC(NPERP),MEKWHO(NVLP,NPERP)
15
16   C Print table heading for the peak periods:
17          DO 100 I = 1,NPPS
18           PERIOD = NPP(I)
19           DO 100 J = 1,4
20   100      PERNMP(I,J) = PERNAM(PERIOD,J)
21          PRINT 110, ((PERNMP(I,J), J=1,2),I=1,NPPS)
22   110    FORMAT (///T20,'TOTAL MARGINAL COST (CENTS/KWH)'
23         1        /T20,31('-')//
24         1        5X,'ON-PEAK PERIODS'//' VOLT.  GENER.  TRANS.',
25         2        '  ENERGY/TOTAL'/' LEVEL',10X,'& DIS. ',8A6)
26          PRINT 120, ((PERNMP(I,J),J=3,4),I=1,NPPS)
27   C fill in the table for the Peak periods:
28   120    FORMAT (23X,8A6)
29          DO 160 VL = 1,NVL
30           DO 130 I = 1,NPPS
31            PERIOD = NPP(I)
32            MEKWHP(I) = MCEKWH(VL,PERIOD)
33   130      TOTMC(I) = MCKWHG(VL) + MCKWHT(VL) + MCEKWH(VL,PERIOD)
34           PRINT 140, VL,MCKWHG(VL),MCKWHT(VL),(MEKWHP(I), I=1,NPPS)
35   140     FORMAT (I4,F9.3,F7.3,4F12.3)
36           PRINT 150, (TOTMC(I), I=1,NPPS)
37   150     FORMAT (20X,4F12.3)
38   160    CONTINUE
39   C Print the table for the off Peak Periods:
40          NOFFPP = NPER - NPPS
41          OFFPP = 0
42          DO 190 PERIOD = 1,NPER
43           IF (PRPEAK(PERIOD) .EQ. 'PEAK') GO TO 190
44           OFFPP = OFFPP + 1
45           DO 170 I = 1,4
46   170      PERNMO(OFFPP,I) = PERNAM(PERIOD,I)
47           DO 180 VL = 1,NVL
48   180      MEKWHO(VL,OFFPP) = MCEKWH(VL,PERIOD)
49   190    CONTINUE
50          PRINT 200, ((PERNMO(I,J), J=1,2), I=1,NOFFPP)
51   200    FORMAT (//5X,'OFF-PEAK PERIODS:  TOTAL MARGINAL COST (= ',
52         1        'ENERGY COST)'//' VOLTAGE',3X,10A6)
53          PRINT 210, ((PERNMO(I,J), J=3,4), I=1,NOFFPP)
54   210    FORMAT ('  LEVEL',4X,10A6)
55          DO 220 VL = 1,NVL
56   220     PRINT 230, VL,(MEKWHO(VL,I), I=1,NOFFPP)
57   230    FORMAT (I4,4X,5F12.3)
58          RETURN
59          END
PRT     COMPLETED..
```

REVENUE
(and associated subprograms)

```
P.S.REVENUE
 1  C THIS PROGRAM ("REVENUE") MODIFIES A TARIFF TO PRODUCE DESIRED REVENUES
 2  C Variable and Subroutine Names:
 3  C  NPERP    maximum allowed NUmber of PERiods (a PARAMETER variable)
 4  C  NCCLP    maximum allowed Number of Customer CLasses (a PARAMETER variable)
 5  C  PER      the current PERiod
 6  C  POS      a DEFINE function that = .TRUE. iff its argument is POSitive
 7  C             (actually, iff it is > -10..-6)
 8  C  PRINTQ   [for "PRINT?"] PRINTQ(1) = .TRUE. iff lines "B" and "C" are
 9  C             to be PRINTed for the "customer charge adjusted" section of the
10  C             table, PRINTQ(2) = .TRUE. iff line "D" is to be printed, and
11  C             PRINTQ(3) = .TRUE. iff lines "B" and "C" are to be Printed for
12  C             the "off-peak price adjusted" section of the table
13  C  P        Prices
14  C  SALES    SALES
15  C  NCUST    Number of CUSTomers
16  C  DESREV   DESired REVenues
17  C  CSCHRG   CuStomer CHaRGes
18  C  SALREV   REVenue attained from SALes at the current prices
19  C  PCRED1   PerCent REDuction used for line "B" in the "cust. chg." section
20  C  PCRED2   PerCent REDuction used for line "C" in the "cust. chg." section
21  C  PCRED3   PerCent REDuction used for line "D" in the "cust. chg." section
22  C  PCRED4   PerCent REDuction used for line "B" in the "Price off peak" section
23  C  PCRED5   PerCent REDuction used for line "C" in the "price off peak" section
24  C  CUSCHG   modified CUStomer CHarge (for line "A" of "cust. chg.")
25  C  PONP     modified Price On Peak
26  C  POFFP    modified Price OFF Peak
27  C  OUTCC    array containing the OUTput for the Cust. Chg. section -
28  C             the second subscript gives the row (eg 1 = "A", 2 = "B")
29  C  OUTPOF   OUTPut for the Price OFFf peak section - like OUTCC
30  C  OUTPON   OUTPut for the Price ON Peak section - like OUTCC
31  C  ACTREV   ACtual REVenue that would be attained under the unmodified tariff
32  C  FIRRUN   = 'YES' iff the current run is the FIRst RUN
33  C  FIRCHG   = 'YES' iff any change would be the FIRst CHanGe ("change"
34  C             meaning user-produced change ["$NEW ..."])
35  C  NPER     Number of PERiods
36  C  NCSCLS   Number of CuStomer CLasses
37  C  PRDATA   subroutine that PRints the DATA
38  C  WCHGS    = 'YES' iff the user wants to make CHanGeS
39  C  HEADNG   subroutine that prints the table HEADING and ACTREV
40  C  CC       Customer Class
41  C  CSCHGS   subroutine that fills OUTCC
42  C  POFFPK   subroutine that fills OUTPOF
43  C  PONPK    subroutine that fills OUTPON
44  C  OUTPUT   subroutine that prints the rows of the table for one customer
45  C             class (ie OUTCC,OUTPOF,OUTPON)
46  C  KEY      subroutine that prints the KEY
47  C  LET      array with the LEtters 'B','C','D'
48        PARAMETER NPERP=3, NCCLP=3, NPER2P = NPERP + 2
49        IMPLICIT INTEGER (A-Z)
50        INTEGER PER
51        LOGICAL POS,PRINTQ(3)
52        DOUBLE PRECISION P(NPERP,NCCLP),SALES(NPERP,NCCLP),NCUST(NCCLP)
53       1                 ,DESREV(NCCLP),CSCHRG(NCCLP),SALREV,
54       2                 PCRED1,PCRED2,PCRED3,PCRED4,PCRED5,
55       3                 CUSCHG,PONP,POFFP,OUTCC(NPER2P,4),
56       4                 OUTPOF(NPER2P,3),OUTPON(NPERP),ACTREV(NCCLP)
```

```
 57         NAMELIST /NEW/NPER,NCSCLS,DESREV,P,SALES,NCUST,CSCHRG
 58         DEFINE POS(X) = INT(X*1000000) .GE. 0
 59
 60         FIRRUN = 'YES'
 61         FIRCHG = 'YES'
 62   C read and print initial data:
 63         PRINT 10
 64   10    FORMAT (/' PLEASE FURNISH INITIAL DATA')
 65         READ, NPER,NCSCLS
 66         READ, ((P(I,J), I=1,NPER), J=1,NCSCLS),((SALES(I,J), I=1,
 67       1       NPER), J=1,NCSCLS),(NCUST(J), J=1,NCSCLS),
 68       2       (DESREV(J),J=1,NCSCLS),(CSCHRG(J), J=1,NCSCLS)
 69         PRINT  20
 70   20    FORMAT (//' INITIAL DATA:'//)
 71         CALL PRDATA
 72   C make changes and print revised data:
 73   30    PRINT 40
 74   40    FORMAT (///' DO YOU WANT TO CHANGE THE DATA?')
 75         IF (FIRCHG .NE. 'YES') PRINT 50
 76   50    FORMAT (' (PRECEEDING CHANGES REMAIN IN EFFECT)')
 77         READ 60, WCHGS
 78   60    FORMAT (A6)
 79         IF (WCHGS .EQ. 'YES') GO TO 80
 80         IF (FIRRUN .EQ. 'YES') GO TO 140
 81         PRINT 70
 82   70    FORMAT (//' GOOD BYE THEN'//)
 83         STOP
 84   80    IF (FIRCHG .EQ. 'YES') PRINT 90
 85   90    FORMAT (/' ENTER THE NEW VALUE(S) AS IN THIS EXAMPLE:'/
 86       1         ' (END LINES AT COMMAS AND NEVER TYPE IN COLUMN',
 87       2         ' ONE - IT IS IGNORED)'/
 88       3         ' $NEW DESREV(2) = 800E6, P(1,2) = .02,'/
 89       4         '   .01, .005'/' $END'/)
 90         IF (FIRCHG .NE. 'YES') PRINT 95
 91   95    FORMAT (/' ENTER THE NEW VALUES AS BEFORE')
 92         FIRCHG = 'NO'
 93   100   READ (5,NEW,ERR=110)
 94         GO TO 130
 95   110   PRINT 120
 96   120   FORMAT (/' THERE WAS AN ERROR IN THOSE CHANGES - PLEASE TRY ',
 97       1         'AGAIN')
 98         GO TO 100
 99   130   PRINT 135
100   135   FORMAT (//' REVISED DATA:'//)
101         CALL PRDATA
102   C compute and print results by customer class:
103   140   NPERP2 = NPER + 2
104         NPERP1 = NPER + 1
105         NPERM1 = NPER - 1
106         DO 145 CC = 1,NCSCLS
107          ACTREV(CC) = CSCHRG(CC)*NCUST(CC)
108          DO 145 PER = 1,NPER
109   145     ACTREV(CC) = ACTREV(CC) + P(PER,CC)*SALES(PER,CC)
110         CALL HEADNG
111         DO 170 CC = 1,NCSCLS
112          DO 150 I = 1,3
113   150     PRINTQ(I) = .FALSE.
```

```
114            SALREV = 0
115            DO 160 PER = 1,NPER
116    160       SALREV = SALREV + P(PER,CC)*SALES(PER,CC)
117            CALL CSCHGS
118            CALL POFFPK
119            CALL PONPK
120            CALL OUTPUT
121    170    CONTINUE
122           IF (FIRRUN .EQ. 'YES') CALL KEY
123           FIRRUN = 'NO'
124           GO TO 30
125
126           SUBROUTINE PRDATA
127
128           PRINT 10, NPER,NCSCLS,((P(I,J),J=1,NCSCLS),I=1,NPER),((SALES
129          1         (I,J),J=1,NCSCLS),I=1,NPER),(NCUST(J),J=1,NCSCLS),
130          2         (DESREV(J),J=1,NCSCLS),(CSCHRG(J),J=1,NCSCLS)
131    10     FORMAT (/' NUMBER OF PERIODS:',T30,I3,T50,'NPER'/
132          1         ' NUMBER OF CUSTOMER CLASSES:',T30,I3,T50,'NCSCLS'//
133          1        T25,'CUSTOMER CLASS (J)'/
134          1        T7,'PERIOD (I)',T21,'1: IND.  2: COM.  3: RES.'/
135          1        /' PRICES (CENTS/KWH):',T50,'P(I,J)'/
136          1        6X,'1: ON PEAK'2P3F9.2/
137          1        6X,'2: INTERM.',3F9.2/
138          1        6X,'3: OFF PEAK',F8.2,2F9.2/
139          1        /' SALES (BILLION KWH):',T50,'SALES(I,J)'/
140          1        6X,'1: ON PEAK',-9P3F9.2/
141          1        6X,'2: INTERM.',3F9.2/
142          1        6X,'3: OFF PEAK',F8.2,2F9.2/
143          1        /' NUMBER OF CUSTOMERS:',T50,'NCUST(J)'/
144          1        16X,0P3F9.0/
145          1        /' DESIRED REVENUE (MILLION DOLLARS):',T50,'DESREV(J)'/
146          1        16X,-6P3F9.2/
147          1        /' CUSTOMER CHARGES ($/MONTH):',T50,'CSCHRG(J)'/
148          1        16X,0P3F9.2)
149           RETURN
150
151           SUBROUTINE CSCHGS
152
153           CUSCHG = (DESREV(CC) - SALREV)/NCUST(CC)/12
154           DO 10 PER = 1,NPER
155    10      OUTCC(PER,1) = P(PER,CC)
156           OUTCC(NPER+1,1) = CUSCHG
157           IF (POS(CUSCHG)) GO TO 40
158           PRINTQ(1) = .TRUE.
159           PCRED1 = 1 - DESREV(CC)/SALREV
160           PCRED2 = (SALREV - DESREV(CC))/(P(NPER,CC)*SALES(NPER,CC))
161           DO 20 PER = 1,NPER
162            OUTCC(PER,2) = (1 - PCRED1)*P(PER,CC)
163    20      OUTCC(PER,3) = P(PER,CC)
164           OUTCC(NPER,3) = (1 - PCRED2)*P(NPER,CC)
165           OUTCC(NPER+1,2) = 0
166           OUTCC(NPER+1,3) = 0
167           OUTCC(NPER+2,2) = PCRED1
168           OUTCC(NPER+2,3) = PCRED2
169           IF (POS(.5 - PCRED2)) GO TO 40
170           PRINTQ(2) = .TRUE.
```

```
171            PCRED3 = (SALREV-DESREV(CC)-P(NPER,CC)*SALES(NPER,CC)/2)/
172           1         (SALREV-P(NPER,CC)*SALES(NPER,CC))
173            DO 30 PER = 1,NPERM1
174     30      OUTCC(PER,4) = (1-PCRED3)*P(PER,CC)
175            OUTCC(NPER,4) = P(NPER,CC)/2
176            OUTCC(NPER+1,4) = 0
177            OUTCC(NPER+2,4) = PCRED3
178     40     RETURN
179
180            SUBROUTINE POFFPK
181
182            POFFP   = (DESREV(CC)-SALREV+P(NPER,CC)*SALES(NPER,CC)-
183           1          12*CSCHRG(CC)*NCUST(CC)) / SALES(NPER,CC)
184            DO 10 PER = 1,NPERM1
185     10      OUTPOF(PER,1) = P(PER,CC)
186            OUTPOF(NPER,1) = POFFP
187            OUTPOF(NPER+1,1) = CSCHRG(CC)
188            IF (POS(POFFP)) GO TO 40
189            PRINTQ(3) = .TRUE.
190            PCRED4 = 1 - (DESREV(CC)-12*CSCHRG(CC)*NCUST(CC)) /
191           1         (SALREV-P(NPER,CC)*SALES(NPER,CC))
192            PCRED5 = 1 - (DESREV(CC)-P(1,CC)*SALES(1,CC)-12*CSCHRG(CC)*
193           1         NCUST(CC)) / (SALREV-P(1,CC)*SALES(1,CC)-P(NPER,CC)*
194           2         SALES(NPER,CC))
195            DO 20 PER = 1,NPERM1
196     20      OUTPOF(PER,2) = (1-PCRED4)*P(PER,CC)
197            OUTPOF(NPER,2) = 0
198            OUTPOF(NPER+1,2) = PCRED4
199            OUTPOF(NPER+2,2) = CSCHRG(CC)
200            OUTPOF(1,3) = P(1,CC)
201            DO 30 PER = 2,NPERM1
202     30      OUTPOF(PER,3) = (1-PCRED5)*P(PER,CC)
203            OUTPOF(NPER,3) = 0
204            OUTPOF(NPER+1,3) = PCRED5
205     40     RETURN
206
207            SUBROUTINE PONPK
208
209            PONP   = (DESREV(CC)-SALREV+P(1,CC)*SALES(1,CC)-12*CSCHRG(CC)*
210           1         NCUST(CC)) / SALES(1,CC)
211            OUTPON(1) = PONP
212            DO 10 PER = 2,NPER
213     10      OUTPON(PER) = P(PER,CC)
214            RETURN
215
216            SUBROUTINE OUTPUT
217
218            DIMENSION LET(4)/'  ','  B','  C','  D'/
219            PRINT 10, CC,(OUTCC(I,1),I=1,NPERP1),(OUTPOF(I,1),I=1,NPERP1),
220           1         (OUTPON(I),I=1,NPER)
221     10     FORMAT (/I2/'  A',2P3F5.2,0PF7.2,5X,2P3F5.2,4X,0PF7.2,2P3F5.2)
222            DO 50 J = 2,3
223             IF(PRINTQ(1).AND.PRINTQ(3)) PRINT 20, LET(J),(OUTCC(I,J),I=1,
224           1      NPERP2)
225           1    ,(OUTPOF(I,J),I=1,NPERP1)
226     20      FORMAT (A3,2P3F5.2,0PF7.2,2PF4.0,1X,2P3F5.2,2PF4.0)
227             IF (PRINTQ(1) .AND. .NOT. PRINTQ(3))
```

```
228          1    PRINT 20, LET(J),(OUTCC(I,J),I=1,NPERP2)
229            IF (.NOT.PRINTQ(1) .AND. PRINTQ(3))
230          1    PRINT 40, LET(J),(OUTPOF(I,J),I=1,NPERP1)
231   40       FORMAT (A3,27X,2P3F5.2,2PF4.0)
232   50      CONTINUE
233           IF (PRINTQ(2)) PRINT 20, LET(4),(OUTCC(I,4),I=1,NPERP2)
234           RETURN
235
236           ENTRY KEY
237
238           PRINT 60
239   60      FORMAT (///' KEY:'//' A:  THE FIRST LINE OF EACH CUSTOMER CLASS '
240          1,'(''A'') SHOWS WHAT THE'/5X,'TARIFF WOULD BE IF THE ''ADJUSTED'
241          1,' CHARGE'' WERE SET TO YIELD THE'/5X,'DESIRED REVENUE FOR THAT'
242          1,' CUSTOMER CLASS'/' B:  THE SECOND LINE (''B'') APPEARS WHEN '
243          1,'THE ADJUSTED CHARGE IN ''A'''/5X,'BECOMES NEGATIVE.  IT SHOWS'
244          1,' A TARIFF WITH THE ADJUSTED CHARGE'/5X,'SET EQUAL TO ZERO AND '
245          1,'THE OTHER CHARGES REDUCED BY A COMMON'/5X,'PERCENTAGE'/' C:  '
246          1,'LINE ''C'' IS LIKE ''B'' EXCEPT THAT ONLY THE PRICE DURING THE'/
247          1 5X,'PERIOD WITH LEAST DEMAND IS REDUCED'/' D:
248          1,'IF IN ''C'' THE PERCENT REDUCTION OF THE OFF-PEAK PRICE'
249          1,' IS'/5X,'GREATER THAN 50%, A FOURTH LINE (''D'') APPEARS, IN'
250          1,' WHICH THE'/5X,'CUSTOMER CHARGE IS SET EQUAL TO ZERO, THE OFF-PE
251          1AK PRICE IS'/5X,'REDUCED BY 50% AND THE OTHER PRICES ARE REDUCED',
252          1' BY A COMMON'/5X,'PERCENTAGE')
253           RETURN
254
255           ENTRY HEADNG
256
257           PRINT 70, (ACTREV(CC), CC=1,NCSCLS)
258   70      FORMAT (///' RESULTS:'
259          1             //' ACTUAL REVENUE (MILLION DOLLARS):'/16X,-6P3F9.2
260          1             //' ADJUSTED',6X,'CUSTOMER',15X,'PRICE',18X,'PRICE'/
261          1             '   CHARGE:',6X,'CHARGE',14X,'OFF  PEAK',15X,'ON PEAK'/
262          2             /' C  PRICE(CTS/KWH)  CUST. (%   PRICE(CTS/KWH) ',
263          3             '(%)  CUST. PRICE(CTS/KWH)'/
264          4             ' U    ON  INT.  OFF CHARGE RED-  ON  INT.  OFF',
265          5             '      CHARGE  ON  INT.  OFF'/
266          6             ' S  PEAK',6X,'PEAK ($/MO) UC.) PEAK',6X,'PEAK ',
267          7             4X,'($/MO) PEAK',6X,'PEAK'/)
268           RETURN
269
270           END
PRT     COMPLETED..
```

TYPICAL–BILL
(and associated subprograms)

```
@PRT,S P•S.TYPICAL-BILL

P•S.TYPICAL-BILL
1  C THIS PROGRAM ("TYPICAL-BILL") COMPUTES TYPICAL ELECTRIC BILLS
2  C The M/P statements in P•S.BILLMAP indicate the subroutines used
3  C Variable and Subroutine Names:
4  C   BILLP     PROC stored in P.S.BILLPPROC
5  C   NROWSP    maximum Number of ROWS allowed in the typical bill table
6  C               when there are no "Peak" tariffs (a PARAMETER variable)
7  C   NROWPP    maximum Number of ROWs allowed in the typical bill table
8  C               when there are "Peak" tariffs (a PARAMETER variable)
9  C   PEAKQ     [for "PEAK?"] = .TRUE. iff there is a "PEAK" tariff
10 C   KWHSAM    = .TRUE. iff the KWH level of the current row of the table
11 C               is the SAMe as in the previous row
12 C   KWSAME    = .TRUE. iff the KW level of the current row of the table
13 C               is the SAME as in the previous row
14 C   PCPKSM    = .TRUE. iff the PerCent on Peak level of the current row
15 C               is the Same as in the previous row
16 C   BILL      array of the BILLs for all the tariffs for the levels of the
17 C               current row
18 C   PCPKA     Array with the levels of PerCent on PeaK for all the rows
19 C   TYPETF    array containing the TYPES of the TariFFs (eg 'F')
20 C   NAMETF    array containing the NAMES of the TarIFFs
21 C   KWHA      Array containing the levels of KWH for all the rows when there
22 C               are no "Peak" tariffs
23 C   KWA       Array containing the levels of KW for all the rows when there
24 C               are no "Peak" tariffs
25 C   KWHPA     Array containg the levels of KWH when there are "Peak" tariffs
26 C   KWPA      Array containing the levels of KW when there are "Peak" tariffs
27 C   NROWS     Number of ROWS in a table with no "Peak" tariffs and later
28 C               the Number of ROWS in the actual table to be Printed
29 C   NPROWS    Number of ROWS in a table with "Peak" tariffs
30 C   NTARIF    Number of TARIFFs
31 C   TYPETR    TYPE of the current TaRiff
32 C   NCHAR     Number of CHARacters in the name of the current tariff
33 C               (=6 except for the ninth tariff when it equals 5 [to fit on
34 C               the Page])
35 C   NOTRF     NO. of the current TaRiFF
36 C   NAMETF    array with the NAMEs of the Tariffs
37 C   BL        array with the BLock specifications: BL(I,J,K)=the kth "x" of
38 C               the documentation for the ith tariff, where j always = 1 except
39 C               when the ith tariff is a "hopkinson" tariff. Then J=1 for the kwh
40 C               charge and j=2 for the kw charge.
41 C   P         array with the Price specifications, with subscripts like "BL" but
42 C               for the "p"s of the documentation rather than the "x"s
43 C   NBLS(I,J) = Number of BLocKS (ie prices) for the ith tariff, J as for "BL"
44 C   PCPEAK    PerCent on PEAK of the current row of the table
45 C   KW        KW level of the current row of the table
46 C   KWH       KWH level of the current row of the table
47 C   COST      COST (ie bill) for the current tariff at the current levels
48 C   FORH      subroutine that fills BL and P for an 'F' OR 'H' tariff
49 C   PEAK      subroutine that reads the prices on & off Peak for a "PEAK" tariff
50 C   EXPAND    subroutine that reads the specifications for an EXPANDer tariff
51 C   PEAKP     ENTRY Point in PEAK that determines the effective Price per Kwh
52 C               from the prices on & off Peak by their average weighted by the
53 C               % on Peak
```

```
 54  C  EXPNDB  ENTRY point in EXPAND that calculates BL from the tariff
 55  C              specifications and KW
 56  C  COSTSB  the variable COST is calculated in this Subroutine
 57          INCLUDE BILLP,LIST
 58          PARAMETER NROWSP=200, NROWPP=200
 59          LOGICAL PEAKQ/.FALSE./KWHSAM,KWSAME,PCPKSM
 60          REAL BILL(NTARFP),PCPKA(NROWPP)
 61          DIMENSION TYPETF(NTARFP),NAMETF(NTARFP),KWHA(NROWSP),KWA(NROWSP),
 62       1              KWHPA(NROWPP),KWPA(NROWPP)
 63
 64  C read the levels for the table:
 65          PRINT 5
 66   5      FORMAT (//' PLEASE SUPPLY THE CONSUMPTION LEVELS')
 67          READ, NROWS,(KWHA(I),KWA(I),I=1,NROWS),NPROWS,(KWHPA(I),KWPA(I),
 68       1          PCPKA(I),I=1,NPROWS)
 69  C read the tariff information:
 70          PRINT 10
 71   10     FORMAT (/' HOW MANY TARIFFS ARE THERE?')
 72          READ, NTARIF
 73          PRINT 20
 74   20     FORMAT (/' WHAT TYPE IS THE FIRST TARIFF? (TYPE ''?'' FOR ',
 75       1          'A LIST OF CHOICES).)
 76   30     READ 40, TYPETR
 77   40     FORMAT (A1)
 78          IF (TYPETR .NE. '?') GO TO 60
 79          PRINT 50
 80   50     FORMAT (/' YOUR CHOICES ARE:'/' FIXED BLOCK'/' HOPKINSON'/
 81       1          ' PEAK'/' EXPANDER BLOCK'/' (YOU NEED ONLY ENTER',
 82       2          ' THE FIRST LETTER OF THE NAME)'/' NOW WHAT TYPE',
 83       3          ' IS THE FIRST TARIFF?')
 84          GO TO 30
 85   60     NCHAR = 6
 86          DO 110 NOTRF = 1,NTARIF
 87           IF (NOTRF .EQ. 9) NCHAR = 5
 88           TYPETF(NOTRF) = TYPETR
 89           PRINT 70, NCHAR
 90   70      FORMAT (/' WHAT IS THE (',I1,' CHARACTER) NAME OF THE TARIFF?')
 91           READ 80, NAMETF(NOTRF)
 92   80      FORMAT (A6)
 93           IF (TYPETR.EQ.'F' .OR. TYPETR.EQ.'H') CALL FORH
 94           IF (TYPETR .NE. 'P') GO TO 90
 95           CALL PEAK
 96           PEAKQ = .TRUE.
 97   90      IF (TYPETR .EQ. 'E') CALL EXPAND
 98           IF (NOTRF .EQ. NTARIF) GO TO 110
 99           NOTRF1 = NOTRF + 1
100           PRINT 100, NOTRF1
101  100      FORMAT (/' WHAT TYPE IS THE NEXT TARIFF (NUMBER',I2,')?')
102           READ 40, TYPETR
103  110     CONTINUE
104  C Print the table heading:
105          IF (PEAKQ) GO TO 130
106          NROWS = NROWS
107          PRINT 120, (NAMETF(I), I=1,NTARIF)
108  120     FORMAT (///7X,'TYPICAL ELECTRIC BILLS'///'  KWH  KW',T25,'BILL'/
109       1          10X,8(1X,A6),1X,A5)
110          GO TO 150
```

```
111  130    NROWS = NPROWS
112         PRINT 140, (NAMETF(I), I=1,NTARIF)
113  140     FORMAT (///9X,'TYPICAL ELECTRIC BILLS'///'  KWH  KW  % ON',T25,
114       1          'BILL'/11X,'PEAK ',8(1X,A6))
115  150    DO 230 NOROW = 1,NROWS
116  C compute the bills for this row:
117          IF (PEAKQ) GO TO 160
118          KWH = KWHA(NOROW)
119          KW = KWA(NOROW)
120          GO TO 165
121  160     KWH = KWHPA(NOROW)
122          KW = KWPA(NOROW)
123          PCPEAK = PCPKA(NOROW)
124  165     IF (NOROW .EQ. 1) GO TO 170
125          KWHSAM = PEAKQ.AND.KWH.EQ.KWHPA(NOROW-1) .OR. .NOT.PEAKQ.AND.
126       1           KWH.EQ.KWHA(NOROW-1)
127          KWSAME = PEAKQ.AND.KW.EQ.KWPA(NOROW-1) .OR. .NOT.PEAKQ.AND.
128       1           KW.EQ.KWA(NOROW-1)
129          PCPKSM = PCPEAK .EQ. PCPKA(NOROW-1)
130  170     DO 190 NOTRF = 1,NTARIF
131           TYPETR = TYPETF(NOTRF)
132           IF (NOROW .EQ. 1) GO TO 180
133           IF (TYPETR.EQ.'F'.AND.KWHSAM .OR. (TYPETR.EQ.'H'.OR.TYPETR.EQ.
134       1        'E').AND.KWHSAM.AND.KWSAME .OR. TYPETR.EQ.'P'.AND.KWHSAM
135       2        .AND.PCPKSM) GO TO 190
136  C (If the levels relevant to the current type of tariff are the
137  C  same as for the last row, don't bother to recompute BILL(NOTRF))
138  180      IF (TYPETR .EQ. 'P') CALL PEAKP
139           IF (TYPETR .EQ. 'E') CALL EXPNDB
140           CALL COSTSB
141           BILL(NOTRF) = COST + .005
142  190     CONTINUE
143  C Print the row:
144          IF (PEAKQ) GO TO 210
145          PRINT 200, KWH,KW,(BILL(NOTRF),NOTRF=1,NTARIF)
146  200     FORMAT (I5,I4,9F7.2)
147          GO TO 230
148  210     PCPK = PCPEAK*100 + .5
149          PRINT 220, KWH,KW,PCPK,(BILL(NOTRF),NOTRF=1,NTARIF)
150  220     FORMAT (I5,I4,I5,2X,8(F6.2,1X))
151  230    CONTINUE
152         PRINT 240
153  240    FORMAT (//' AUF WIEDERSEHEN'//)
154         STOP
155         END
PRT    COMPLETED..
@PRT,S P*S.BILLMAP

P*S.BILLMAP
1      IN P*S.TYPICAL-BILL,.FORM,.PEAK,.COSTSB,.EXPAND
PRT    COMPLETED..
@PRT,S P*S.BILLPPROC

P*S.BILLPPROC
1   BILLP PROC
2  C THIS PROC IS INCLUDED IN THE ROUTINES FOR TYPICAL-BILL (see P*S.TYPICAL-
   BILL)
3          PARAMETER NTARFP=9, NBLP=10, NBLMIP=NBLP - 1
```

```
  4        IMPLICIT INTEGER (A-Z)
  5        REAL BL,P,PCPEAK,COST
  6        COMMON /BILLBL/NOTRF,BL(NTARFP,2,NBLMIP),NBLS(NTARFP,2),P(NTARFP,
  7       1                 2,NBLP),PCPEAK,KW,KWH,COST,TYPETR
  8   END
PRT    COMPLETED..
@PRT,S P*S.FORH

P*S.FORH
  1  C THIS SUBROUTINE IS REFERENCED BY TYPICAL-BILL (see P*S.TYPICAL-BILL)
  2  C (KWHKW = 1 iff the current charge is the kwh charge and = 2 iff the
  3  C  current charge is the kw charge)
  4        SUBROUTINE FORH
  5        INCLUDE BILLP,LIST
  6        KWHKW = 1
  7        IF (TYPETR .EQ. 'H') PRINT 10
  8   10   FORMAT (/' FIRST CONSIDER THE KWH CHARGE')
  9   20   PRINT 30
 10   30   FORMAT (/' PLEASE ENTER THE UPPER LIMITS OF THE BLOCKS, ',
 11       1      'STARTING WITH THE LOWEST'/' (FOR A FLAT TARIFF ',
 12       2      'ENTER A BLANK LINE)')
 13        READ (-,40) DUMMY
 14   40   FORMAT (A6)
 15        DO 50 I = 1,100
 16   50    READ (0,-,ERR=60) (BL(NOTRF,KWHKW,J), J=1,I)
 17   60   NBL = I
 18        NBLS(NOTRF,KWHKW) = NBL
 19        NBLMI = NBL - 1
 20        IF (NBL .EQ. 1) GO TO 80
 21        READ (0,-) (BL(NOTRF,KWHKW,J), J=1,NBLMI)
 22        PRINT 70
 23   70   FORMAT (/' PLEASE ENTER THE PRICES OF THE BLOCKS',
 24       1      ' (IN THE SAME ORDER)')
 25        GO TO 100
 26   80   PRINT 90
 27   90   FORMAT (/' PLEASE ENTER THE PRICE')
 28   100  READ, (P(NOTRF,KWHKW,J), J=1,NBL)
 29        IF (TYPETR.NE.'H' .OR. KWHK,.NE.1) RETURN
 30        KWHKW = 2
 31        PRINT 110
 32   110  FORMAT (/' NOW CONSIDER THE KW CHARGE')
 33        GO TO 20
 34        END
PRT    COMPLETED..
@PRT,S P*S.EXPAND

P*S.EXPAND
  1  C THIS SUBROUTINE IS REFERENCED BY TYPICAL-BILL (see P*S.TYPICAL-BILL)
  2  C (EBL is the array with the block size specifications)
  3        SUBROUTINE EXPAND
  4        INCLUDE BILLP,LIST
  5        REAL EBL(NTARFP,1,NBLP)
  6        PRINT 10
  7   10   FORMAT (/' PLEASE ENTER THE SIZES OF THE BLOCKS,',
  8       1      'ADDING A MINUS SIGN (''-'')'/' TO EXPANDER BLOCKS')
  9        READ, EBL(NOTRF,1,1)
 10        DO 20 I = 1,100
```

```
 11  20       READ (0,-,ERR=30) (EBL(NOTRF,1,J), J=1,1)
 12  30      NBL = 1
 13           NBLS(NOTRF,1) = NBL
 14           NBLM1 = NBL - 1
 15           READ (0,-) (EBL(NOTRF,1,J), J=1,NBLM1)
 16           PRINT 40
 17  40      FORMAT (/' PLEASE ENTER THE PRICES OF THE BLOCKS')
 18           READ, (P(NOTRF,1,J), J=1,NBL)
 19           RETURN
 20
 21           ENTRY EXPNDB
 22           NBL = NBLS(NOTRF,1)
 23           FACTOR = 0
 24           DO 60 NOBL = 1,NBL
 25             IF(EBL(NOTRF,1,NOBL) .GT. 0) GO TO 50
 26             BL(NOTRF,1,NOBL) = BL(NOTRF,1,NOBL-1).FACTOR + KW*ABS(EBL(
 27          1                         NOTRF,1,NOBL))
 28             GO TO 60
 29  50         BL(NOTRF,1,NOBL) = BL(NOTRF,1,NOBL-1).FACTOR + EBL(NOTRF,
 30          1                         1,NOBL)
 31  60         FACTOR = 1
 32           RETURN
 33           END
PRT      COMPLETED..
@PRT,S P*S.PEAK

P*S.PEAK
  1   C THIS SUBROUTINE IS REFERENCED BY TYPICAL-BILL (see P*S.TYPICAL-BILL)
  2   C (PONP(I) and POFFP(I) are the Prices ON and OFF Peak for the Ith
  3   C  tariff [both are 0 if the Ith tariff is not a "peak" tariff]
  4          SUBROUTINE PEAK
  5          INCLUDE BILLP,LIST
  6          REAL PONP(NTARFP),POFFP(NTARFP)
  7          PRINT 10
  8  10      FORMAT (/' PLEASE ENTER THE ON- AND OFF-PEAK PRICES')
  9          READ, PONP(NOTRF),POFFP(NOTRF)
 10          NBLS(NOTRF,1) = 1
 11          RETURN
 12
 13          ENTRY PEAKP
 14   C (A "peak" tariff with prices PONP and POFFP is exactly the same
 15   C  as a flat tariff [with one block] with "effective" price:)
 16          P(NOTRF,1,1) = PCPEAK*(PONP(NOTRF)- POFFP(NOTRF)) + POFFP(NOTRF)
 17          RETURN
 18          END
PRT      COMPLETED..
@PRT,S P*S.COSTSB

P*S.COSTSB
  1   C THIS SUBROUTINE IS REFERENCED BY TYPICAL-BILL (see P*S.TYPICAL-BILL)
  2   C (KWHKW is as in FORM [see P*S.FORM] and NKWHKW is the Number of
  3   C  KWH [iff KWHKW=1] or KW [iff KWHKW=2] and NOBL is the NO. of the
  4   C  current Block)
  5   C (By the time this subroutine is referenced, all the possible types
  6   C  of tariffs have been put into a common form - the fixed-block.  The
  7   C  prices off- and on-peak have been merged into one flat rate, the
  8   C  expander blocks have been expanded to a known size and the upper
```

```
 9   C  limits of the blocks computed: we now just calculate the cost,
10   C  going around twice for a hopkinson tariff changing from kwh to kw.)
11   C ("FACTOR" is thrown in only so that the special case NOBL=1 [when
12   C  FACTOR=0] can be treated in the same way as the other times [when
13   C  FACTOR=1])
14          SUBROUTINE COSTSB
15          INCLUDE BILLP,LIST
16          KWHKW = 1
17          NKWHKW = KWH
18          COST = 0
19   10     NBL = NBLS(NOTRF,KWHKW)
20          FACTOR = 0
21          DO 30 NOBL = 1,NBL
22           IF (NKWHKW.LT.BL(NOTRF,KWHKW,NOBL) .OR. NOBL.EQ.NBL) GO TO 20
23           COST = COST + P(NOTRF,KWHKW,NOBL)*(BL(NOTRF,KWHKW,NOBL)-
24        1        BL(NOTRF,KWHKW,NOBL-1)*FACTOR)
25           FACTOR = 1
26           GO TO 30
27   20      COST = COST + P(NOTRF,KWHKW,NOBL)*(NKWHKW-BL(NOTRF,KWHKW,NOBL-1)
28        1       *FACTOR)
29           GO TO 40
30   30     CONTINUE
31   40     IF (TYPETR.NE.'H' .OR. KWHKW.NE.1) RETURN
32          KWHKW = 2
33          NKWHKW = KW
34          GO TO 10
35          END
PRT    COMPLETED..
```

METER–COST

```
P*S.METER-COST
     1  C THIS PROGRAM CALCULATES BREAK-EVEN METER COST and was written by
     2  C    C. Cicchetti
     3          DIMENSION PPRC(6),OPRC(6),PPH(6),OPPH(6)
     4          WRITE(6,100)
     5  100     FORMAT(///' INPUT DATA:'/
     6         1' METER LIFE, INTEREST RATE, ADDITIONAL OTHER BILLING,'/
     7         2' ANNUAL SALES SHIFTED IN KWH, NUMBER OF PEAK PERIODS,'/
     8         2' PEAK PERIOD RUNNING COSTS, PEAK PERIOD HOURS,'/
     9         2' NUMBER OF OFF-PEAK PERIODS, OFF-PEAK RUNNING COSTS,'/
    10         2' OFF-PEAK PERIOD HOURS, NEW CAPACITY AVOIDED, LRIC,'/
    11         4' NUMBER OF CUSTOMERS'///)
    12          READ, XL,XI,OC,ASS,NPPS,(PPRC(I),I=1,NPPS),(PPH(I),I=1,NPPS),
    13         1        NOPPS,(OPRC(I),I=1,NOPPS),(OPPH(I),I=1,NOPPS),
    14         2        XNIA,XLRIC,XNC
    15  C (Calculate Running Cost on-Peak and Off-peak;)
    16          SUM1 = 0
    17          SUM2 = 0
    18          DO 3 I = 1,NPPS
    19           SUM1 = SUM1 + PPRC(I)*PPH(I)
    20  3        SUM2 = SUM2 + PPH(I)
    21          RCP = SUM1/SUM2
    22          SUM1 = 0
    23          SUM2 = 0
    24          DO 6 I = 1,NOPPS
    25           SUM1 = SUM1 + OPRC(I)*OPPH(I)
    26  6        SUM2 = SUM2 + OPPH(I)
    27          RCO = SUM1/SUM2
    28  C (Print out the inPuts and the Running Costs just calculated)
    29          WRITE(6,11) XL,XI,OC,ASS,RCP,PCO,XNIA,XLRIC,XNC
    30  11      FORMAT(///' METER LIFE',F47.5/' INTEREST RATE',F44.5/
    31         1' ADDITIONAL OTHER BILLING COSTS',F27.5/
    32         2' ANNUAL KWH SALES SHIFTED',F33.5/
    33         3' RUNNING COST ON PEAK',F37.5/' RUNNING COST OFF PEAK',F36.5/
    34         3'  (BOTH COSTS ARE AVERAGES WEIGHTED BY HOURS, NOT BY SALES)'/
    35         4' ANNUAL KW OF NEW CAPACITY AVOIDED',F24.5/
    36         5' LONG RUN INCREMENTAL COST OF A NEW KW',F20.5/
    37         6' NUMBER OF CUSTOMERS',F38.5)
    38  C CALCULATE ANNUAL BENEFITS OF DIURNAL PRICING
    39  C RUNNING COST SAVINGS
    40          RCS = ASS*(RCP-RCO)
    41  C  CALCULATE CAPACITY COST SAVINGS
    42          CCS = XNIA*XLRIC
    43          BEN = PCS + CCS
    44  C  CALCULATE CRF
    45          CRF = (XI*(1.+XI)**XL)/(((1.+XI)**XL)-1.)
    46  C CALCULATE BREAK-EVEN METER COSTS
    47            TOC = OC*XNC
    48           BEMC = ((BEN-TOC)/CRF)/XNC
    49          WRITE(6,21) BEMC,BEN,CRF
    50  21      FORMAT(///' BREAK-EVEN METER COSTS',F19.5/' BENEFITS',F33.5/
    51         1' CAPITAL RECOVERY FACTOR',F18.5)
    52  C IF METER COSTS ARE KNOWN CALCULATE BENEFIT-COST RATIO
    53  C SET ZZZ EQUAL TO 1 IF METER COSTS ARE KNOWN
    54          WRITE(6,200)
```

```
55  200    FORMAT(///' PUT IN 1. IF METER COSTS ARE KNOWN AND 2. IF NOT KNOWN
56         1'/' SPACE AND PUT IN COST PER METER')
57         READ (5,20) ZZZ,XMC
58  20     FORMAT()
59         IF (ZZZ .NE. 1.) XMC = BEMC
60         BCR = BEN/(((XMC*CRF)+OC)*XNC)
61         WRITE (6,12) XMC,BCR
62  12     FORMAT(///' METER COSTS', F17.5/' BENEFIT COST RATIO',F10.5)
63         WRITE (6,30)
64  30     FORMAT(///' TYPE IN KILOWATT HOURS SALES ON PEAK AND'/
65        1' KILOWATTS OF PEAK CAPACITY'///)
66         READ, SOP, XKAP
67         WRITE (6,31) SOP,XKAP
68  31     FORMAT(///' KWH SALES ON PEAK:',F20.2/' KW OF PEAK CAPACITY:',
69        1F18.2)
70         COSTS = ((XMC*CRF) + OC) * XNC
71  C   CALCULATE SHIFT IN KWH WHEN KW ARE NOT CHANGED
72         ASSN = COSTS/(RCP - RCO)
73         PAS = ASSN/SOP*100
74         WRITE (6,40) ASSN, PAS
75  40     FORMAT(' PEAK ENERGY SAVING:',F19.2,'    PERCENTAGE:',F11.5)
76  C   CALCULATE REDUCTION IN KW WHEN KWH ARE NOT SHIFTED
77         XNIAN = COSTS/XLRIC
78         PNS = XNIAN/XKAP*100
79         WRITE (6,41) XNIAN,PNS
80  41     FORMAT(' PEAK CAPACITY AVOIDED:',F16.2,'    PERCENTAGE:',F11.5)
81  C   BOTH SHIFT BY AN EQUAL PERCENTAGE
82         PSS = COSTS/(SOP*(RCP-RCO) + (XKAP*XLRIC))*100
83         WRITE (6,50) PSS
84  50     FORMAT(' PERCENTAGE PEAK ENERGY & POWER SAVING:',F25.5///' ADIOS'/
85        1        /)
86         END
PRT    COMPLETED..
```

LOAD

```
P*S.LOAD
 1  C THIS PROGRAM ("LOAD") DRAWS LOAD AND LOAD DURATION CURVES
 2  C The MAP statements in P*S.LOADMAP indicate the subroutines used
 3  C The statements in P*S.LOADCOMPILE compile those routines
 4  C Variable and Subroutine Names:
 5  C   BEGIN    PROC in F*S.BEGINPROC with beginning (eg type) statements
 6  C   LDDUR    = .TRUE. iff the current graph is a LoaD DURation curve
 7  C   XCOORD   array with X or horiz. COORDinates of points to be graphed
 8  C   IMAGE    array containing the IMAGE of the date of a holiday
 9  C   DEVSET   GRAPH package routine to SET plotting DEVice = plotter
10  C   NGRAPH   Number of the current GRAPH
11  C   YEAR     YEAR in which the data was taken
12  C   NHOL     Number of HOLidays
13  C   DATE     subroutine which reads DATE in arg. 1 and puts # of month in arg. 2
14  C              and # of day of month in arg. 3
15  C   MONHOL   array with #s of the MONths of the HOLidays
16  C   DAYHOL   array with #s of the DAY of the month of the HOLidays
17  C   CALNDR   subroutine that fills DAYYR and WKEHOL and sets value of NDAYYR
18  C   NDAYYR   Number of DAYS in the yeaR
19  C   DAYYR(i,j) = # of the DAY of the YeaR of the jth day of the ith month
20  C   WKEHOL(I)   = .TRUE. iff the ith day of the year is a WeeKEnd or
21  C                  HOLiday
22  C   DATA     load DATA for each day of the year and hour of the day
23  C              [DATA(i,j) = load during hour j of the ith day of the year]
24  C   WCHGS    = 'YES' iff user Wants to make CHanGeS in the curve (flatten it)
25  C   WTABLE   = 'YES' iff user Wants a TABLE printed
26  C   FIRCHG   = 'YES' iff any change in the current curve would be the FIRst CHangi
27  C   OUT      first letter of the choice of OUTput (ie curve)
28  C   OUTPUT   array containing loads (y-coord.s) to be OUTPUT in the graph
29  C     NOTE:  "prepares" in the following means "fills OUTPUT for"
30  C   DLOADC   subroutine that prepares a Daily LOAD Curve
31  C   PEAKD    subroutine that prepares a PEAK Day load curve
32  C   MONTHS   subroutine that prepares an average monthly load curve if the
33  C              arg. is 'AVEMON' and otherwise prepares a monthly load
34  C              duration curve
35  C   YLDDUR   subroutine that prepares a Yearly LoaD DURation curve
36  C   URSORT   MACC Utility Routine that SORTs the first arg. 2 elements of
37  C              arg. 3 in descending order (when arg. 1 = 3)
38  C   GRAPH    MACC routine that GRAPHs arg. 5 points, with x-coords in arg. 1
39  C              and y-coords in arg. 3, using arg. 11 as graph title
40  C   NOUT     Number of points to be OUTPUT in the graph
41  C   TITLE    array filled in the subroutine (eg DLOADC) which prepares OUTPUT
42  C              and containing the appropriate graph TITLE
43  C   NGRAPH   Number of the current GRAPH
44  C   TABLE    subroutine that prepares and prints the TABLE for a load duration
45  C              curve
46  C   CHANGE   subroutine that CHANGEs points to flatten graph
47  C   RERUN    = 'YES' iff the user wants to RERUN the program (draw another
48  C              graph)
49  C   MONNAM   MONth Names [the name of the ith month is in MONNAM(1,i)
50  C              and MONNAM(2,i)]
51          INCLUDE BEGIN,LIST
52          LOGICAL LDDUR
53          DIMENSION XCOORD(8784),IMAGE(12)
54          CALL DEVSET('PLTTR')
```

```
 55          NGRAPH = 0
 56          DO 40 I = 1,8784
 57   40      XCOORD(I) = I
 58          PRINT 50
 59   50     FORMAT (/' PLEASE ENTER THE YEAR THE DATA WAS TAKEN, THE NUMBER',
 60         1   ' OF HOLIDAYS'/' THAT YEAR, AND THE DATES OF THOSE HOLIDAYS',
 61         2   ' (EACH ON A SEPARATE LINE)')
 62          READ, YEAR,NHOL
 63          DO 57 I = 1,NHOL
 64           READ 55, IMAGE
 65   55      FORMAT (12A6)
 66           CALL DATE(IMAGE,MONHOL(I),DAYHOL(I))
 67   57     CONTINUE
 68          CALL CALNDR
 69          PRINT 60
 70   60     FORMAT (/' PLEASE SUPPLY THE DATA')
 71          READ, ((DATA(DAY,HOUR), HOUR=1,24), DAY=1,NDAYYR)
 72   70     WCHGS = 'NO'
 73          WTABLE = 'NO'
 74          FIRCHG = 'YES'
 75          PRINT 80
 76   80     FORMAT (/' WHAT OUTPUT WOULD YOU LIKE? (TYPE ''?'' FOR A LIST',
 77         1         ' OF CHOICES)')
 78   85     READ 90, OUT
 79   90     FORMAT (A1)
 80          IF (OUT .NE. '?') GO TO 110
 81          PRINT 100
 82   100    FORMAT (/' YOUR CHOICES ARE:'/' DAILY LOAD CURVE'/
 83         1         ' PEAK DAY LOAD CURVE'/
 84         2         ' AVERAGE MONTHLY LOAD CURVE (EXCLUDING WEEKENDS AND',
 85         3         ' HOLIDAYS)'/' MONTHLY LOAD DURATION CURVE'/
 86         4         ' YEARLY LOAD DURATION CURVE'/
 87         5         ' (YOU NEED ONLY ENTER THE FIRST LETTER OF THE NAME)'
 88         6         /' NOW WHAT OUTPUT WOULD YOU LIKE?')
 89          GO TO 85
 90   110    LDDUR = OUT.EQ.'M' .OR. OUT.EQ.'Y'
 91          IF (.NOT.LDDUR) GO TO 150
 92   120    PRINT 130
 93   130    FORMAT (/' DO YOU WANT A TABLE?')
 94          READ 140, WTABLE
 95   140    FORMAT (A3)
 96          IF (WCHGS .EQ. 'YES') GO TO 155
 97   C (If the graph to be plotted is just a flattened graph, there is
 98   C  no need to reprepare the graph)
 99   150    IF (OUT .EQ. 'D') CALL DLOADC
100          IF (OUT .EQ. 'P') CALL PEAKD
101          IF (OUT .EQ. 'A') CALL MONTHS('AVEMON')
102          IF (OUT .EQ. 'M') CALL MONTHS('MLDDUR')
103          IF (OUT .EQ. 'Y') CALL YLDDUR
104          IF (LDDUR)
105         1   CALL URSORT(3,NOUT,OUTPUT,DUMMY,DUMMY,0,DUMMY)
106   C (points are in chronological order until URSORT rearranges them
107   C  for a load duration curve)
108   155    CONTINUE
109          CALL GRAPH (XCOORD,'INTGR',OUTPUT,'LINEAR',NOUT,'NONE'
110         1  ,'SOLID','HOUR$$','LOAD$$','NORMAL',TITLE,'FULL','NORMAL')
111   C (see GSP documentation for meaning of all these arguments)
```

```
112          NGRAPH = NGRAPH + 1
113          PRINT 170, NGRAPH,(TITLE(I),I=1,7)
114   170    FORMAT (/' GRAPH NUMBER',I3,' DRAWN:',2X,7A6)
115   190    IF (WTABLE .EQ. 'YES') CALL TABLE
116          PRINT 200
117   200    FORMAT (/' DO YOU WANT THE CURVE FLATTENED?')
118          READ 140, WCHGS
119          IF (WCHGS .NE. 'YES') GO TO 210
120          CALL CHANGE(FIRCHG)
121          FIRCHG = 'NO'
122          IF (LDDUR) GO TO 120
123          GO TO 155
124   210    PRINT 220
125   220    FORMAT (/' DO YOU WANT TO RUN AGAIN?')
126          READ 140, RERUN
127          IF (RERUN .EQ. 'YES') GO TO 70
128          PRINT 230
129   230    FORMAT (/' SO LONG'//)
130          STOP
131          END
PRT     COMPLETED..
@PRT,S P*S.LOADMAP

P*S.LOADMAP
  1        IN P*S.LOAD,.CALNDR,.DLOADC,.PEAKD,.MONTHS,.YLDDUR,.TABLE,.CHANGE
  2        IN P*S.DATE
  3        LIB IRP-DC*LIB
PRT     COMPLETED..
@PRT,S P*S.LOADCOMPILE

 P*S.LOADCOMPILE
   1       @PDP,SFX P*S.BEGINPROC,P*S.BEGINPROC
   2       @FOR,SZC P*S.LOAD
   3       @FOR,SZC P*S.CALNDR
   4       @FOR,SZC P*S.DLOADC
   5       @FOR,SZC P*S.PEAKD
   6       @FOR,SZC P*S.MONTHS
   7       @FOR,SZC P*S.YLDDUR
   8       @FOR,SZC P*S.TABLE
   9       @FOR,SZC P*S.CHANGE
PRT     COMPLETED..
@PRT,S P*S.BEGINPROC

P*S.BEGINPROC
   1  BEGIN PROC
   2  C  THIS PROC IS INCLUDED IN THE ROUTINES FOR LOAD (see P*S.LOAD)
   3        IMPLICIT INTEGER (A-Z)
   4        LOGICAL WKEHOL
   5        REAL DATA,OUTPUT
   6        COMMON /CMN/YEAR,NDAYYR,NOUT,NHOL,MONHOL(17),DAYHOL(17),TITLE(9),
   7       1          DAYYR(12,31),WKEHOL(366),DATA(366,24),OUTPUT(8784)
   8       2          ,MONNAM(2,12)
   9        DATA MONNAM/'       JANUARY',' FEBRUARY',' ',' MARCH',' ',
  10       1      ' APRIL',' ','    MAY',' ',' JUNE',' ',' JULY',' ',
  11       2      'AUGUST','  SEPTEMBER','   OCTOBER','   NOVEMBER',
  12       3      '    DECEMBER'/
  13    END
PRT     COMPLETED..
```

```
WPRT,S P*S.CALNDR

P*S.CALNDR
  1   C   THIS SUBROUTINE IS REFERENCED BY LOAD (see P*S.LOAD)
  2   C   Variables particular to this routine:
  3   C   FIRSNY   # of the FIRst SUNday of the Year (eg 4=Jan. 4 for 1975)
  4   C              (because there are 7 days/week and leap years every 4 years this
  5   C              number repeats itself every 7x4=28 years. for 1960,1988...
  6   C              it is 3, and in general for year N it is the Ith number in
  7   C              the array FIRSNY, where I = MOD(N,28) + 1)
  8   C   DAYPMO   # of DAYS Per MOnth
  9   C     [all other variables are used to hold values of subscripted
 10   C       variables temporarily - they are used where subscripts are illegal]
 11          SUBROUTINE CALNDR
 12          INCLUDE BEGIN,LIST
 13          DIMENSION FIRSNY(28),DAYPMO(12)
 14          DATA FIRSNY/3,1,7,6,5,3,2,1,7,5,4,3,2,7,6,5,4,2,1,7,6,4,3,2,1,6,5,
 15         1            4/
 16         2     DAYPMO/31,28,31,30,31,30,31,31,30,31,30,31/
 17         3     WKEHOL/366*.FALSE./
 18          NDAYYR = 365
 19          IF (MOD(YEAR,4) .NE. 0) GO TO 3
 20   C (these next two statements executed only for a leap year)
 21          NDAYYR = 366
 22          DAYPMO(2) = 29
 23   3      DAY = 0
 24   C (by simply stepping through the days of the year, fill DAYYR:)
 25          DO 5 I = 1,12
 26           DAYSMO = DAYPMO(I)
 27           DO 5 J = 1,DAYSMO
 28            DAY = DAY + 1
 29   5        DAYYR(I,J) = DAY
 30   7      SUB = MOD(YEAR,28) + 1
 31          FIRSUN = FIRSNY(SUB)
 32   C (FIRSUN is the # or the FIRst SUNday of the relevant year [YEAR])
 33          IF (FIRSUN .NE. 1) WKEHOL(FIRSUN-1) = .TRUE.
 34   C (unless the year starts on Sunday, the day before FIRSUN is a
 35   C  SAturday and hence a weekend)
 36          WKEHOL(FIRSUN) = .TRUE.
 37   C (now starting with FIRSUN add 6 and 7 successively to the DAY #
 38   C  thus hitting all Saturdays and Sundays:)
 39          DAY = FIRSUN
 40          DO 10 I = 1,54
 41           DAY = DAY + 7
 42           IF (DAY-1 .LE. NDAYYR) WKEHOL(DAY-1) = .TRUE.
 43           IF (DAY .GT. NDAYYR) GO TO 20
 44   10      WKEHOL(DAY) = .TRUE.
 45   C (having hit all the weekends, get the holidays:)
 46   20     DO 30 I = 1,NHOL
 47           MON = MONHOL(I)
 48           DAYMON = DAYHOL(I)
 49           DAYY = DAYYR(MON,DAYMON)
 50   30      WKEHOL(DAYY) = .TRUE.
 51          RETURN
 52          END
 PRT     COMPLETED..
```

```
@PRT,S P•S.DATE

P•S.DATE
  1   C THIS SUBROUTINE IS REFERENCED BY MARGINALCOST AND LOAD (see
  2   C P•S.MARGINALCOST and P•S.LOAD)
  3   C   DATEIM(I) = Ith character in the DATE Image stored in IMAGE
  4   C   MONNM(I) = first I characters in the MONth NaMe
  5           SUBROUTINE DATE(IMAGE,MONNO,DAY)
  6           IMPLICIT INTEGER (A-Z)
  7           DIMENSION IMAGE(12),DATEIM(72),FORMT(3)/'(',' ','X,I2)'/
  8          1          MO(12)/'JA','F','MAR','AP','MAY','JUN','JUL',
  9          2                 'AU','S','O','N','D'/
 10          3          ,MONNM(3)
 11           MONNO = 0
 12           DAY = 0
 13           DECODE (IMAGE,10) DATEIM
 14    10     FORMAT (72A1)
 15           DO 20 I = 72,1,-1
 16    20      IF (DATEIM(I) .NE. ' ') GO TO 30
 17    30     IM2 = I - 2
 18           ENCODE (COLUMN,40) IM2
 19    40     FORMAT (I6)
 20           FORMT(2) = COLUMN
 21           READ (0,FORMT,ERR=80) DAY
 22           DO 50 J = 1,3
 23            MONNM(J) = 6H
 24    50      FLD(0,6*J,MONNM(J)) = FLD(0,6*J,IMAGE(1))
 25           DO 60 I = 1,12
 26            DO 60 J = 1,3
 27    60       IF (MONNM(J) .EQ. MO(I)) GO TO 70
 28           RETURN
 29    70     MONNO = I
 30    80     RETURN
 31           END
PRT     COMPLETED..
@PRT,S P•S.MONTHS

P•S.MONTHS
  1   C THIS SUBROUTINE IS REFERENCED BY LOAD (see P•S.LOAD)
  2   C Variables particular to this routine:
  3   C   FIRDAY   # of the day of the year that is the FIRSt DAY of the month
  4   C   LASDAY   # of the day of the year that is the LASt DAY of the month
  5   C   MVCFST   a routine in the library IRP-DC•LIB which is here used
  6   C            to Move the Characters of the month name into TITLE
  7   C   NODAYS   NO. of DAYS in the month, excluding weekends and holidays
  8           SUBROUTINE MONTHS(WHICH)
  9           INCLUDE BEGIN,LIST
 10           DIMENSION IMAGE(12)
 11           PRINT 10
 12    10     FORMAT (/' WHICH MONTH WOULD YOU LIKE?')
 13           READ 15, IMAGE
 14    15     FORMAT (12A6)
 15           IMAGE (12) = '1'
 16           CALL DATE(IMAGE,MONTH,DAYMO)
 17           FIRDAY = DAYYR(MONTH,1)
```

```
 18         IF (MONTH .NE. 12) LASDAY = DAYYR(MONTH+1,1) - 1
 19         IF (MONTH .EQ. 12) LASDAY = NDAYYR
 20         IF (WHICH .EQ. 'AVEMON') GO TO 30
 21   C for a monthly load duration curve ---
 22         NOUT = 0
 23         DO 20 DAY = FIRDAY,LASDAY
 24          DO 20 HOUR = 1,24
 25           NOUT = NOUT + 1
 26   20      OUTPUT(NOUT) = DATA(DAY,HOUR)
 27         TITLE(1) = 'MONTHL'
 28         TITLE(2) = 'Y LOAD'
 29         TITLE(3) = ' DURAT'
 30         TITLE(4) = 'ION CU'
 31         TITLE(5) = 'RVE FO'
 32         TITLE(6) = 'R'
 33         CALL MVCFST(MONNAM(1,MONTH),2,TITLE(6),2,12)
 34         TITLE(8) = '$$'
 35         RETURN
 36   C for an average monthly load curve ---
 37   30    DO 40 HOUR = 1,24
 38   40     OUTPUT(HOUR) = 0
 39         NODAYS = 0
 40         DO 55 DAY = FIRDAY,LASDAY
 41          IF (WKEHOL(DAY)) GO TO 55
 42          NODAYS = NODAYS + 1
 43          DO 50 HOUR = 1,24
 44   50      OUTPUT(HOUR) = OUTPUT(HOUR) + DATA(DAY,HOUR)
 45   55    CONTINUE
 46         DO 60 HOUR = 1,24
 47   60     OUTPUT(HOUR) = OUTPUT(HOUR)/NODAYS
 48         NOUT = 24
 49         TITLE(1) = 'AVERAG'
 50         TITLE(2) = 'E MONT'
 51         TITLE(3) = 'HLY LO'
 52         TITLE(4) = 'AD CUR'
 53         TITLE(5) = 'VE FOR'
 54         TITLE(6) = MONNAM(1,MONTH)
 55         TITLE(7) = MONNAM(2,MONTH)
 56         TITLE(8) = '$$'
 57         RETURN
 58         END
PRT    COMPLETED..
@PRT,S P*S.PEAKD

P*S.PEAKD
  1   C THIS SUBROUTINE IS REFERENCED BY LOAD (see P*S.LOAD)
  2         SUBROUTINE PEAKD
  3         INCLUDE BEGIN,LIST
  4         REAL PEAKLD
  5         PEAKLD = 0
  6   C (find PEAKLD = PEAK LoaD and PEAKDY = # of the PEAK DaY:)
  7         DO 10 DAY = 1,NDAYYR
  8          DO 10 HOUR = 1,24
  9           IF (DATA(DAY,HOUR) .LE. PEAKLD) GO TO 10
 10           PEAKLD = DATA(DAY,HOUR)
```

```
11              PEAKDY = DAY
12   10       CONTINUE
13            DO 20 HOUR = 1,24
14   20        OUTPUT(HOUR) = DATA(PEAKDY,HOUR)
15            NOUT = 24
16   C (find the date of the peak day:)
17            START = PEAKDY/30 + 1
18            DO 30 MONTH = START,12
19             DO 30 DAYMO = 1,31
20   30         IF (DAYYR(MONTH,DAYMO) .EQ. PEAKDY) GO TO 40
21   40       PRINT 50, (MONNAM(I,MONTH),I=1,2),DAYMO,PEAKLD
22   50       FORMAT (//' THE PEAK DAY IS',2A6,I3,'; THE PEAK LOAD IS',F10.3)
23            TITLE(1) = 'LOAD'
24            TITLE(2) = 'CURVE'
25            TITLE(3) = ' FOR'
26            TITLE(4) = MONNAM(1,MONTH)
27            TITLE(5) = MONNAM(2,MONTH)
28            ENCODE (TITLE(6),60) DAYMO
29   60       FORMAT (I3)
30            TITLE(7) = ' '
31            TITLE(8) = '73'
32            RETURN
33            END
PRT     COMPLETED..
@PRT,S P*S.DLOADC

P*S.DLOADC
1    C THIS SUBROUTINE IS REFERENCED BY LOAD (see P*S.LOAD)
2             SUBROUTINE DLOADC
3             INCLUDE BEGIN,LIST
4             DIMENSION IMAGE(12)
5             PRINT 10
6    10       FORMAT (/' WHICH DAY WOULD YOU LIKE?')
7             READ 15, IMAGE
8    15       FORMAT (12A6)
9             CALL DATE(IMAGE,MONTH,DAYMO)
10            DAY = DAYYR(MONTH,DAYMO)
11            DO 20 HOUR = 1,24
12   20        OUTPUT(HOUR) = DATA(DAY,HOUR)
13            NOUT = 24
14            TITLE(1) = 'LOAD'
15            TITLE(2) = 'CURVE'
16            TITLE(3) = ' FOR'
17            TITLE(4) = MONNAM(1,MONTH)
18            TITLE(5) = MONNAM(2,MONTH)
19            ENCODE (TITLE(6),30) DAYMO
20   30       FORMAT (I3)
21            TITLE(7) = ' '
22            TITLE(8) = '73'
23            RETURN
24            END
PRT     COMPLETED..
```

```
@PRT,S P•S.YLDDUR

P•S.YLDDUR
  1   C THIS SUBROUTINE IS REFERENCED BY LOAD (see P•S.LOAD)
  2   C Variables particular to this routine:
  3   C   TOTKWH   TOTal energy demanded throughout the year
  4   C   PEAKLD   PEAK LoaD
  5   C   LOADF    LOAD Factor [ = ratio of average to peak load]
  6             SUBROUTINE YLDDUR
  7             INTEGER SUBSCR
  8             INCLUDE BEGIN,LIST
  9             REAL TOTKWH,PEAKLD,LOADF
 10             SUBSCR = 0
 11             DO 10 DAY = 1,NDAYYR
 12               DO 10 HOUR = 1,24
 13                 SUBSCR = SUBSCR + 1
 14     10          OUTPUT(SUBSCR) = DATA(DAY,HOUR)
 15             NOUT = SUBSCR
 16             PEAKLD = 0
 17             TOTKWH = 0
 18             DO 20 DAY = 1,NDAYYR
 19               DO 20 HOUR = 1,24
 20                 TOTKWH = TOTKWH + DATA(DAY,HOUR)
 21                 IF (DATA(DAY,HOUR) .LE. PEAKLD) GO TO 20
 22                 PEAKLD = DATA(DAY,HOUR)
 23     20      CONTINUE
 24             LOADF = (TOTKWH/(NDAYYR*24))/PEAKLD
 25             PRINT 30, TOTKWH,PEAKLD,LOADF
 26     30      FORMAT (///' TOTAL ENERGY DEMANDED:',1PE12.5,', PEAK LOAD:',
 27           1        1E12.5/'  LOAD FACTOR:',1PE12.5)
 28             TITLE(1) = 'LOAD D'
 29             TITLE(2) = 'URATIO'
 30             TITLE(3) = 'N CURV'
 31             TITLE(4) = 'E FOR'
 32             ENCODE (TITLE(5),40) YEAR
 33     40      FORMAT (I4)
 34             TITLE(6) = ' '
 35             TITLE(7) = ' '
 36             TITLE(8) = '33'
 37             RETURN
 38             END
PRT      COMPLETED..
@PRT,S P•S.TABLE

P•S.TABLE
  1   C THIS ROUTINE IS REFERENCED BY LOAD (see P•S.LOAD)
  2   C Variables particular to this routine:
  3   C   MAXOUT   the MAXimum of the loads in the graph OUTput
  4   C   MINOUT   the MINimum of the loads in the graph OUTput
  5   C   ROWPC    array with the PerCents in the 1st column of the table
  6   C   INC      the INCrement in % between the rows
  7   C   ROWLVL   the level of load (2nd column) of a ROW of the table
  8   C   TENTRY   Table ENTRY for 3rd column
```

```
 9          SUBROUTINE TABLE
10          INCLUDE BEGIN,LIST
11          REAL MAXOUT,ROWPC(25),MINOUT,INC,ROWLVL,TENTRY
12          MAXOUT = OUTPUT(1)
13          PRINT 10
14   10     FORMAT (/' ENTER THE % INCREMENT BETWEEN ROWS OR THE % VALUES',
15       1         ' OF THE ROWS')
16   C (read the ROWPCs - since we don't know how many there will be,
17   C  keep trying to read more and more until an error [tried to read
18   C  too many] occurs:)
19          READ, ROWPC(1)
20          DO 20 I = 2,100
21   20      READ (0,-,ERR=30) (ROWPC(J), J=1,I)
22   30     NROWS = I - 1
23          READ (0,-) (ROWPC(I-J), J=1,NROWS)
24          IF (ROWPC(1) .LE. 1) GO TO 50
25   C (if %s are entered on a scale of 100, divide them by 100:)
26          DO 40 I = 1,NROWS
27   40      ROWPC(I) = ROWPC(I)/100
28   50     IF (NROWS .NE. 1) GO TO 70
29   C (if the % increment has been specified, compute the row %s: ---)
30          MINOUT = OUTPUT(NOUT)
31          INC = ROWPC(1)
32          ROWPC(1) = 1.00
33          DO 60 I = 2,25
34           ROWPC(I) = ROWPC(I-1) - INC
35           DONE = 1000*(ROWPC(I)*MAXOUT - MINOUT)/(MAXOUT-MINOUT)
36           IF (DONE .LE. 0) GO TO 65
37   C (this last statement would be "IF(ROWPC(I)*MAXOUT.LE.MINOUT) GO TO 65"
38   C  except that "the test for equality of non-integers may not be
39   C  meaningful". This way, if ROWPC(I)*MAXOUT is less than
40   C  MINOUT by greater than 1/1000 of the difference between MAXOUT and
41   C  MINOUT, we GO TO 65. Note: "DONE" is an integer.)
42   60     CONTINUE
43   65     NROWS = I
44   70     PRINT 80
45   80     FORMAT(//' % OF PEAK LOAD',4X,'LOAD',4X,'% OF TIME LOAD EXCEEDED')
46   C (compute and print the table row by row [this is a little sticky]:)
47          I = 0
48          DO 120 ROWNO = 1,NROWS
49           ROWLVL = MAXOUT*ROWPC(ROWNO)
50           START = I + 1
51           DO 90 I = START,NOUT
52           DONE = 1000*(OUTPUT(I) - ROWLVL)/(MAXOUT - MINOUT)
53   90      IF (DONE .LE. 0) GO TO 100
54           TENTRY = 1.00
55           PRINT 110, ROWPC(ROWNO),ROWLVL,TENTRY
56           GO TO 130
57   100     TENTRY = (I - 1.)/NOUT + .00005
58           PRINT 110, ROWPC(ROWNO),ROWLVL,TENTRY
59   110     FORMAT (2PF9.0,0PF16.2,2PF16.2)
60   120    CONTINUE
61   130    PRINT 150
62   150    FORMAT (/)
63          RETURN
64          END
PRT    COMPLETED..
```

```
@PRT,S P*S.CHANGE

P*S.CHANGE
 1  C THIS SUBROUTINE IS REFERENCED By LOAD (see P.S.LOAD)
 2  C Variables particular to this routine:
 3  C   P        Percent flattening desired (on a base of 1)
 4  C   Q        = 1 - P
 5  C   AVEOUT   AVErage value of the loads OUTput
 6  C   OLDQ     OLD value of Q from previous change of current graph
 7  C (This routine changes all the loads of the current graph [in array
 8  C   OUTPUT] from X to (1-P)*X+P*AVEOUT = Q*X+(1-Q)*AVEOUT.  The reason
 9  C   for using Qs rather than Ps is that a flattening specified by a Q
10  C   of Q1 followed by one of Q2 is exactly the same as a flattening
11  C   of Q1*Q2 - thus if a second change in a graph is desired to be of Q3
12  C   with respect to the original graph, a second change of Q3/OLDQ follow-
13  C   ing the previous change of OLDQ gives a net change of OLDQ*(Q3/OLDQ) =
14  C   Q3, as desired.  Note that since flattening does not change AVEOUT,
15  C   [ie the average value of the changed curve = average value of original
16  C   curve] AVEOUT does not have to be recomputed for second and subsequent
17  C   changes, when FIRCHG .ne. 'YES'.)
18          SUBROUTINE CHANGE(FIRCHG)
19          INCLUDE BEGIN,LIST
20          REAL P,Q,AVEOUT,OLDQ
21          PRINT 10
22   10     FORMAT (/' BY WHAT PERCENTAGE DO YOU WANT THE CURVE FLATTENED?')
23          IF (FIRCHG .NE. 'YES') PRINT 15
24   15     FORMAT (' (RELATIVE TO THE ORIGINAL CURVE - PREVIOUS '
25        1          ,'CHANGES ARE IGNORED)')
26          READ, P
27          IF (P .GE. 1) P = P/100
28          Q = 1 - P
29          IF (FIRCHG .NE. 'YES') GO TO 25
30          AVEOUT = 0
31          DO 20 I = 1,NOUT
32   20      AVEOUT = AVEOUT + OUTPUT(I)
33          AVEOUT = AVEOUT/NOUT
34          GO TO 27
35   25     Q = Q/OLDQ
36   27     DO 30 I = 1,NOUT
37   30      OUTPUT(I) = Q*OUTPUT(I) + (1-Q)*AVEOUT
38          OLDQ = Q
39          END
 PRT    COMPLETED..
```

Index

About the Authors

Charles J. Cicchetti, formerly Director of the Wisconsin Office of Emergency Energy Assistance, has resumed his position as Associate Professor of Economics at the University of Wisconsin at Madison. He received his undergraduate training at Colorado College and his Ph.D. from Rutgers University. Between 1969 and 1972 he was a Research Associate at Resources for the Future in Washington, D.C. He has published books on forecasting the demand for outdoor recreation, the Alaska Pipeline, and the problems of regulating the electric power industry.

William J. Gillen received the B.A. and M.A. degrees in Economics from George Washington University and the J.D. degree from the University of Wisconsin. He has been a consultant on utility pricing matters to several private organizations and state and federal agencies. His publications and expert testimony have been in the areas of benefit-cost analysis, oil import restrictions, utility regulation and environmental litigation.

Paul Smolensky has worked for several years on mathematical, statistical and computational aspects of utility pricing. He received his AB from Harvard, summa cum laude, and is currently pursuing his doctorate in mathematical physics at Indiana University.